TEN CREATIVE STAGES TO CONFIDENT THINKING

JAMES R. FISHER, JR., PH.D.

OTHER BOOKS BY
JAMES R. FISHER, JR., PH.D.

- Confident Selling
- Work Without Managers: A View From The Trenches
- The Worker, Alone! Going Against The Grain
- Confident Selling For The 90'S
- Purposeful Selling For The 21St Century
- The Taboo Against Being Your Own Best Friend
- Meet Your New Best Friend
- Six Silent Killers: Management's Greatest Challenge
- Corporate Sin: Leaderless Leaders & Dissonant Workers
- In The Shadow Of The Courthouse—A 1940'S Memoir as a Novel
- The Velvet Glove & Iron Fist
- The Short Inscrutable Life & Terrible Fate of the Domesticated Lion, Zimba/Human Cruelties of a Similar Kind

Continued…

Continuation of
OTHER BOOKS BY
JAMES R. FISHER, JR., PH.D.

- Ascent of the Working Woman
- Self-Confidence – The Elusive Challenge
- Who Put You in the Cage?
- DEVLIN, a psychological novel
- Nowhere Man in Nowhere Land
- Near Journey's End
- A Look Back to See Ahead
- Confident Thinking
- Time Out for Sanity
- Confidence in Subtext
- A Way of Looking at Things!
- A Way of Thinking about Things!
- Postmodern Worker Exposed
- The Fisher Paradigm

Dedicated to the memory of my daughter
the late Jeanne Marie Fisher and to her
son, Taylor Michael Fisher
With special thanks to George Edward Daly
Calgary Alberta Canada

When young, we trust ourselves too much; and we trust others too little when old. Rashness is the error of youth; timid caution of age. Manhood is the isthmus between the two extremes, the ripe and fertile seas of action when, only, we can hope to find the head to contrive, united with the hand to execute.

Caleb Colton, Nineteenth century English Clergyman

Trust men and they will be true to you; treat them greatly and they will show themselves great.

Ralph Waldo Emerson, Nineteenth century American poet and essayist

ACKNOWLEDGEMENTS

I T IS NO exaggeration that this project would not have gotten off the ground if it were not for the tireless efforts of George Edward Daly of Alberta, Canada. To give you a sense of what I am saying, my first draft of this book was written in 2003. George Daly has provided the technical support needed for this project to develop legs. But more importantly, he has been responsive to my ideas and provided me with valuable feedback over the years. This is the first time we have worked closely on a project and I suspect it won't be the last.

Confident Thinking is a book in a series on social, industrial and cultural psychology and organizational development.

I would also like to thank Chris Carlin, my Kindle editor at Amazon. com, who guided me through the process of updating and coordinating all my works for Amazon's Kindle library, and to Dr. Donald Farr for making people on the Farr (e-mail) Network aware of and supportive of my works.

TABLE OF CONTENTS

AUTHOR'S NOTE

THIS BOOK REPRESENTS the distillation of my experience with people at all levels of society, people who have demonstrated the ability to lead and to influence others. They have one thing in common: they think confidently. It is not by chance that 80% of the productive effort of any project is accomplished by 20% of the people. It is why the old maxim, *"If you want to get something done, assign it to the busiest person in the room,"* resonates.

Nevertheless, confident people are not immune to disappointment, surprise, failure, or even tragedy. They simply do not allow such circumstances to derail them, or provide an excuse for being stuck. They soldier on. They embrace misfortune, rather than retreat from it, with more resolve than ever to make a difference.

Personally, trials and tribulations have shown me the way to unlock the "will within," to serve as friend and not as enemy to myself; to see life as a whole, not as disparate parts.

Although the stages described here may appear elementary, they require resolve to carry them out. I don't say this smugly, but humbly as they have led to a creative and happy life for me, if not always an untroubled one.

These stages have been my own best friend, when I had few others. They have helped me to rebound when it seemed I was down for the count. Walt Whitman's cry, *"I am great,"* is not conceit, but that of every human spirit crying out to be heard to release the potential within.

The key to thinking confidently is keeping the rhythm of the heart and mind in harmony with one's essence and personality. These stages are meant to assist in making life worth living, knowing it takes more energy to be stuck than to go with the flow. It is true that we get in our own way more often than other people do. Alas, we are prone to erect barriers against non-existent threats, and to assume antagonisms simply because we have misread intentions. With *Confident Thinking*, you will be disinclined to entertain such false assumptions while your attitude will promote synergism. When that happens, the sky is your only limit.

James R. Fisher, Jr., Ph.D.
Tampa, Florida
July 4, 2017

CONFIDENT THINKING: A BRIDGE TO CONFIDENT ENGAGEMENT OF THE SELF

Confidence: self-trust is the essence of heroism.
—**Ralph Waldo Emerson**

Thinking is the talking of the soul with itself.
—**Plato**

To be empirical is to be guided by experience, not by sophists, charlatans, priests, and demagogues.
—**Philip Kerr**, American Novelist

KEYS TO DOING BUSINESS IN THE 21ST CENTURY

CONFIDENT THINKING IS a book that prepares a person to see situations clearly, so that problems may be defined accurately and the persistent confusion between self-demands (ego) and job demands (role) can be avoided. Everyone is in the selling business, whether it is the selling of an idea, a product or the value of their services. To that end, several keys are critical to success and satisfaction. These may be summarized as:

CONFIDENT THINKING

Confident Thinking engenders guiding sellers past their arrogance,

1

averting an adversarial contest with buyers by framing selling situations in a positive light with an opportunity to make a difference.

Confident Selling is a book I wrote during the confrontational climate of the 1970s, when the favorite bromide was "winning through intimidation." I rejected that premise then as counterproductive and counterintuitive, as I reject it now.

Confident Thinking in the selling situation is structured around intuitive listening, not talking; about observing, not demanding; being a student, not a schoolmaster; paying full attention to what the potential buyer says, judiciously separating "wants" from "needs," then tactfully moving the buyer towards what he needs, and can afford to satisfy his wants.

The most audacious proposition to *Confident Thinking* is that the obstacle to success in selling is the seller, not the buyer. Lack of confidence is quickly sensed by the buyer, which scuttles any likelihood of a sale. A corollary to this proposition is that everyone is engaged in creative selling regardless of profession or trade or the relationship. Thus success hinges on thinking confidently.

These rules of engagement were not gleaned from scholarly texts, but from life. Nor were they realized from staring into the mirror repeating, "I am confident, I am confident, I am confident." Confidence is garnered naturally as sellers and buyers move forward in a mutually beneficial partnership.

The much discussed game of selling is a stroll in the park if sellers have their feet planted firmly on the ground, and not creating unnecessary barriers to success. Failure is a product of the seller defining the selling situation poorly.

Confident Thinking can also be cultivated by judiciously dealing with problems within existing accounts. Competitors hear similar complaints to what you encounter routinely. Sensitivity to these issues can be raised during the selling narrative to get the buyer's attention, and then used in the problem solving to generate new business. The more insightful the seller is of the buyer's environment, the more attentive the buyer will be. This intelligence may include:

- Understanding the customer's business, history, culture, and operations.
- Recording complaints.
- Recording how complaints are handled.
- Recording time between reporting and addressing complaints.
- Recording complexity and chronic nature of complaints.
- Identifying source of these chronic problems.
- Assessing customer operating competence, and what can be done to improve that competence.
- Recording service history and relationship to those in charge.

Confident Thinking alerts the seller to every possible nuance of the sales call, and is pivotal to an exploration and evaluation of the buyer's current level of satisfaction. It represents listening with a "third ear," or the thinking level. "Listening" on this plain is essential, as a buyer seldom says what he means, but always means what he says.

SELLERS

Sellers, like everyone else, are handicapped when it comes to listening: 40 percent of our development is learning to talk; 60 percent is learning to read.

Listening is taken for granted. It is as if the skill could be acquired by osmosis. Consequently, most sellers, as with most people, are poor listeners. Listening demands those rare human characteristics: focus, attentiveness, emotional maturity and self-discipline.

With maturity comes control; with control comes *Confident Thinking*; and with that comes the advantage of perceptive listening.

So, for a situation to "listen well," the seller must listen with his whole body. This means using eyes, ears, hands, and posture as components of listening to display interest and attention. A word of caution: thinking too much can get in the way of how the situation feels, which is key to perceiving the situation accurately.

Although we are poor listeners, research indicates that most communication <u>before</u> the age of the Internet was 75 percent verbal and only 25 percent written. Now that everyone is tweeting, and texting, as well as writing e-mails that is all changing. Social networks in cyberspace are eclipsing those of face-to-face relationships, and changing the nature of human bonding.

Complicating the matter further, despite the emphasis previously on verbal, research indicates that 85 percent of communication person-to-person is taken through the eyes (nonverbal communication), and only 15 percent through the ears. In other words, it is not so much what we say person-to-person but how we say it that registers.

For sellers, this is daunting. They must see clearly, hear thoughtfully, and react suitably, trusting their minds and bodies to be alert to the vagaries in the situation. From the moment sellers come in contact with buyers, they must find their way past the white noise that is screaming in their ears. They must wear the personality of the place, and assess its geography and demography as if it were a garment. They must also become the place and space as if it resides in their subconscious. If this sounds absurd, think again.

Confident Thinkers feel everything before they think of anything. Feelings are facts in the selling situation as cognitive biases of the seller and buyer are on display if not formally addressed as such.

From their initial contact with the receptionist, security guard or secretary to the people they meet in the course of their contacts they are information gatherers. These data give them a sense of the place and space and what these psychosocial indicators are trying to tell them to enhance their confidence and competence.

Is the social climate of the buyer's environment relaxed, tense, anxious, frantic or self-important? The walls of the lobby talk. What are they saying? How is the lobby furnished? Does the lobby say, "Welcome," or does it say, "We don't need any." Is the lobby furnished for comfort and counsel, or is it saying we don't like visitors?

Emerson understood the language of silence. *"Who you are speaks so loudly I cannot hear what you're saying!"* Nothing in a place of business is a matter of chance. Everything is crying out to be understood. What it "feels like" is likely to be "what it is."

Sellers can check first impressions against what they experience as they meet the buyer and his people. Without perhaps realizing it, the seller's mind is busy processing information: (1) potential; (2) climate; (3) personnel; (4) opportunity; (5) treatment; and (6) readiness of the buyer for an order.

CONFIDENT LISTENING

A baseball player may get a hit only every third or fourth appearance at the plate, which is considered good, but he expects to hit every time. He contributes whenever he puts the ball into play, or advances the runner with a fly out or ground out. Likewise, the success ratio of sellers is likely to be even chancier, but they, too, are contributing when they move the selling dialogue closer to a sale.

These considerations are flooding sellers' minds. They must be ready, and trust their minds to process the information efficiently. They will if they are *Confident Thinking* students as are Major League baseball players' students of hitting knowing hitting a baseball is the hardest thing in sports.

The dedicated student becomes the *Confident Thinker* when he trusts his wits in the selling moment to not fail him, not unlike the baseball player. Once in the batter's box, he goes with the flow, stops consciously thinking, and allows instinct to take over. Trust me, it will not fail! Conversely, you can think too much, try to memorize a pitch, lose your natural flow, as well as your confidence and rhythm when being challenged. Then, seller and baseball player can become each other's own worst enemy.

The *Confident Thinker* knows valleys go with peaks, failure leads to success, and that most learning takes place on nonproductive plateaus, not while on the dizzying heights of hitting streaks. Ultimately, sellers need to trust their wits and training to put them in their *confident zone*, going with the flow with the mind and body working as one.

That will happen if sellers are open to experience, and sensitive to everything. No matter how the sales call goes, it is a learning experience. There is no such thing as a bad at bat in baseball or a bad sales call. Each is a learning experience and a new insight into what works and what does not in this professional journey. As long as the seller has the buyer's best interests at heart, sellers and buyers will be connected with good will evolving naturally.

We are all products of our programming. We cannot escape it. It will not get in our way if we accept and adjust to it with the understanding that problems and struggle are germane to all endeavors, but especially to selling and therefore should be embraced not avoided. That is the business of maintaining perspective.

CONFIDENT AND REALISTIC PERSPECTIVE

Once I was traveling with one of my men, who became engaged in an animated conversation with a man at a large construction site. The man was well dressed and friendly. He asked my associate for his business card. They exchanged cards and my associate nearly fainted.

The gentleman was chairman of the board of a Fortune 100 company. Large potential accounts intimidated my associate in general. This puzzled me because he was highly talented. It was the reason I was traveling with him. If only he could get his arms around his problem, I thought, he could be successful, but what was the problem?

The problem showed itself here. While first being intimidated by the stranger, the two of them talked on animatedly with each other for some time, as I walked away to give them some privacy.

Later, I asked him what had happened. His comment was matter-of-fact, "He's a Civil War buff like I am. We just hit it off:"

"I could see that," I said, "but what about you nearly fainting?"

No reply.

"He asked you to call on him in New York City, right?"

"Yes," he answered, "he's got some stuff he wants to show me."

"I don't think so," I said.

"No?"

"No," I repeated. "What other reason might he have?"

This completely threw him. He could not fathom a man of such status interested in working with him, personally. Yet, he allowed the CEO to display his Civil War knowledge without interruption, feeding the CEO lines to fuel his continuing commentary.

"You listened," I reminded him. "Didn't you notice?" I persisted. "You hardly spoke at all, feeding him questions that kept him excitedly on theme. You were selling. You could have embarrassed him but you didn't. You perceived him correctly. He likes being on stage, and considers himself a Civil War buff when we both know he isn't one compared to your repertoire."

Here was a seller who was easily intimidated by position power. This resulted in him making rote calls on high-end buyers while concentrating on low-enders without clout.

Even with the flicker of bias, the buyer senses it. My associate's demons did not show here because he was in a neutral zone (construction site) engaged in casual conversation on a subject of common interest (the American Civil War) with no decision-making requirement.

Did my associate experience an epiphany? I would like to say, yes, but that was not the case. He took his rapport with the CEO to be a fluke, and never followed up on a call to the man in New York City.

If a seller fails to recognize his cognitive biases, he cannot control them, and therefore may be penalized for them. Biases cannot be willed away because they are part of us, but they can be controlled. *This means accepting ourselves as we are, warts and all, while being aware and accepting of others as we find them.* Every interpersonal exchange no matter how incidental has the potential for hidden contamination when biases are not recognized and controlled, but instead summarily denied.

BEING AWARE AND ACCEPTING OF PERSONAL DEMONS

Success has a chronology as if it were a ticking clock telling us the time of day, only its chronology is telling us whether we are likely to succeed or fail in our appointed quest. Going through the mind of the buyer in the sales interview or the employer in the job interview is this chronology in descending order:

Am I comfortable with this person?

- Can I see my people and myself working with this person?
- Will this person's talent fit comfortably with what we are already doing?
- Is this person technically qualified?

This is 180 degrees out of phase with how the seller is trained and how the buyer imagines he thinks. Indeed, it is 180 degrees out of phase with how the job seeker prepares for the position interview and how the employer believes he evaluates personnel. How could this be?

Clash between personalities are emotional for buyer and seller, interviewer and interviewee. Buyers and employers, sellers and job seekers are not trained in emotional intelligence, but in cognitive or thinking intelligence, and so dutifully they plod straight ahead. Often, failure in this arena is mask in hyperbole or rationalizing.

The myth persists that competence matters most, when as improbable as it may seem competence is more often a subjective bias than an objective value. That is why high-tech salespeople are often poor sellers. They believe the mind is dominant, when emotion invariably controls the game. Stated another way, it is the buyer's competence the seller uses to mutual advantage by writing the script and then letting the buyer take center stage as its author.

The seller who recognizes this progression will work his magic by creating comfort, developing trust, establishing rapport, and finally, securing a solid account. Benefits will then accrue to both buyer and seller.

If the seller isn't able to establish a trusting climate the buyer is likely to become resentful towards sellers in general, stereotyping them as untrustworthy exploiters. Despite all the rhetoric to the contrary, comfort, fit, and competence are in sequential order and this never changes. It is a matter of subjective trust.

CONFIDENT UNDERSTANDING OF THE CHRONOLOGY OF SUCCESS

Traditional sales training focuses on the company, its products, and the seller's technical competence, failing to see these as ancillary requirements to the seller's psychological proficiency. The seller must be able to read buyers. To be able to read buyers, he must first be able to read himself. Technical competence is essential, but will produce nothing if the seller is unable to establish rapport with buyers.

My initial orientation was intensive technical training in chemical technology, company products and services, but not an hour on how to approach buyers other than to wow them to death with the company's place in the industry and its technical competence.

That, incidentally, is how confidence became the script and narrative of my first book, *Confident Selling* (1971).

As customer, these same "technical dandies" endeavored to dazzle me with their technical brilliance without ever asking me what I needed. They assumed they knew without any probing, conducting the sales interview as "buying consultants," not as sellers at all. When that happens, it is a case of "self-demands" (ego) overriding the "role demands" (the job) of the selling situation.

It is impossible for the selling situation to be defined clearly when self-demands rule—"Do you see who I am? I am a buying consultant."—over role demands—"What do you need? How can I help you?"

It is because of this misplaced emphasis that *Confident Thinking* is

9

focused on the seller—on the person who intends to persuade someone to think or behave differently—not on the buyer.

When the seller is leading with his chin and worried about how he is being perceived, the buyer becomes a mirror to that obsession and sees only the buyer's wants and not the buyer's needs.

With role demands (the job at hand), the focus is on the buyer, but not as an obstacle. Selling handbooks imply the buyer is an obstacle—that artificial contrivances must be employed to get the order by emphasizing the penalty for delay, limited availability, a time-bound special offer—none of which require reading the buyer's current mood or pressing needs.

The buyer provides many clues to readiness to buy during the course of a sales call if the seller remains attentive. The seller who is tied up with contrived approaches is hardly likely to recognize these signals, being preoccupied with making the sale, and not on solving the buyer's problem.

Sellers and buyers are not adversaries. They are partners. Partners must first be comfortable and trusting of each other before they can move on to the problem-solving. When the seller assaults the buyer with charm and knowledge, overwhelming him with his war dance, any success, at best, will be short lived. *The seller needs to build a bridge of trust to establish a pathway to loyalty.*

Given these parameters, is it any wonder that the introvert is more likely to be successful in selling in this 21st century? Introverts are unlikely to have a mesmerizing dance to camouflage a fragile ego; or harbor the necessity to appear as Mr. (or Ms.) Know-it-all. They simply treat all buyers with respect; and for this attention, they generate respect. Introspection is in their toolkit so that they see, listen, and act in accordance with the situation which is well defined.

CASE STUDY: WOODY ALLEN SYNDROME

Nalco Chemical Company assembled its young managers at the remote and rustic setting of Starved Rock State Park in LaSalle-Peru, Illinois for a historic conference. Nalco was a small company on the move.

It was the mid-1960s. It had taken Nalco Chemical Company thirty years from its inception to reach $60 million in sales, but was now soaring in post-World War II international business. The question being asked: could Nalco reach $1 billion dollars in sales? The question produced an electric climax. Little did participants know that company sales would soar well into the multi-billions of dollars in much less time than it took to reach $60 million.

In that atmosphere, after dinner one evening, the national sales manager was holding court in a corner of the huge meeting room, surrounded by his adoring acolytes. They were four deep, spellbound by his every word.

He was the prototype of the charismatic leader, six five, 260, tall, dark and handsome with a crew cut, a news anchor's voice, and a hearty laugh that made the glassware quiver on the meeting room tables. He had been a bomber pilot at 19 in WWII and before that a Big Ten football player at Purdue. His command of language electrified like fireworks in the mind. No wonder he was treated like a prophet.

My friend and I were not part of the group. We were sitting diagonally across the room a distance of 50 feet away sipping coffee observing this scenario. Finally, my friend said, **"I'll** never make it with this outfit."

I asked him why. "Can you imagine me being Tex?" I started to laugh. I got the giggles so bad I was getting a stomach ache.

This caused the mountain across the room, to stop in mid-sentence. All heads turned towards us accusingly as if we were infidels. I had interrupted the soliloquy of the mountain. Obediently, I raised my hand, palm up, in apology, with heads first looking at me with scorn, then turning back in unison to the droning staccato of their leader.

My friend said, "What was that all about?"

"I had the incredible thought of Tex trying to be you," I said. My friend was small of stature, slim of physique, quiet with a small shrill sounding voice that was not much above sotto voce, and an introspective disposition. Although he was only thirty, he was already losing his hair, wore thick glasses that made him look like

Woody Allen, and seemingly, moved with exertion.

He was offended. "Thanks a lot! I needed that!"

"Oh, no!" I added. "I meant no offense."

"Look at him," I said, "he's a poster boy extraordinaire, true, but only two-dimensional. You're the real deal, flesh and blood in three dimensions. You've outsold the poster boy when he was in the field ten to one. That's a fact." I made it my business to know such things.

My friend had no idea how Tex had climbed the executive ladder. He didn't want to know. He took what he saw as the personification of excellence. It wasn't. He didn't know that Tex never sold, or that he had a mentor who had greased his skids. The irony is that his mentor was the mild mannered executive vice president who closely resembled my friend. Apparently, the vice president felt he needed the charismatic fire that Tex exuded to complement his own low-key personality.

My friend left me that night wounded still believing I had stuck a sword in his side, and then twisted it. Obviously, he recovered. He did leave the company, joined a competitor, and no surprise to me, and rose to become CEO. I've always wondered if he found himself a Tex as a direct report.

The Woody Aliens of the world, rule, but often off stage. There is no reason to emulate what we are not, or to apologize for what we are.

THE POWER OF CRITIQUES

The simple habit of critiquing every sales call—good, bad or indifferent—drawing on immediate impressions, can be of greater benefit than any book read, guru favored, or training program attended. Ultimately, the sales strategy that works for each one of us is self-invented.

When the customer visit is fresh in the seller's mind, a few words scribbled in a diary can become priceless later. Our written words leap out at us with patterns, themes, chronic problems, and opportunities revealed in cold appraisal. The mind is cool and the heart is calm once it is restored to its normal rhythm. Time is not only a healer, then, but a revealer as well.

Words stare back that had been written in the heat of the moment revealing hidden meanings. They transmit messages to the mind to make known what lies beyond the hurt, wounded pride, humiliation, confusion, defeat, embarrassment, or, indeed, euphoria, each experienced during a surprisingly successful sales call. These puzzling pieces form patterns to reveal clear pictures of what works and what doesn't, when and why. Seeing the sales call in cool retrospective can become like footprints, tracking along the road to success. Anyone, of course, in any field can use this disciplined strategy to advantage.

A WORK IN PROGRESS: NAPKIN MANIA AND ITS USES

When I was a field sales manager traveling with one of my more receptive men, I would critique the sales call immediately afterwards, as we would retire to a coffee shop, writing on napkins a summary of my observations.

He confessed to me in a letter years later that he retained this stack of napkins, which had grown to several inches high. "I've referred to your napkin mania over the years," he said, "and now find I use the mania to train my people."

My aim with the napkin sales critique was to impress on the seller the fact that we carry our geography with us, and no one more so than the buyer. By keeping these napkin notes, and obviously referring to them from time to time, this seller-now-manager appreciated them as clues to buyer motivation, which he now was sharing with his people.

The implicit behavior in any operation may be interpreted as favoring some type of culture: that is, a culture of comfort, complacency or contribution. Data observed will be consistent with one of these cultures, while the buyer's conduct may or may not be. The seller's job is not to pass judgment on the culture, or the buyer, but to use that information in the best interest of a buying decision.

There is always the matter of how the buyer wants to be perceived. Again, the buyer's geography may be consistent or not with the cultural context, geography and demographics of his particular workplace. Keeping notes on this clarifies the matter considerably with many possible options of how best to utilize it.

Books, certificates, mementoes, honors, trophies, personal albums, type and condition of furniture, location of office, and its arrangement all have meaning to the buyer. It can be quickly gleaned as to whether this is a workplace or a shrine. Without a word being said, the seller can undress the buyer as a person. Capturing the essence of a place avoids bouncing off the walls of resistance in unproductive chatter and being no wiser for the punishment. Buyers, like all of us, telegraph their identities. The *Confident Thinker* covets this intelligence to mount their case.

A WORK IN PROGRESS: HE WHO HESITATES IS NOT ALWAYS LOST!

When I was a seller calling on a General Electric facilities manager with my area manager, his office reminded me of such a personal shrine. Not only were university degrees prominently on display but an honorary degree as well.

Before I could adjust to this exhibit, he declared, "Son, give me your spiel," then turned his swivel chair around with his back facing us and proceeded to clip his fingernails. Not only was this rude, but his office, I thought, was pretentious to the extreme. I had a fiery disposition, which I kept under control by my note taking among other devices. My mind raced as I scribbled in my notebook, looking up and thinking the furnishings were more appropriate for a chief executive officer than a facilities manager.

For fully ninety seconds, I did not say a word and motioned to my area manager with my hand to support my silence. He nodded. Ninety seconds of silence in a sales call is an eternity. Finally, the buyer turned his chair around, and in a stern voice, as if he were a principal addressing a troubled student, said, "What seems to be your problem, young man?"

I replied, "Apparently, we caught you at a bad time. I would like to reschedule when you have time to give us your full attention."

He came back with a curious grin just short of a smile, but an expression clearly devoid of anger, "What if that is never?"

I fed those exact words back to him; "What if that is never?"

Again, I sat in silence. Meanwhile, my area manager was dying. But I was unwavering. Looking the GE manager in the eye, I waited.

He shook his head, looked to my area manager for support, who turned away, put down his nail clipper, and said, "Set it up with my secretary."

I said, thank you and we left.

The critique of that call was simple: prospect arrogant, cut his nails, no respect, office his shrine, need to find another way, find George, made appointment but seems little point in following up.

My area manager looked over my shoulder at my scribbling, and said, "How do you make sense of that?" I said I always enlarge upon these notes at the end of the day in my motel room, and, yes, they make sense, and are helpful.

Before my next GE call, I did some intelligence gathering, and found that the facilities manager was not George, or the person who could buy. The facilities manager was an administrator in power plant facilities, a paper pusher who processed requests from the line, but had no clout in operations.

Two other bits of information were learned as well: he was intimidated by technical people, and was embittered having been passed over for promotion several times. This was learned from the chief engineer who was "George." I was allowed to call on him on the subsequent call. I didn't get an order on that call, but he was quite accommodating, and the prospects looked good.

What was the source of the information on "George" and the nail clipper?

A telephone call was made to the director of engineering. He was asked technical questions on power plant operations, politely referring me to the chief engineer. I have found executives are quite amenable to sloughing off such queries to men in their line of command.

Over time, I realized the higher the position in the hierarchy the more aware office holders are of the power of public relations. Customer complaints that arrive on a CEO's desk send reverberations throughout the company. I made it clear to the director of engineering that I was encountering difficulty. It worked. Every seller knows this but, in my experience, few use it as a tool to make the correct connections.

Clearly, the nail clipper was not a friend of the chief engineer's, and the latter showed no hesitation to pour scorn on the reputation of this manager. This alerted me to the fact that this facility of some 10,000 employees stretching over two square miles of plant facilities was a culture of innuendo, nitpicking, personality assassination, and rumor, or the culture of complacency, masquerading as the culture of contribution.

It took me several years to fully realize how prevalent this was, but the pattern was there in my notes in those early days of my career. Few things are as they seem, and when they aren't, it behooves the seller to use his ingenuity to find out why.

THE CASSANDRA EFFECT

In Greek mythology, Cassandra was the daughter of Priam, King of Troy. She was endowed with the gift of prophecy from the god Apollo. The problem for Cassandra was that she was never believed. Something of that nature has been my experience in this business of *Confident Thinking* and *Confident Selling*.

It was natural for me to use this strategy as I had created the terms. Yet, I am not surprised that my colleagues those many years ago saw my success as a matter of luck and pluck, and not skill at all as it was considered counterintuitive.

Admittedly, the emphasis in *Confident Thinking* is counterintuitive as it insists the way to the seller's success is to embrace his fears, for then the buyer will have little recourse but to suspend his suspicions and trust him. The veil of distrust vanishes when we first trust ourselves. It is called sincerity.

When I made presentations on this approach to sales professionals and managers many years ago, it was considered too abstract and too much of a radical departure from traditional adversarial selling, or selling by intimidation. The palpable reality today in the selling equation is not the buyer, as adversary, but the seller, who inadvertently establishes imaginary barriers or obstacles to his selling success.

Adversarial selling involves overwhelming the buyer with benefits, finessing objections, and seeking the order with a manipulative close, at variance with this intuitive approach. Selling, today, with enlightened buyers is a process with the outcome a natural flow that finds the seller and buyer on the same page with a similar objective, the solving of a problem.

The audience for *Confident Selling* did not appear until 1970 when my book of that title was first published. Now, in the early 21st century *Confident Thinking* becomes the bridge to *Confident Selling,* which means the *Cassandra Effect* is being tested once again. The old adage appears to still apply, when the student is ready, the teacher will arrive. He is here.

CONFIDENT THINKING
CREATIVE STAGE ONE

BELIEVE IN YOURSELF COMPLETELY HAVE FAITH IN YOUR ABILITY TO DO WHAT YOU DESIRE AND DESIRE WHAT YOU DO!

A wise man will desire no more than he may get justly, use soberly, distribute cheerfully, and leave contentedly. The passions and desires, like the two twists of a rope, mutually mix one with the other, and twine inextricably round the heart; producing good, if moderately indulged; but certain destruction if suffered to become inordinate.

Richard E. Burton, Nineteenth Century American Author

THE REGIMENTATION

FROM OUR EARLIEST memory we are doing what others tell us to do and what these significant others tell us is important, not only to do but what to think. Consequently, there is little time to know the rhythm of our own hearts.

Added to this is the constant bombardment of television, which subliminally and aggressively engages our attention, creating desire for what is packaged in a way to make "whatever" most wanted. If this were not enough, we are now exposed to the Internet, and handheld electronic devices with digital games that have nonsense caricatures of aggression, intended to energize our animal instincts, to crush, plunder, destroy, and punish those characters the electronic designers have declared the enemy. All this is such innocent fun until it becomes translated into community violence, insensitive to life, limb and property.

If this were not enough, noise has been declared music; noise that its creators insist is art. This destroys our eardrums and bombards our senses with bad language and even worse images offensive to the nature of human, loving, caring, and innocent beings.

The discordant constant is that we grow old, never finding time to grow up, seeking refuge in noise, games, drugs and other excesses, remaining unreceptive to the music of Mother Nature; singing birds, chirping insects, the patter of rain, or clouds dancing in the sky.

We are made a stranger to ourselves almost from the moment of birth, responding to the agenda of others, who claim they have our best interests at heart, when all too often it is only their own. They place us in a cage of their good intentions, and we wonder why we cannot smile or find the gumption to walk out of it. There are many clues as to why.

We are thirsty sponges for all this attention, for all this instruction, for all this noise and pontification. We think our motivation is love when it is only counter dependence. It differs little with the wild birds who are fed by tourists, eventually losing their instinct to forage for their own food. We absorb it all, without complaint or comprehension, docile and agreeable unable to be otherwise.

We are amorphous tissue and bone molded into form susceptible to the popular norms of our time supplied in nurturing care by those we love, respect, fear and admire as if we have no will of our own.

Consequently, much of our early training has a tinge of anxiety to it, not because of what and who we are, which is not clear to us, but because significant others unwittingly cause us to be anxious.

They have their reputation, which is already established, and we are meant in our innocence to protect that reputation by proxy as willing indiscriminate sponges, giving attention to their biases and then treating them as if our own. So, the first breakdown in belief in self is suffered before we know what that means.

Much is made when we first walk, talk, or show mental or physical dexterity. Likewise, concern is shown when we seem self-centered with little evidence of altruistic inclination. We are expected to be or approximate mirror images of our DNA elders.

Self-interest and aggression are discouraged, when self-interest and aggression are the foundation of confident thinking in terms of belief in oneself.

Well-meaning though these significant others may be, they introduce us to a cultural disease: "compare and compete". It has crippled our civilization producing dull, imitative, insensitive, mediocre, burned-out and stereotyped individuals who are devoid of initiative, imagination, originality and spontaneity.

Great art, philosophy, music, literature and science have been created by the exception not the rule. Albert Einstein turned physics on its head after it had been coasting for 300 years. Technology has replaced art, philosophy, music, literature and science with all that is deemed new piggybacking on what was invented long before.

So, almost from the beginning of our consciousness, we are aware of how well someone else does something and how poorly we do the same. Our attention is not only other-directed but approval as well. We must search for what is important instead of allowing it to surface naturally in us, something that is buried deep in our soul, crying out to be heard.

We are instructed to be friendly, not shown how to be our own best friend. We are told how important love is but exposed to the constant drum roll of sex and eroticism, which has little to do with love. We are told to seek freedom from fear but never to embrace it, which is the only way freedom can be realize. We are told to seek perfection, but creativity is derived from our imperfection. We are reminded that to be alone is the nature of loneliness and leads to depression, when one is never alone if comfortable in one's own company. We are told greed is need, when it is insatiable want. Greed can never be satisfied, but need can. We are conditioned to fear death, when it is life we fear. How could we fear death when it is unknown? We are conditioned to be polite, never to be candid, insinuating it is better to lie, thereby alienating us from own selves.

THE BREAKING FREE

We are constantly reminded that we ought to become this or that, and not to be satisfied with just being ourselves. We're counseled that progress is our most important product. This never gives us time to be content, and being content is the only place happiness can be found. Yet "happiness" has become a pejorative that we should avoid like the plague, even while it is celebrated. We must constantly be "becoming," never arriving.

Becoming lives alongside the illusion o-f progress. It is ambitious, yearns to be loved, depends on the approval of others, feels emotionally drained, craves rewards, and performs for pay, dancing to the company tune, while living on borrowed time with borrowed money.

On the other hand, "being" lives comfortably in our own skin. Reality is its home, where it owes nothing to others; nothing to achieve to earn their approval; no need to demonstrate our wor-thiness of their attention; nowhere to go but where we are, no concern about "Big Brother's" watchful eye, and no head in any dimension of society higher than our own. Our friends and relatives, peers and acquaintances compete and compare with us, as do our parents, teachers and siblings. Competing starts at an early age. It first happens in our home, then in school, then on the playground, as we quickly establish the relativity of skills among our playmates. Unfortunately, such assessments are based on narrow parameters of our potential. If magnified early on, we may never grow into ourselves. What others decide we are may not be best for us or even true. We may end up reproving ourselves for the neglect of our potential.

If we are slow of foot or hand, don't see well, or don't have good hand-eye coordination, peers will be quite perceptive of these shortcomings, and painfully so, choosing us last when in games, or not choosing us at all. In a strange way, this may become our salvation, as we have little choice but to become acquainted with ourselves.

The pitfall, however, is that we may drift towards others equally spurned but without insight into their gifts. This is not a time to brood or think of ourselves as losers, or be obsessed with the winners who rejected us. We are all winners only different.

The bigger game is taking place inside us. It has a rhythm and range, a character and composition unique to us and to those whom we have drifted. The mark of our individuality is stamped on us, and we have the opportunity to find out what it is telling us.

When we become preoccupied with others, who and what they are, compared to who and what we are, adolescent jealousy may surface. Realistically, some allowance must be made for this angst when we are young.

Jealousies will eventually go away, but envy never dies. To envy someone is to willingly poison our heart, inflicting a lasting scar on our psyche, an embittering lifetime mindset.

Among individuals so inclined, there is a tendency from the youngest age, throughout one's entire life, to exaggerate the coveted qualities of others, whatever they may be, always at the expense of those we possess, but take for granted.

One thing is certain; great people also have great weaknesses. No one escapes his or her weaknesses. No one. Great people make headlines when their greatness becomes public knowledge. We expect our heroes to be less human than we are, when they tend to be more than human, meaning more flawed. They are more self-interested, greater risk takers, and more ambitious. They fight constant wars with their demons and these battles sublimate into greatness. It is because not despite their demons that they are great.

Some buy into their own celebrity, basking in their greatness, taking their genius to be self-evident when the talent they possess is God given, as it is with us all. God has a sense of humor. He inserts in their bonnet unsavory temptations that play on their self-ignorance and lead to their undoing.

People of tremendous ability must also battle tremendous demons. If these demons are not monitored, they inevitably lead to disaster and despair.

Greatness is the play of the angels and demons of our nature clashing in creative verve. Without this thunder, nothing of consequence would find the light of day. So, it is advisable for us to be charitable to the most gifted among us, because the war these people fight every day is a war that would humble most of us very quickly.

People we deem "great," who manage to somehow earn such recognition, are the same people who learn at an early age to hide what they are not. They bury their misgivings, their fears of being inadequate, frauds or pretenders, yet, at the same time, excelling despite themselves. They are always as surprised as we are at their success.

Fame makes them easy targets for sycophants who magnify their strengths and minimize their weaknesses. That is why celebrities are often found to have clay feet, buying into their celebrity as a manifestation of themselves when it is only a facade. The focus while on strengths away from weaknesses belies the fact that celebrities are more like us than you might imagine.

They step out of the ordinary to appear extraordinary, succeeding in promoting idolatry, envy and jealousy. We compare ourselves and compete with an image that is not only unreal but also surreal. We are seduced by an image of a person we don't know and most likely will never meet, at the expense of discovering and developing our precious uniqueness.

In a celebrity culture, nothing is what it seems as others define everything that should matter, making strangers rich and famous and adoring them for the attention. Celebrity worship is a sickness, but it becomes a cultural norm when the majority subscribes to it.

DESIRE IN THE DOUBLE BIND JUNGLE OF WANT

Confident Thinking recognizes that we must cut through this baffling obsession to discover what we desire. Desire is a most noble aspect of confident thinking. It is made problematical by the fact that we often want what we don't need, and need what we don't want. When desire is driven by want, there is never enough. Want, as greed can never be fulfilled. It always wants more.

Want is a hole in the psyche, a prison of self-en-cage-ment. Want is the road to self-destruction. Often, want is never satisfied until it destroys everyone and everything that is near and dear. Want is the constant mantra of the advertiser, the pundit, the television guru, and the criminal. Want is the separation of the soul from the body the bottomless pit between yesterday and tomorrow with no bridge to today.

Want is the double bind and wishful behavior of the imma- ture individual running into unquenchable demand.

This occurs when we look for others to fight our battles, to carve our paths for us through the hostile wilderness of life. Conversely, when we volunteer to do for others what they might best do for themselves; we make them dependent and enduring emotional cripples. This is so because we weaken their resolve and devalue them as persons. The same holds true for us if we allow someone else to carry our burden. Only we can carry our load, for we created it by our choices.

The double bind of want destroys. This is the double bind that fills our hospitals with lifestyle complaints. This is the double bind that enslaves the mind. This is the double bind that has delusions of grandeur.

- The enslaved mind is *passive-receptive*. It sees itself becoming a "big shot", whereas a free mind is active-productive and creative.

- The enslaved mind takes; the free mind gives.

- The enslaved mind pleads to get its way; the free mind takes the initiative.

- The enslaved mind seeks security by conforming; the free mind is non-attached.

- The enslaved mind is obsessed with the superiority-infe- riority mindset; the free mind has no desire to impress and puts no one on a pedestal.

- The enslaved mind has placed its center-of-gravity in others; the free mind's center-of-gravity is within.

- The enslaved mind follows rules to the nth degree no matter how ridiculous; the free mind uses its discretionary powers to validate the rules.

- The enslaved mind imitates; the free mind improvises.

- The enslaved mind is impressed by appearances; the free mind sees only reality, which cuts through the facade.

The double bind of the enslaved mind is like a coyote chasing two rabbits at once, going in opposite directions, whereas the free mind is like water that can flow into and around everything regardless of shape or size. It fits into anything.

The free mind can best be illustrated by the fact that it manipulates circumstances as called for, as well as things, but not people. The free mind refuses to trap itself in old forms, traditions, customs, and programming. It understands that its programming is the culprit that enslaves.

So, it follows that want is the ultimate punishment of self-haters. They strive "to please others," and never do, with little inclination to understand much less please themselves. Want is a cagey game of self-deception, thinking they are pleasing themselves when they attempt to be envied as they have envied, or try to emulate someone they admire at the expense of being themselves, whom they hate. They are perfect fodder for the advertiser, the con, the flatterer, the sycophant, and the bully.

Need is fundamental to existence and is fed by natural desire. We need food, shelter, clothing, human contact, love and work, but want separates us into groups, classes, categories, and classifications. Advertisers know this, housing developers know this, social architects of culture know this, and so we imitate those we envy most by conforming to their tastes, only on a reduced economic scale often at the expense of our heritage, customs, culture, and nature.

Now, every large city looks the same, every village the same, every new community the same. Every place looks like every other place; everyone dresses like everyone else dresses, everyone eats what everyone else eats, everyone works where everyone else works doing what everyone else is doing, and everyone mates and marries or relates to others like everyone else does.

Even the least expensive car looks like the most expensive car; the least expensive clothes look like the most expensive clothes. When need becomes synonymous with want, there is no longer originality, no longer authenticity, no longer real contact with anything that is real. It is an artificial existence spinning out of control in an artificial world spinning into oblivion, and no one seems to notice because the focus is always on the spinning and not on the spinner.

There is no possibility of Confident Thinking when what we are doing is not what we desire to be doing, but is only what we think we want to do, believing want is legitimate when want is always someone else's idea that we bought into a long time ago and now think it is part of us. The evidence of the falsity of want with natural desire is when we are never happy where we are. If we needed to be doing something else, desire would place overwhelming pressure on us to be doing it.

Don't confuse organizational pyramid climbers with doers. Climbing is a full-time and all-out proposition in which there is no time to do, only time to take credit for what others do. Climbers are obsessed with getting to the top. They are hungry and full of want. They were born wanting; they live for want fulfillment; and they will die wanting still more. If you were to ask them, what their purpose in life is, they would say, "to get to the top." But that is not a purpose. That is a want. They do not know nor want to know why they climb. They just do.

Doers do not seek anything. They are builders. They create and shape their own world inside themselves, which has little resemblance to the world outside. They could be billionaires but it was never their desire to be billionaires. It was their desire to create something good for the world. They explore, discover, produce and build out of the fullness and independence of their desire. They live in a state of excitement as they press to the horizon to discover the unfolding of the unknown. They believe in themselves and that is their secret.

James R. Fisher, Jr., PhD.

CONFIDENT THINKING
CREATIVE STAGE TWO

**BELIEVE IN WHAT YOU ARE DOING
BELIEVE YOU POSSESS THE ABILITY
TO SOLVE YOUR OWN PROBLEMS
BELIEVE OTHERS CAN SOLVE THEIR
PROBLEMS WITH YOUR HELP**

From the big dawn until now, every single advance in civilization was made by an individual acting outside of the influence of the social controls of the tribe.

—William L. Livingston III,
American Inventor and Author

THE HAZARDS OF A SECOND HAND LIFE

IT IS SO easy to become the victim to our own destiny by falling into a job, a career, a lifestyle, a relationship, or situation that has little to do with what we desire and are capable of doing.

It is so easy to go with the flow and never take inventory of where we are, or how we got there. It is as if it just happened. Knowing and taking charge is preamble to understanding what gives satisfaction, pleasure, and purpose. Psychic energy may be enslaved to incentives to seek gain without the pain of making choices.

It is so easy to fill our consciousness with everyone else's information until there is no space left for our essence. The more astute approach is to treat the mind as an unwritten transcript unfolding to a life as we write it.

It is so easy to imagine others have answers to our life and how it should be directed, packing our minds with facts, sermons, lectures, and solutions. This is reflected in television talking heads and evangelists. We are looking for answers in all the wrong places, confusing what we want with what we need. Psychologist Adam Phillips puts it succinctly:

> *Whenever we have too much. It is because there is too little of what we need; whenever we have too little it is because there is too much of what we don't need.*

We have had a surfeit of television confections, now a surfeit of information on the Internet. Nothing makes for excess more than the excessive; nothing is more addictive than habit. The Internet and the wonder of handheld electronic devices are now superseding the habit of television. We have replaced one excess with another.

It is so easy to run into the wall of bad habits and to depend on outside authority to figure out what is wrong, relying on this dependency to come up with miraculous solutions. But within each of our problems is the right solution for us. It will not be the right solution for another person's problem because that person is not walking in our moccasins or putting its foot into our stream. Others can help us define our problem but they cannot solve it for us. Nor would it wise for us to rush to a solution without first examining the problem. Conversely, we cannot own other people's problems, because it weakens them and their resolve to make the effort to solve them.

IT STARTS WITH AWARENESS

Most everyone reaches a point in their life when they sense that their conditioning is not serving them. Beliefs adopted without questioning their bases can lead to deep -rooted misconceptions. These misconceptions perpetuate bad habits. People tell themselves that they must change; that they must root out their misconceptions, but then they turn to a guru.

It doesn't work that way. We cannot alter ourselves until we are first aware, then accepting, and self-directing ourselves through a series of choices to unlearn what we have learned, or mistaken for certainties. We must de-condition ourselves and break free of our dependency. Bad habits are not something we grow out of but something we grow into. They tell us more about ourselves than we want to know.

If we are smokers, we must avoid others who smoke, or situations that recreate the dependency. We cannot expect the problem to be resolved by wearing a patch, taking a pill, or making a New Year's resolution. This is kidding ourselves. We must destroy the compulsion to smoke before the old crutch has a chance to re-ignite.

The same goes for alcohol, or any other dependency. The dependency has become a friend, a void-filler, when there is no other. A person who gives up drinking or smoking or taking drugs is suddenly and shockingly faced with emptiness. The smoker doesn't know what to do with his hands; the drinker doesn't know how to spend his leisure time; and the recreational drug taker doesn't know how to deal with routine.

Wearing a patch, taking a pill, or drinking non-alcoholic beverages doesn't work because the addicted person is filled to the brim with old conditioning and these bad habits. Before anything can be done, this old garbage must be dumped. Otherwise, these pain-free prescriptions are being poured into an already overflowing cup, and therefore have little effect other than cosmetic. We must help ourselves.

We must never feel we are unable to help ourselves. Never. We must never believe we are in a situation that is too overwhelming, or too demanding that we feel helpless and lonely, fearful and despairing, because if we do, it will be. And then we are lost.

Do you know when panic sets in? Panic sets in when we lose confidence in ourselves, listen to everyone with answers to our dilemma, and begin to run in all directions for an escape from the threat of pressing events. We become obsessed with self. We peel this onion in a bed of self-pitying tears, until there is nothing left to peel, only to discover the onion has no center, like our self. There is no core. There is only the anxiety produced in the peeling, which gets us further and further from the source of the problem, which is lack of self-trust.

UNLEARNING EMOTIONAL DEPENDENCE

Where do we find self-trust? We find it in helping others with similar problems, not lecturing or judging them, that we become more accepting and trusting of ourselves. Through service to others, life becomes personally fulfilling and satisfying.

It is not in running from fear that peace is found, but in embracing what we fear. The eye of the hurricane is the location of total calm. Likewise, the quiet mind free of thought and the chaos of the world around is where peace is found. What prevents us from getting to that center?

A frenzied technological life has made things more important than people, where illusion is more appealing than direct experience, where life is lived increasingly mythically in cyberspace. Long before the technological revolution, Thoreau saw people of his era, the early nineteenth century, living lives of quiet desperation. Sociologist Peter Berger coined the expression, "the homeless mind" to depict the dilemma facing modern man. Does modern life condemn us to this desperation, this homelessness? Is there no escape? Are we perennial victims of a hostile world, or does each of us have an equal chance for happiness regardless of the accident of our birth, wealth, learning, race, religion or nationality?

The short answer is that most everyone can find their way if they will unlearn whatever habits perpetuate their dismal outlook on life and engage in work that gives them personal satisfaction. Anthropologist Karen Armstrong points out that the scientific and secular culture, the heart of modernity, have dismantled traditional values that had been our anchors. Despite this, self-realization is possible and even probable.

One of the blessings of the mind is that what pleases us the most in work is something that we are interested in and can do reasonably well. All honest work is worthwhile, and when the match between the worker and the work is positive, it is love made visible.

A belief in what we are doing allows us to go beyond the destructive dichotomy of success and failure. Most of us gravitate to where we are most comfortable and content. We get there often through a circuitous route, but we do get there. Once we get there, the only thing that can destroy us is the driving need to get ahead and become somebody else. Some people are so blinded by this illusion that they cannot imagine anything else but an endless struggle to get ahead. There is no time for contentment, and therefore there is no capacity for peace.

When we imagine we are failures, it is usually because we decide we have not risen as high as Jane or Joe. We live in the compare and compete world of what Yeats describes as, "the rag-and-bone-shop of the heart."

Again, to keep us always on edge and ill-at-ease, we spend more than we make, living beyond our means, burning the candle at both ends, pressing hard to outrun boredom. Success is a thing, like a new car, a new house, a new career, a new mate, a new job, a new location, always a thing, but never an improved sense of reality. We are trapped in a cage of our own making the victim of wishful thinking, believing that there is an idealized state just beyond where we are and where we belong.

What does this have to do with believing in what we do? The answer is everything. The heart is more reliable than the head when it comes to choosing a career. There is a simple formula that may prove useful:

First, look at your greatest interest, not analytically, but as a matter of record, of the patterns your life has demonstrated. The early interests of an individual have much to say about what that great interest will be. Conditioning may have driven him away from those interests, suggesting he ought to be a medical doctor rather than a writer, only because most doctors are known to make a good living, while writers can struggle. This suggestion can create confusion along with self-negation. A person can change only if he embraces the demons of his past and accepts them for what they are, the remnants of an imperfect childhood, now to be left behind. The individual is in charge. Always remember, the child is the father of the man. The child lives within but the man must now think as an adult, not as a child. He must now solve problems by defining them clearly putting aside childish behavior and the aimless ways of youth. His interests are real and will speak loudly to him, if he will simply listen to them.

Second, validate your true interests by considering how much time you give to these interests daily, weekly, and monthly. The time committed establishes a representative pattern consistent with these interests. There is a certain security in our interests. So much so that it is difficult to persuade us to reason against them even if they are harmful. Such interests come to mind as reckless lifestyles where prudence has no traction. Interests launch all virtues and vices into motion. Self-interests and the pursuit of them has been the main revolution of our society since its conception. Interests have made some people quick witted and others blind. When our interests are at variance with our occupation, any premise that would seek to rationalize them satisfies a hollow heart. So, there must be balance between interests and how they benefit or defeat our purpose as contributing human beings.

Third, identify your primary and secondary interests, and establish the amount of time you have devoted to their pursuit; categorize them in terms of your satisfaction from greatly to moderately to occasionally satisfying. Ask yourself what was particularly satisfying and how sustaining was the satisfaction? It is as if first principles reign supreme when it comes to interests because interests that fail to sustain us, no matter how much we delight in them, will ultimately drain us.

Be ready for surprises because few people realize how much time they spend on nonsense interests, interests that could derail a satisfying and productive career.

Oftentimes, sensible and flippant concerns seem to be on a collision course. Things done are done because "I have to" rather than "I need to." There is a natural reluctance "to take charge," preferring "to go with the flow," and drift into a lifestyle and work without direction or purpose or consequence. A facetious belief is that college must follow high school, when many have no real interest in academia and book learning, per se. It is wasteful, of money, time and energy, which could all be directed toward worthier pursuits.

GETTING BEYOND THE MASKS WE WEAR

We currently live in a culture in which formal education is considered the only sure road to a life worth living. It is understood in economic terms: a high school graduate will make 50 percent more than a student who doesn't finish high school; a high school graduate with some college will make 30 percent more; a college graduate 50 percent more than that, and so on. Yet, we have tens of thousands of well-educated people unhappily doing what they were educated to do, but dislike the doing. Something is wrong with this picture.

The learning of a trade has been lost in the equation. Yet, we need craftsmen today more than ever before. It is not that education is bad for anyone. It is simply that education is intended to prepare the individual to be a solid and contributing member of society, and not simply a working, consuming stiff

Something strange happens when "outside" pressure for doing something is replaced by something "inside," which governs the choices we make. The governor activated from "within" takes charge and confronts life aggressively.

Consider this against the feeling of deprivation that can gnaw at us; "I'm not where I should be, doing what I should be doing". Without awareness, a person can start leaning, expecting, envying, comparing, and literally begging for attention. Such a person has suppressed his own interests and negated his own initiative to put other people's heads higher than his own. He has drifted into a *passive-receptive* approach to life, looking at what others are doing, what others have, and how others are treated, taking several steps backward instead of a confident step forward into an active-productive and self-generating adult role.

This impasse can be managed successfully by simply changing the orientation of our mind from self-demands or being ego-driven to role demands, or being reality driven. When a person chooses to think confidently, he feels expansive and receptive to the challenges ahead because he has actively chosen the path of self-reliance.

Yet, the moment he starts to compare and feels driven to compete with someone else, whose head he puts higher than his own, and the chill of deprivation leads to a sense of defeat. He is suddenly defensive and feels inadequate. It never occurs to him that he can never be "that other person," nor can that other person ever be him. They are foreign to each other.

A game of trivial pursuit has commenced within the human heart, between essence and personality. Essence is that unique "something" that is the special talent that we possess independent of others. It is unique to us and no one else. It may be a faculty for math, music, art, caring, drawing, dancing, language, carpentry, or throwing some kind of ball in sport.

Personality is the many masks that we wear in life to get by; to gain attention, recognition, win approval, to belong, or a myriad of other longings, so that we may fit in. We are first, last and always a social animal.

Still, we can become lost in this chase. The bright beautiful girl who wants to be accepted plays down her intelligence. The handsome young Adonis neglects his talents and relies on his good looks. If this were only an adolescent tic, it would be one thing, but gifted people often downplay their gifts ultimately to lose them through dissipation and obsequious toadying. The wealthy among us are known to collect trophies—trophy mates, trophy celebrities — to enhance their status, and then to treat them as things to be manipulated as if they were works of inanimate art.

If the most important thing in life is to be well liked, personality will prevail at the expense of essence. Innate talent is to be used, not suppressed, even if it means enduring envy and jealousy. That doesn't mean you gloat, or bring attention to your gifts, or punish others with them, but simply that the masks you wear should not seek to deny your talent.

Satisfaction never comes from meeting others' needs at the expense of our own. Selfless generosity comes only when our heart and head are in the right place, and that is when we are expressing our essence, not suppressing it.

Believing in what we are doing seldom arrives directly, like an epiphany, but evolves as if building blocks put in place over time, when the activities on the surface seem unrelated. High school typing was one for me. I took it only on a lark, and it has proven invaluable through my many careers, especially now as a writer. Likewise, although I am light years away from science, which was my first career, I still take comfort in the harmony and balance that it provides in the painting of words across a page out of scrambled thoughts.

Often, along the way, certain people introduce us to ourselves. This was the case of a professor of mine. It was after class one day, a literature course, when he asked me my major. I told him it was chemistry. He informed me I should be in the humanities, and offered to recommend me for the Honors Program. I balked, wanting to continue pursuing my career in chemistry. Many years later, I would become a writer, the work I most cherish.

As a chemist, I went from the chemical lab into chemical sales engineering, and then into corporate management. My work found me traveling the world, then something dormant in my soul kicked-in: nothing made sense to me anymore. There had to be more to life. I was at a crossroads.

In my early thirties, I retired to think, read, and write, only to find that 1 lacked the skill and training for commercial success as a writer. Had I taken my professor's advice, I might have developed such skills much earlier.

But here is the *"Catch 22,"* I would have had the skills but nothing interesting to write about. My working life to that point, a door opened by chemistry, provided the material.

The reason for sharing this personal history is that often there is not a direct relationship between activities and interests, or the ultimate impact on the work you most desire to do.

Another situational activity, common to students in college, is working part time in restaurants, as waiters and waitresses. They have to deal with the public, developing a tolerance for bad manners, and occasional abusive verbal treatment, all the time being professional and in control. This provides a classroom for dealing with power from a powerless position. It can prove invaluable for understanding people who feel powerless, should they become lawyers, teachers, medical doctors, psychologists, public servants, politicians, or corporate managers. No working experience is valueless, if it is remembered and later used.

In terms of interest, certain activities can be of instrumental (means to an end) value, but not necessarily of terminal (ends in themselves) value. Typing was an instrumental value, but at the time, apparently unrelated to the terminal value of being a writer. A pattern develops with values that either enhances or diminishes essence. Reading is also an instrumental value that enhances the business of writing. What might diminish such essence? Perhaps not liking to work in isolation from others, or to do the pure research and reading required.

You can be gifted with the ability to manipulate words and to think conceptually, but lack the discipline to dedicate time and energy to the writing, finding solace instead in telling everyone you'll one day write, but you never do. It is easy to fall into one of these holding patterns of "gonna do's" or "gonna be's", without ever escaping them.

Consider the restaurant business. It provides transitional jobs for people on their way to doing other things. But you can get stuck in such a job and never find your way out until it is too late.

The window of opportunity is never a wide-open window, not even in opportunistic times. It often is only opened a crack, revealing

37

the sunlight. If the skills demanded are not honed early, then opportunities decline at a precipitous rate. Race, religion and ethnicity are often given as the reasons why some people never make satisfactory progress. But if that is so, the only way to remove such obstacles is to deal with them head on, not to be undermined by them. The rationalizing inertia is never convincing.

Those caught in this vice of self-deception play games with their psyche, saying they are going to do something about the situation, but always tomorrow, until eventually time runs out and nobody wants them, even for what they have been doing, because they are too old.

What can you do about it? The beauty of life is that as long as you have your health you have your wealth.

WINDOW OF EMOTIONAL HEALTH TO SECOND CHANCES

In possession of your emotional health, it is never too late to take charge whether you are thirty, forty, or beyond. If the energy is there, and the will is there, and the need is real, then there is always hope. Second chances are common in our culture.

Second chances often evolve from escaping the confinement of our egos and finding real satisfaction in the service of others. Nothing compares with such satisfaction. Serving others makes life worthwhile.

The reason is fundamental. Our wants can never be fulfilled. The job is never big enough, the income, the automobile or automobiles never exclusive enough. Our domicile is never fashionable enough or in the right neighborhood. Want has no bounds. There are never enough adoring friends, or enough people who envy us. More is always wanted.

An emotionally self-reliant person is not driven by ego, but by the desire to serve and create a better world. The focus is on what he can give, not get.

To be clear on this point there is nothing wrong with being affluent or being a wealth creator. Nor is there anything wrong with wishing to create a better world for members of one's family. The problem occurs when the wealth creators become twisted in the process. Some are quite successful in earning a good living, building a business or profession, and managing family affairs, and otherwise conducting themselves in public and private affairs above reproach.

Such individuals can appear to be self-reliant, while being emotional dependent. This can be manifested in alcoholism, workaholism, tyrannical behavior, or some other emotional aberration. The climate is tense for everyone in this person's emotional sphere. Unfortunately, the last person to realize this is the person himself.

We are what we do, and what we do is the real answer to what we mean and intend. Actions not only speak louder than words; actions are statement of our mental health.

The corruption of good intentions can occur when parents have the affluence to give their children everything, but lack the will to imbue them with responsibility and accountability. Excuses are made when their children's actions don't compute with their words. Juvenile records can be expunged when they get into trouble with the law. Teachers can be enticed to play favorites when parents give generously to their children's schools. Homework assignments can be plagiarized or parents can do the work to guarantee their children get good grades.

A life without struggle or risk and pain has little chance for growth and development.

A life without consequences has even less chance for the emotional health of self-reliance.

Parents who have struggled finding their way to success, and want their children to bypass this pain, risk, and doubt, are on their way to creating an emotionally dependent monster. Their child will likely always look for an easy way out when, ironically, the easiest way out is that of hard work and a focused goal. To compensate for a life empty of meaning, they are also likely to accumulate toys of distraction, but they will never have enough to fill the emotional void. It becomes a dizzying decline into a bottomless pit ending in ultimate despair.

Therefore, affluent parents are doing their children a disservice by denying them the opportunity to discover their own way. This includes through inevitable failure. Some children have been held hostage by their parent's wealth, threatened with the blackmail of disinheritance if they don't toe the mark and walk the walk according to their parents' dictates. Nobody ever does. The problem is not failure; the problem is the golden parachute to break the fall of consequential action. As such, no learning takes hold. Failure is life's best teacher equally relevant to the rich as to the poor.

In our culture, about 10 percent of the population of 300 million has developed emotional self-reliance. Perhaps the bailout strategy of parents is a major reason why. Parents are afraid their children will commit the same mistakes that they did: fail a grade, get fired from a job, be evicted from an apartment, file bankruptcy, suffer a divorce, and be caught cheating, be kicked out of a movie theatre for raucous behavior, and yet they survived and grew up, imperfectly so. Failure is not the problem. An unexamined life is the problem, an examination that always gives the examiner a second chance.

For argument purposes, the flip side is the person who has no wealth cushion, no parents with clout, no influential authority figure. Because of this, he feels discriminated against. I came from such an environment. In fact, my parents and their friends forthrightly said I would suffer discrimination in the community purely because I was an Irish Roman Catholic boy.

I encountered some religious bias, but didn't let it get in my way. I can thank the good Sisters of St. Francis for this. They guided me expertly through my first eight years of education, treating me fairly, consistently, firmly, and decisively when I stepped out of line. If they played favorites, I didn't notice. The Nuns, however, gave me a wide berth and didn't direct my learning or behavior with a draconian hand. This measure of psychological and emotional self-reliance, resulted in my taking the initiative, sometimes with negative consequences. For example, going to the blackboard to solve a problem while another student was still pondering it, only to appropriately receive a dressing down for that behavior.

My mother, who was my mentor and chief supporter, made it clear to me at an early age that I would have to make my own way, and that if I fell I would have to pick myself up because there would be no one else to do it. She talked of college when there was never enough money week-to-week to pay the bills. She placed a governor in me, which fit my temperament while casting no aspersions that I was special, only that I had the ability to think and act independently, and didn't have to lead a secondhand life. Owing to her efforts, I have had an amazingly easy life, not because I am so gifted, but because the self-reliant person habitually minimizes the dangers ahead of him, whereas the one lacking in such self-sufficiently habitually exaggerates them.

Individual temperament is most important to a person because it sets the overall climate in which he plays out his particular game of life. For example, I am high strung and my mother did not try to temper this complexity, but made it clear that to compensate for it I must always think ahead, always be better prepared than anyone else, and never rest on my laurels. "Life is not all about you," she said, "life is all about what you do."

Should a person make short shrift of his life, when things don't break his way, he may assume the unwitting role of the victim and become his own executioner. This can happen when a person stakes his identity and aspirations on someone else's agenda. When things come apart, he is apt to blame his woes on the ambitions of the other, failing to realize he was willingly playing the other's game, and not finding his own.

The inability to see is a condition of having blinders on, spiraling out of focus, so that we stereotype those assumed to have wronged us, while pointing fingers everywhere but at ourselves. No one else is responsible for what happens to us but ourselves. Therefore, if any wrong is done, it is because we have either willed it on ourselves or consciously-unconsciously walked into circumstances that made it inevitable. It may be convenient to blame others, or to sense a conspiracy against us when the only enemy we must master is lurking in our own hearts. It is a constant struggle every day between essence (what we are) and personality (what we pretend to be).

THE MATTER OF RIGHTS AND PRIVILEGES

Matters get a bit dicey when we treat rights and privileges as the same. We have the right to life, liberty and the pursuit of happiness.

Becoming an educated citizen is a privilege. A good paying job is a privilege. The opportunity to become affluent is a privilege. A productive life is a privilege.

None of these are rights. None of them are guarantees. You must earn them. No one can make a privilege a right.

Self-educated philosopher Charles **D.** Hayes informs us that education is something you take. It is not given to you. *"Intellectual maturity,"* he writes in *The Rapture of Maturity* ((2004), *"is a function of deliberate learning, not of age. True adulthood is not possible without it."* You can go through twelve or sixteen years of education and never be educated.

There is little respect for rights. They are taken for granted. Privileges separate us into doers and dreamers, the self-reliant and the self-dependent.

You would think the privilege of receiving a free public education would be esteemed, even revered. Yet, tens of thousands of elementary and high school students skip school every day; tens of thousands fail to finish high school altogether, while tens of thousands fail to complete their college education. Too often those that do attend school religiously hurl abuse at their teachers, cheat, cut corners, use electronic devices to secure the answers, or simply idle their time away plotting some kind of mischief to achieve the diploma or degree with as little learning as possible.

Reality of this abuse of privilege doesn't settle in until middle age when it is too late for damage control. This damage is never because of a lack of privilege, nor indeed, of a lack of potential, but rather the failure to apply the effort to harness the potential, which everyone in a democratic has that right to do.

DISORDER AS LIFESTYLE EXCESS

More than anything else that gets in the way of believing in what we are doing is lifestyle. It is the disorder of lifestyle that derails us. While we may confuse privilege and right, this confusion can be easily compounded when lifestyle becomes therapy.

Someone once said there are two kinds of people: those who love what they do and those who hate what they do.

The fortunate 20 percent minority, those who are prepared to meet life's demands independently, self-reliantly, demonstrate love in everything they do. Individuals receive emotional as well as economic sustenance in the process.

The unfortunate 80 percent majority, those looking for excuses why they have failed to make satisfactory progress, are inclined to withhold commitment and avoid responsibility in everything they do. They look for fulfillment outside of work in countless distractions, seduced by consummate consumerism as therapy, obsessed with toys of distraction. It is believed the route to happiness is in the possession of satisfying things, but happiness is not only a feeling, but a mindset. Philosopher Alan W. Watts claims once we define happiness we lose it. John Lennon states it another way:

> *Life is what happens to you when you're busy making other plans.*

So, it is as well with happiness.

It is no accident that 80 percent of the productive work accomplished in an organization is the product of this 20 percent minority. This engaged minority is not worry about what it will get, but is committed to what it can give.

Meanwhile, lifestyle keeps the luxury boat and luxury car business going. Lifestyle is also evident in eating, drinking, smoking, partying and playing to the point of excess, the key word being, to "excess." None of this is inherently bad in and of itself, but becomes self-destructively so when it becomes obsessive and addictive. What one does one becomes.

Lifestyle excess also involves cheating sleep, staying up too late and getting up too early, not getting enough rest, working too hard, partying too much, and not getting enough exercise. The lack of sleep impairs the brain's ability to regenerate new brain neurons, slowing learning and thinking ability. To compensate for sleep deprivation, lifestyle excess turns to the drugstore or promiscuity for artificial stimulation and rejuvenation. Scientists consider sleep deprivation a possible contributor to Alzheimer's disease.

Another downside of lifestyle as excess is the soaring medical insurance costs for organ malfunction: heart disease, emphysema, liver and kidney failure. The 20 percent of insurance subscribers who have their act together and are emotionally self-reliant are paying the bills for the 80 percent who are emotional dependent and retreat into the disorder of lifestyle excesses. We have yet to understand how Obamacare, which goes into effect as this is being written, will have on these costs.

Corporations are overburdened with these *passive-receptive* dependent workers. General Motors, for one, is now operating mainly on life support, largely because of its health insurance burden for current and retired personnel. This cost is reflected on the price tag of every vehicle off the assembly line, straining competition with foreign models. This does not include the skyrocketing costs of absenteeism, because of lifestyle excess, which is a multi-billion dollar corporate expense. Alas, were it not for the multi-billion dollar bailout of GM by the government in 2008, GM could very well be out of business.

To believe in what you are doing you need to see clearly where you are. If you are burning the candle at both ends, you are not seeing clearly. You are in a cage of your own making. Rather than alerting you to this fact, chances are you are, blaming the condition on everyone but yourself, justifying lifestyle excess as necessary therapeutic relief. This only drives you deeper into the cage.

This process of self-en-cage-ment starts innocently and with little awareness as you secure a new crutch. Since the lifestyle excess option fails to move you closer to self-reliance, the pressure mounts and the vise tightens. It drives you deeper into excess. If something doesn't give, the spirit can break down and the body can give out. You can lose your self-confidence, your optimism and the very ability to cope. The life you so desired is heading off the rails.

Coping becomes a full-time job, as there is little energy to perform. Daily pain is a reminder you are living a lie. All because you have failed to recognize you are the problem and the problem solver.

The self-help industry with all its books and gurus, well-meaning though its intentions, has unwittingly promoted self-deception by denying the reality that the sufferer must cure himself. Once the dream dies that we are immortal and can do anything to excess without consequences, despair sets in, a despair we must embrace. It is the only cure for illusion. Without this wakeup call, we never grow up. In the end, time runs out on adolescence, the youth must die to give birth to the man. That is the problem. We don't want to grow old and so we are not interested in growing up.

When a person is in great pain, he needs a map to find his way out of it, not a formula, method, or system of "do's and don'ts." He doesn't need some authority figure to provide him with positive and negative commands. He doesn't need a guru or personal trainer. He needs to acknowledge he is the problem and must free up his mind to make choices that will put him on the road to recovery. Where will he find this map?

Each of us has an intuitive feeling deep inside us that has intelligence far beyond our cognitive minds. This gut intelligence provides the map when the mind is quiet and free of thought. The map can spring alive during a hot shower or a long solitary walk or working in the garden or home workshop.

It comes out of the silence and all the person has to do is listen, for inside each of us beyond the chaotic noise outside is a sanctuary of peace. The problem is finding our way to this center, and then once there, holding on to it. This requires a free mind to acknowledge that the problem exists with the will to find our way out of this wilderness.

Our problems are never outside of us. They are linked to the way we think, feel, behave and relate to others. Whenever we get ourselves into a lifestyle mess, we can count on being self-imprisoned in excess. That is where the culprit lies. Group or individual therapy may prove helpful, but it is not enough. Looking for a convenient socially approved quick fix is why recidivism is so high in these addiction relieving step programs. They are looking for answers in all the wrong places.

You cannot solve the problem with the same thinking that created it. Step programs employ the same linear logic, chronological time; offer the same incentives, and iterate the same mantras and support jargon only in a different key.

The incentive to join a step program involves a gradual coaxing of the psyche to behave differently, which it never does. If you are a binge eater, compulsive gambler, or addictive to sex, alcohol or drugs, the mind must first change its mental chemistry before you will behave and continue to behave differently.

As high as 90 percent of smokers, for example, who quit smoking by wearing a patch, or committing to a step program, resume smoking at some time in the future. Those who quit cold turkey are much less likely to ever smoke again. The first thing smokers who have quit think of having in a crisis is a cigarette to calm their nerves. The patch wearer is likely to give in whereas the cold turkey quitter is not. The reason is because the mind is now programmed differently.

Quitting cold turkey involves making a choice. When choices are made, the mind deals with information radically different than it did before. Step programs avoid making choices by easing the pain and playing a game on the mind with one-step-at-a-time progress. Playing this game the mind always wins because the mind doesn't want to make choices, but to continue thinking, feeling and doing what it has always thought, felt and done. Step programs are a formula and a method, when the mind needs a map. Once the mind has the map, the person knows instantaneously what he must do. Choice is the outcome of the process of deciding.

Lifestyle addiction might require the separation of you from friends and family who reinforce the compromising behavior. This is necessary because it is too radical for a mind to comprehend much less deal with reminders of bad habits. The mind always wants it both ways, the benefit of change with only cosmetic change, continuing to be with the same people that coaxed it into the problematic behavior in the first place.

Nor is it wise to frequent places associated with the behavior. Ambience can be as much a destroyer of a person as people can.

As a problem solver, a person needs to continuously redefine his purpose in life, as circumstances and interests change. What one aspired to at 16 may not be compatible with what one aspires to at 26 or 36. What gives satisfaction and a sense of renewal at 50 or 60 may have again changed radically from what had been preferred before. We never stop growing until we die.

A PERSONAL ASIDE

In my early thirties making a good living as a corporate executive, my life made no sense to me anymore.

I was living in colonial splendor in South Africa facilitating the formation of a new company, when reality caught up with me. The white minority ruled while the non-white majority suffered the dehumanizing policy of apartheid. Imagine a person with Midwestern values from the rural state of Iowa being treated as if royalty with a gardener, house manager, cook, maid and chauffeur.

This departure from reality for the son of a blue-collar working class father was too much. I found myself increasingly coming apart as I experienced this dichotomy. Here I was doing what I thought I wanted to do, but finding my family and myself unhappy. Something was terribly wrong. I resigned feeling I had to take a "time out" despite having a wife and four small children to support, and in the best years of my working career. I took a two-year sabbatical in which I read and thought and wrote.

When I was nearly broke, I went back to school full-time, year-around for six years to earn my master's and doctor's degree in psychology, consulting on the side. I was looking for answers in academia but found none.

During this additional six-year-period of study, my family experienced difficulty adjusting to a lifestyle quite different from what they had become accustomed.

I mention this here because hard choices are never easy. What I did may offend some readers, who put pleasing others above pleasing themselves, but I was living a lie. I listened to my heart because my head no longer controlled me.

I will not make light of the pain, struggle, disappointment, depression and failure that accompanied this radical change. My marriage survived only for another decade. As for my children, they remembered what affluence was like and have found their own way back to some sense of it with their respective roadmaps, not mine.

Once you make the commitment to change, once you back away from worrying about what other people will think, you find you are not the first to go this road less traveled nor will you be the last.

With radical change, there are setbacks, reversals, and much uncertainty. Would I do it again? Yes. Why?

I have never felt such liberation before or such fulfillment since. There is a common belief that you can avoid setbacks, and regrets, if you stick to a course as unhappy or unfulfilling as it may be because there is always retirement. If you subscribe to such an argument, you may never know what could have been. I know a chief engineer of a high tech company who hated his job, but wanted to be a stockbroker. When I asked him why he didn't quit, and become a broker, he said, "I've got another seven years to full retirement." He stuck it out, retired, fell off his roof working on some shingles, and is now an invalid. He never became a stockbroker. It happens. Meanwhile, I am happily employed in my eighth decade working on the second editions of my ten published books.

To mount a departure from what you are doing, whatever it is, choices have to be made. This may mean certain friends have to be cut out of your life, certain experiences discontinued, certain places and people avoided, and certain weaknesses faced without terror. There must be a full acceptance of yourself as you are so that you may see, understand and accept others as you find them, not as you would have them be but as they actually are.

You must get outside the cycle of your self-enslavement, solving problems with different thinking than what created them.

The problem in believing in what you are doing is made more complicated because of emotional dependence on what others may think. In South Africa, I was informed that apartheid was not bad for the Bantu people, who represented 80 percent of the nation's population. Such assurance came from co-workers, American friends, my South African Catholic Church pastor, the nuns teaching my children, my American bosses in the States, and from English and Afrikaans speaking South Africans.

Yet, these Bantu natives had no vote, had to carry a passbook in the city of Johannesburg, and could be jailed without charge for 60 to 90 days if their green card was not up to date, or they failed to have it with them.

Then one day my Bantu gardener whom I considered a friend was murdered. His murder was treated as if the family dog had been killed. It came crushing down on me that I was living a lie. Suspended in luxury, I was brain dead in toxic waste. My instinct for survival kicked in. I resigned.

Confident Thinking is realistic thinking seeing clearly "what is" without blinders. It is the will to do what is proper, fair and right. You do this by listening to your own drummer, your own best friend; sometimes your only friend. You hear others talking about you and it hurts, but that is because there is a certain truth to what they say that registers within.

For it is in the heart that truth resides, our moral center, which cannot be touched by the evil tearing at our conscious minds. Once in charge, you can do what you want to do, be what you want to be with no apologies. You will encounter others on this same road less traveled, doing what they believe in as well. No one walks in your shoes; or understands the rhythm of your heart, no one else but God, and that god is the "god within," what the Greeks called "*entheos,*" and which we have anglicized to the word "enthusiasm."

CONFIDENT THINKING
CREATIVE STAGE THREE

DEVELOP A SELF-IMAGE
PSYCHOLOGY OF SUCCESS
SEE YOURSELF AS SUCCESSFUL
LEARN TO PERSEVERE
KNOW WHEN TO TAKE A "TIME OUT"

Every man who knows how to read has it in his power to magnify himself, to multiply the ways in which he exists, to make his life full, significant and interesting.

—Aldous Huxley, English Novelist

MODERN MAN REDUX

THE MODERN MAN looks after himself, because no one else does. He eats the food that would not destroy his body with cholesterol, he drinks sparingly and never to excess, he keeps his muscles fit, he pursues advancement in his career by saying the right things to his bosses, he covets new technological electronic innovations to take the strain off his life, and he is sensible.

The Modern Man stands out in a crowd as one marked for advancement, certain to prosper in progress. He is nobody's fool, not afraid of work, a person with aptitude for decision-making and taking charge, and an independent thinker.

Somehow, however, his career, his future, and the success he so cherished has collapsed with the finality of an outdated computer system because he has never gotten around to doing what he truly loves. His confidence is a sham. He is on life support and doesn't know it.

Success is one of those ambiguous words. We equate success with financial security, celebrity prominence, athletic prowess, political clout, intellectual acumen, artistic genius, scientific distinction, and military hegemony. There is a pattern here.

Success has most eyes on financial independence, as if there ever was such a thing. This is the perspective of those without it, seldom of those with it. Bill Gates, Rick Waggoner, and Tom Ford are some of the hardest working people, as was the late Steven Jobs, and they need not work at all.

Retirement is an aberration outside their vocabulary. The fact that they could sit back on billions or millions and vegetate for the rest of their lives never occurs to them. They choose not to twiddle their thumbs because life for them is action not about being passive. Life is about being involved in doing something that extends influence beyond the narrow scope of self.

Organizational pyramid climbers are not doers. They are only interested in getting to the top. They are hungry for power, but why? It is because they believe power is there for the taking. It never occurs to them to ask for what purpose? They seek a certain position to make a certain income to acquire certain possessions, but there is no doing in the climbing, only checking off the boxes required of each step of the way in the climb.

Doers first see themselves doing long before they get the opportunity to do. They have a mental blueprint (map) of where they are going and why. This is so because they create and shape their own world inside themselves before it finds its way into the outside world as an extension of themselves. This is so because they have a balance between their conscious mind and their unconscious mind.

The conscious mind

Is aware of what it is doing. For example, you are reading this page, and aware of your immediate surroundings, the clothes you are wearing, the people around you, the sounds, the conversations, and the distractions whatever they may be. The conscious mind has limited storage facilities and handles information one or two pieces at a time. The conscious mind can focus attention so acutely that other incoming stimuli may be temporarily blocked. For example, someone says, "hi," as you read and you don't hear them.

The unconscious mind

Is not consciously aware of what you are doing right now. It has an exceptional storage capacity and handles large quantities of very diverse information. The unconscious holds the record of your life experiences. Thoughts can be easily brought to conscious awareness that are stored in the subconscious. This includes old addresses, phone numbers, e-mails, names of high school teachers, where you were last Friday night. Thoughts that seem to defy being brought into consciousness or thoughts that seem temporarily irretrievable are also stored there. Nothing that was ever experienced is totally lost.

Another distinction between doers and climbers is the matter of *adaptive tension* and *maladaptive tension.* One of the desires of climbers is to get to a place where there is no tension, where they can relax completely, and no one can touch them; where they are finally in charge. It is one of the reasons for entrepreneurs escaping the corporate climate and going on their own to create their own little kingdom. But no one ever escapes tension.

Adaptive tension

Is the balance between the demands of the situation and the body's response to those demands followed by a natural state of relaxation. This is demonstrated when a concerted effort is focused on a project with a rise and subsequent fall in physical tension and emotional anxiety with its completion. A feeling of euphoria is experienced as the body calms down, internal alarms quiet, leaving you feeling relaxed and relieved.

Maladaptive tension

Occurs when no balance is restored. This happens when you retain a level of tension in your body and a level of emotional anxiety that is maladaptive. Tension and anxiety in such an instance do not help you in your coping. You cannot concentrate on the project for worry that you will not complete it on time, or as well as you would desire. You feel you have to be continuously on, and can never relax for fear you will let your guard down and say or do something you will regret. You cannot sleep yet you need your rest to perform well on the project. With maladaptive tension you may experience nervousness, anxiety, restlessness, frustration, and depression as you struggle against the unwanted tension. Before long, you have a headache and need some medicine to cope with this imbalance.

There is a pattern to the ten stages of Confident Thinking and it is that the body and mind are one. We create our own good health by first seeing ourselves healthy (self-imagery), and choosing to do those things that keep mind and body working for us rather than against us. At the moment, we are discussing doers and climbers. Doers accept their weaknesses and for this acceptance, they are strong. Climbers believe that they cannot admit to any weakness or they will be rejected. The converse is true. Doers have learned to function successfully under pressure, not by denying the possibility of failure, or falling short of the mark, but in realizing that failure is the necessary plateau to success (more on this later); that the conscious and unconscious mind represent the complete arsenal to the possible; and that tension is to be embraced and not feared as a natural function of the mind and body working together.

It is difficult for the individual today to find peace of mind in a troubled world. There is a flight from peace in all sorts of aberrations: the virtual reality of cyberspace, senseless survival programs and bizarre confessionals of the most embarrassing and intimate details of personal lives on television.

With only 10 percent of the adult population emotionally healthy and self-reliant, Modern Man fears circumstances that cause no actual immediate physical threat. We fear terrorist attacks, nuclear war, economic collapse, sexual frustration, personal failure, loneliness, cancer, heart attacks, automobile accidents, being robbed, global warming and environmental pollution. We are afraid of not being politically correct, failing in our work, confronting a friend with our anger, talking to a stranger, being rejected by someone we admire, being fired from our job, expelled from our school or excommunicated from our church.

With apologies to Maxwell Maltz of "self-image psychology" fame, here are my interpretations of his twelve ways to correct this obsession with a working self-image that gives us a chance to lead a happy and productive life, not free of tension or anxiety, but in which we do ourselves no harm:

Know yourself as you are.

Don't downplay your strengths and say everyone has them because not everyone does. Don't dwell on your failures at the expense of your successes. Learn to see yourself as you really are in your best moments.

Use your imagination.

Shelley wrote, *"The great instrument of moral good is the imagination."* It is the eye of the soul. Learn to use your mental picturing to visualize yourself in the role and situation that you relish. Make your imagination your best friend.

Life is short, allow relaxation to balance the tension.

Forgive others for their betrayals because holding a grudge only damages your soul, not theirs. Accept others with their faults and relax with your own.

Cultivate that winning feeling moving mountains.

Emerson said, *"Self-trust is the first secret of success."* Have a spirit that relishes the tackling of daunting projects, know that the process has its ups and downs, which are normal, confident that he who stays the course ultimately comes out the winner.

Good habits were to Aristotle the keys to everything.

He said, "Men acquire a particular quality by constantly acting in a particular way." If your habits are working for you, then you are moving towards the fulfillment of your dreams. If you attempt to leaven things with a few bad habits, you are stalking failure. Ovid said, "Habits change into character."

The aim of happiness is good; it must be understood.

It is a mindset. It has nothing to do with who you are or what you have. It is the peace of mind that finds balance between your insides and outsides, your mind and your body, your feelings and your thinking. Happiness is not something you can purchase. It is not something you can consume. It is the something that you are.

Unmasking your person beyond your many masks.

We tend to develop so many different facades, facades that show themselves as if we were actors on stage, first playing this part with some people and another part with others. We can become so conditioned to these masks that we forget the real person lurking beyond them. It is as if these masks are more real than we are, acting as blindfolds to hide us from our potential as a person. We are so much in the business of pleasing others that we never find time to please ourselves. When you learn to see yourself with kind eyes you will have no need for masks.

The greatest of all virtues is kindness.

Compassion is one quality that separates us from beasts. When you have concern for others, you recognize that we are all connected; that the greatest and least of us are the same, that with love anything is possible. Psychiatrist Willard Beecher insists, "Compassion will cure more sins than condemnation."

Accepting yourself as you are shows tolerance.

You may be strong, healthy and successful, but there are no guarantees that your good fortune will not at some time suffer a reversal. Your strong self-image will befriend you and carry you for a time through your troubles, but what happens when you are tired and weak and failing? Do you accept your new circumstances in a human way, or do you blame others? If you reject yourself when you are weak, your strength is not real. Only when you accept your weakness with your strength is your self-acceptance genuine.

Living with your imperfect self and all your mistakes and failures is the mark of a mature person. Learn to laugh at your foibles and find balance and a sense of humor, for your follies. Don't destroy yourself with trying to be what you cannot be, perfect, or unnecessarily criticize yourself
for your occasional blunders. They are part of being human.

Discover your real you.

Find out what that self is and is not. People will constantly say, "You're not acting like yourself," but that is always the self that they expect and not necessarily the self that you are. Strengthen your self-image by learning who and what you are by the baptism of experience. Patterns are in the process of developing as if you are plotting a novel, and all the parts fit nicely together if you will only take the time to listen, observe, and learn. A successful life is truly successful only when you are living your life the way you wish to live it and not according to someone else's plan for you.

Never retire from a useful life.

If you measure everything in chronological time—hours, days, weeks, months, and years—you will be a slave to this arbitrary standard and never realize the beauty of psychological time. It is the time governed by making choices, by being involved, by being completely active in the now, which is the only time that exists because the past is gone and the future is never here. If everything bores you, then you are old at 12 or 16 or beyond. There is no "retirement age" to a fulfilling life. The time to grow up in one field is

> when you retire from another. There are always new challenges to pursue.

The unfortunate thing about these very accessible ways to develop and maintain a satisfying self-image is that we have become for all intent and purposes a *passive—receptive society* finding fulfillment in the exploits of a few while we vicariously experience their achievement behind a book, television or movie screen, computer monitor, or in some magnificent gallery, amphitheater, convention center or sports stadium.

THE PROBLEM WITH A SPECTATOR LIFE

There are many people who hunger for success as celebrity It is a curious dance between the adored and adorers. Celebrities need an audience, while the adulators need an escape from boredom. Even high school and college sports have risen to the level of celebrity gambits. Indeed, what is the appeal of television's "American Idol" other than a fantasy wish dance?

The celebrity culture separates the privileged few that are recognized as the best from the rest of us. Then there are degrees of "the rich and famous" up to the 1 percent that seemingly have it all. The popular magazine People implies that these are the only real people the rest of us are pretenders or invisible. Rather than being angered by this, most of us suffer from a "celebrity complex," having more interest in two-dimensional celebrities seen on some kind of screen than our own three-dimensional families seen in the flesh.

Celebrities within their own ranks go well beyond the matter of financial security. They suffer from a kind of emotional poverty most of us could never imagine much less fathom. Somerset Maugham captures this mania for inclusion in *"The Razor's Edge"* (1944), where people were mortified if not on the guest list of celebrity parties. On the other hand, celebrities cannot be alone. They need an entourage, sycophants for constant reassurance.

Michael Jackson had a veritable army of paid worshipers. Nor is an adoring public enough. Should a celebrity not be included on the guest list of another celebrity's dinner party, well, that would be like taking a mortal wound. Celebrities feel that fame is necessary to ensure self-esteem.

That is why fans are part of the dance as they help to buffer celebrities from reality.

Justice might be blind, but the law isn't. Celebrities have justice. Everyone else has the law. This gives celebrities the implicit right to flaunt the law and to do as they please, while fans are provided an escape from reality adoring them from afar.

It is this carefully cultivated illusion of intimacy between celebrities and fans that has created confusion between public and private worlds. Take the image of Tiger Woods. The number one golfer in the world has suffered a severe blow when his private life clashed famously with his public life. He has apologized for practicing adultery with reckless abandon for years when he was thought to be the ideal family man.

Richard Schickel captures this contradiction in his book, *"Intimate Strangers: The Culture of Celebrity"* (1985). He shows how celebrities shape our worlds and then bend our minds to find us living more in our fantasies than in our own lives. He calls it "the heart of contemporary darkness," and offers a chilling warning about the psychopathic consequences of a nation obsessed with celebrity. When John F. Kennedy and Walter Cronkite reached cult status, he notes, Kennedy as living in Camelot and Cronkite "the most trusted man in America," the symbolic play of celebrity superseded the play of ideas. Such symbolic interaction becomes a trap turning both the adored and adorers into symbiotically connected victims through the medium of flimsy two-dimensional paper shadows or fleeting electronic digital impulses on a screen.

Credentials don't matter. Celebrities become unwitting role models and give advice on national or international issues without privileged information. They have a right to their opinion but should weigh the consequences of expressing it beyond intimate friends.

Jane and Joe Publican create celebrity of the absurd with people's court and Jerry Springer type exhibition programs on television. Then there is television celebrity "news" where dalliances of stars become entertainment. Television journalists attain celebrity status as photogenic personalities with upbeat voices to cover downbeat news, news that shocks and titillates, provokes and angers to keep viewers from muting or changing channels. Life for Jane and Joe Publican is mainly as *passive-receptive* couch potatoes, while perfect strangers known only to them as celebrities enthrall them on the tube.

Modern Man in this upside down world has made celebrities of ordinary Jane and Joe Publicans when they murder and maim, outrage and plunder, corrupt and scandalize drawing attention to themselves. One wonders how much the publicity of the infamous has had in creating this phenomenon.

The fascination for mayhem is the headlines in the morning newspaper and the first item on the nightly television news. Most popular television entertainment programs are about murder and mayhem with the gory details of butchered bodies displayed for the viewing audience, and no one sees this as pornographic.

Jane and Joe Publican see celebrity athletes prominently displaying tattoos and so they quickly run out to mimic them with tattoos of their own. *New York Times* columnist David Brooks finds this ironic as a few generations ago sporting tattoos was a badge of disgrace. Tattoo characters are often of Oriental symbols when the tattooed are unlikely to know the characteristic of a grammatical sentence in their own language.

In this upside down world, Jane and Joe Publican spend as much time watching television and surfing the Internet, as they spend eating and sleeping, or about as much time as they spend at work. Time constraints have complicated this picture further with texting and tweeting. What do you imagine suffers for the attention? Could it be the job and sleep?

Little Jane and little Joe are unlikely to read books for pure pleasure, to visit museums or art galleries, or get acquainted with nature other than on school field trips. They are more likely to have a mobile phone, a Walkman in their ear, or an iPad, iPhone, or laptop at the ready to text and tweet, or surf the Internet. Chances are their parents are equally engaged.

Modern Man has become spectator to life finding passive satisfaction in watching life drift by. The promoters of "The American Idol" had the genius to harness this passivity with remote electronic voting for favorites. Over fifty million voted in the May 2006 *"American Idol"* contest, with electronic voting escalating ever since. Meanwhile, politicians spend millions of dollars to bring out the vote only to have the response fall far short of the mark. This makes it clear what is most important to Jane and Joe Publican. Indeed, according to Brent Bozell and Tim Graham in *"Collision"* (2013), the electronic media stole the presidential election of 2012 with its bias reporting, finding it easy to manipulate a passive audience.

The 2006 World Cup of Soccer, which took place in Germany, had a television global audience of nearly two billion, while hundreds of thousands traveled to Germany to attend the contests. Seventy-five thousand from Sweden, alone, were on hand for the opening match of its national team. Hundreds of thousands watched the contests in huge television screens mounted in open plazas not far from the action, as they were unable to attain seats in the stadium.

Rabid National Football and National Hockey fans pay a king's ransom for season tickets to their favorite team's home games. These fans are not known to be rich, but make the players, owners and television networks rich for their obedient passivity.

The NCAA College Basketball Tournament televised contract with CBS Television in 2010 was for 14-years at $10.8 billion. It is expected to double by that amount by the time a new contract is negotiated.

Economic watchers estimate that several billion dollars is lost in productivity during college basketball's "March Madness" with people calling in sick and playing hooky from work to watch the games on television at home, or at work on their iPads, tweeting or texting each other, betting on the games, or standing around at work talking about them.

Folly is not a matter of devotion to celebrity heroes. Folly is the wishful thinking of emulating these idols at the expense of developing one's own innate talent. Tennis great Arthur Ashe once wrote that a member of his African American race had one chance in 50,000 of ever getting on the professional tennis circuit. The odds of being a doctor, lawyer, engineer, or scientist for those same African American boys and girls were close to one in 100 if the same time and energy committed to sport idolatry were devoted to education.

People see their idols as somebody doing something dramatic, going somewhere exotic, whereas being a doctor, lawyer, engineer, executive, teacher, well, it's not the same, is it? Many little boys want to be NBA, NFL, NHL, or MLB players, which is okay. It becomes a problem when they are consumed with this desire at the expense of what they can do.

When I was a boy, it was Major League Baseball that was the dominant professional sport. We played baseball from sun up to sun down in the summer on the courthouse lawn in Clinton, Iowa, and attended all the Industrial League baseball games in Riverview Stadium, dreaming of the day we would have a minor league contract on our way to the majors. In a town of 33,000, no one has ever made the major leagues as an everyday player, less than a handful as pitchers, and then only briefly at that level.

SELF-IMAGE, SUCCESS AND GENDER PARITY

So, success, indeed, is an ambiguous word. People are disinclined to see success in terms of their essence and personality, circumstance and opportunities. Their rightful self-image is staring them in the face and they are too distracted by all the *passive-receptive* stimuli to recognize themselves in the mirror. Consequently, many drift through life chasing dreams that will never materialize. They want to be somebody, but that person they happen to be is a stranger, and chances are will remain so.

This is not to discourage you from seeing yourself as successful.

It is to send the message success is a deeply personal affair. Success is a condition, not a job, not a particular status or achievement. It is a sense of what you are and can be if you only open your eyes to the fact. Success is love made visible. It is a mindset that suits you.

Think for a moment, what gives you the most satisfaction? What is it you do especially well? We often don't know what we do well until someone tells us. That means we must listen. The inclination is to take ourselves for granted and our special talent as if everyone else has it, too, when not everyone does. Dean Pieper was at Clinton High in my hometown more than a half century ago, running around the track like everyone else in gym class. His gym teacher noted his speed, endurance and the ease with which he ran. He encouraged him to go out for the track team. He did so, and ran the fastest mile in the State of Iowa, and one of the fastest miles in the United States that year, 4:21.6 minutes. He never thought he was especially talented as a runner. His talent provided him with a full scholarship to Northwestern University when otherwise he would not have been able to afford a college education.

There is a hierarchy of what we deem success when we are young. With boys in my day from age four to six, it was skill at playing common games (marbles, checkers); from six to twelve it was physical prowess in running, hitting, shooting, throwing or jumping with some kind of ball; from twelve to eighteen it was organized sport such as football, basketball, track and baseball on high school teams. Separation from doing to observing accelerated once past high school sports. Yet, during all those high school years most students were already spectators to sports.

There are only eleven players on a football team, five on a basketball team, thirty or so in track, and nine on a baseball team. Of course, with the reserves these numbers swell, but still, this is a very small percentage of most high school student bodies.

What is unfortunate is that those who excel in sport can and commonly do neglect other talents that ensure long-term success, freeze framing themselves in eternal adolescence never to mature into responsible and contributing adults to the level of their gifts.

Meanwhile, again in my day, with girls from age four to six, dolls were important; six to eight the focus shifted to social activities and peer relationships; eight to twelve self-awareness brought out competitive instincts academically, social awareness, keying on appearance; twelve to eighteen boys were discovered but subject to parent-teacher approval as 80 percent of academic honors were likely to got to girls.

Again in my era, academic achievement in college proved a reversal of this 80-20 split with 80 percent of the academic honors going to young men. Academia took on precedence because young men, in the main, were to be professionals, not young women. Today, approximately 60 percent of the college student body is women with more than 50 percent of those in professional schools, women, in medicine, education, psychology, law, and the humanities. At the same time, women are 40 percent or more of the students in dentistry, engineering, physics, mathematics and chemistry.

Today, fifty years later, it is a much healthier climate, not only in terms of professional status, but also across the board as high school girls and young women in college are now enjoying parity in sport as well as disciplines formerly dominated by men.

College women have come to assert themselves academically. Nearly 70 percent of female high school graduates attend college compared to less than 60 percent of male high school graduates. Women are over 60 percent of all master degree students and earn better than 50 percent of all master degrees. Today women earn 50 percent of all doctoral degrees, while over 50 percent of medical school students are women with more than 40 percent earning medical degrees. Nearly 50 percent of those earning law degrees are women while the same number are dental students with better than 40 percent receiving dental degrees. Likewise, women earn a majority of the degrees in pharmacy and veterinary medicine. The only disciplines in which they still lag are mathematics, physics, chemistry, and engineering. Even in these disciplines, they have been making tremendous strides in the last quarter century.

Although there seems to be growing parity between white men and women, the same cannot be said for black and Hispanic students. Three quarters of college graduates and professional students among the black and Hispanic population are women, not men.

The success of the *Feminist Movement* has influenced women in giving them permission to succeed on formerly exclusive male turf. The glass ceiling has been fragmented, and somewhat shattered but it has not collapsed. There is inequity in pay and promotion for women despite their credentials and competence.

Still, the focus on college exclusively has generated the myth that after high school it is college or nothing, which is not true. Many positions that are only open to college graduates today could be better served with people with practical experience and special trade school training, not necessarily college degrees. College mania is part of the American syndrome.

Richard Sennett shows in *"Respect in a World of Inequality"* (2003) that people everywhere, men and women alike, want to experience the dignity of work (emotional worth), a sense of carrying their own load (independence), in a system (government) of mutual respect between citizens and the authority. Given this, compensation and character merge into political stability. This goes beyond college degrees to common caring. As it was in my day, it remains the same today, only the self-reliant remain free.

DEALING WITH THE SELF-IMAGE OF DREAMERS

The United States is a reactive society. It was obvious on December 7, 1941 when the Japanese bombed Pearl Harbor. It was again apparent on September 11, 2001 when the projectile of two American commercial planes manned by terrorists destroyed the Twin Towers, killing more than 3,000 innocent American civilians.

Between these two tragedies, there was another shock. The Soviet Union successfully launched Sputnik into space in 1957. Predictably, there followed a hysterical national drive toward science at the exclusion of everything else in our educational system. First there was the new math, then the new science, and then the push to make everyone a college graduate.

Perhaps no more than 20 to 30 percent of the American population is serious about book learning at the scholastic level. Academia involves a commitment to serious book learning at a high level, postponed wage earning, and the likelihood of considerable financial debt. If this were not sobering enough, universities have had to offer remedial courses to compensate for poor secondary achievement of high school students resulting in several colleges and universities more resembling factories in regressive *Machine Age thinking*. Fully 60 percent of college freshmen require some kind of remedial education before they are ready to assume a college academic curriculum.

Pragmatic journalist David Brooks of *The New York Times* suggests, if we intend that everyone be a college graduate that we move to "practical universities" that advocate technical and practical knowledge. This incidentally was the formula a century ago, as I will show shortly. Technical knowledge, Brooks argues, is cookbook knowledge based on what is to be done; practical knowledge is about how you do it. Universities, he says, can provide the technical and the practical can be taught on-line at a fraction of the cost of attending a university.

Liberal arts education has been in effect abandoned, which once functioned as the connection of past civilizations and cultures with our own, enabling us to build towards the future.

A liberal arts college education was meant to give the student an introduction to the many dimensions of society in order to make for a more responsive citizen to the times. Higher education was meant to polish, enhance and enable graduates to enjoy more meaningful lives.

A liberal arts college education was designed to improve the civility of man so that he would be able to live in peace and harmony with people of difference.

A liberal arts college education was meant to promote freedom and the pursuit of happiness by expanding consciousness and tolerance.

A liberal arts college education was meant to make man spiritually aware and socially involved in his community.

A liberal college education was intended to make man an inconspicuous doer, not a conspicuous consumer.

The movers and shakers of American society decided to make the US a professional society as if professionalism were the answer to all our woes. In place of the basic three "R's" (reading, `riting, `rithmetic), high school became a menu of college preparatory courses. This has inadvertently resulted in a "dumbing down" of education to the point that a graduate today is not as well rounded as a high school graduate of the early twentieth century. If you have doubts, here is the high school curriculum of a high school student in Clinton, Iowa in 1900:

First Year
Algebra
Physical Geography English History
Composition
Latin
German Literature

Second Year
Geometry Zoology Botany Civil Government
Latin
German Literature Composition

Third Year
Physics History Geometry
Algebra (Higher)
Geology Latin
German French Rhetoric Composition

Fourth Year
Chemistry
Chemistry Arithmetic
Physiology
American History
Political Economy English Grammar Latin
German
French
Literature
Composition

These additional courses were added to the curriculum 1910-1915:

James R. Fisher, Jr., PhD.

Manual Training
Agriculture
Journalism
Mechanical Drawing
Music
Art
Domestic Science
Commercial Course
Public Speaking

If this seems surprisingly rigorous, Ken Burns featured letters from ordinary soldiers in his televised "The American Civil War: 1860-1865." Soldiers from both sides of the Mason-Dixon Line showed an appreciation of clarity in writing and a facility for composition. For ten years (1970-1980), I was an adjunct professor teaching graduate students in MBA programs for several universities in Florida. The majority of these students were graduate engineers, physicists and chemists who saw a career advantage to earning an MBA. I found less than one in twenty could write a simple declarative sentence. Several had MA's and Ph.D.'s in their technical disciplines.

We have acquired technology and toys of cultural dalliance, but we have lost something when it comes to the liberal arts tradition. We not only have language barriers between ethnic groups, but communication and cultural barriers when professionals leave the security of their jargon.

The academic world is not for everyone. We need scholars, scientists, teachers, doctors, managers, technicians, technologists, nurses, medical specialists, and the educated to man the infrastructure of society. We also need carpenters, road workers, heavy equipment operators, truck drivers, plumbers, pipe fitters, electricians, television and computer repairmen, bakers, butchers, printers, assembly workers, painters, roofers, air conditioning mechanics, bricklayers, salespeople, farm workers, janitors, practical nurses, livestock handlers, cosmetologists, hospital technicians, and surveyors.

Craftsmen need special education and training, but not necessarily four long years in a university that suspends life for them in meaningless nonproductive work, acquiring degrees that have little value added to anyone, leastwise to themselves.

When you force a person into a profession, the person and the profession are compromised.

WHOSE DRUM BEAT DO YOU HEAR?

A friend of mine's father insisted he become a professional man. He preferred to continue farming his family's 2,000 acres of rich Iowa loam soil. His father, a fifth generation farmer, had fought off corporate agribusiness predators during his entire career, and didn't want that to be his son's plight.

Once again, it was a case of the father's good intentions derailing the son's aspirations. Parents do their children unintended injury when they attempt to save them from pain and risk. It was struggle that made the father and struggle would make the son as well.

So, my friend became a dentist, which he hated. He tried to convince his father to allow him to go into agricultural management at Iowa State instead of dentistry at Iowa, thinking he could rally independent farmers to resist corporate takeovers. It might have worked. He had a talent for organization and strategic planning.

Was my friend's life a failure? Only he can answer that. When he failed to convince his father to finance his desired education, he could have rebelled and taken control of his life. He didn't. He could have used his skills to persuade his father to think differently, but he caved in without a fight. He is now retired, looking back on a very unhappy forty years in dentistry, still fantasizing about how it might have been.

The wonder is how many doctors, lawyers, psychologists, engineers, chemists, executives and teachers are not doing what they would prefer to be doing.

My English professor had said I belonged in the humanities and not in science. This incensed my working class father. He saw such students on his trains with long hair, tennis shoes, dirty clothes, reading "weird books." He looked at me. "Can I ask you a question, Jimmy?"

I nodded. "You're not a goddamn fag are you?"

That summed up his view of humanities majors. I was not gay but I had nothing against gayness. That confused and angered him even more. Gender preference was irrelevant. I didn't date because academics meant everything. I was a grind; a poor kid who believed if he ever let up he'd flunk out. So, like my friend who wanted to farm, I stayed in chemistry showing no more courage than he did.

My da couldn't picture his son making a living throwing words around and getting paid for it, or sitting in a classroom throwing ideas around to students who would rather be somewhere else. So, there was certain legitimacy to his concern, which he unfortunately wrapped up in a stereotype.

So, I became a chemist with a facility for theory but not laboratory work, mainly because I am not mechanical. In my day, you had to improvise a good deal of your instrumentation for experiments. Subsequently, I went into chemical sales, not because I was interested in selling, but because I was a failure in the lab and needed to make some money quickly to honor a fellowship to an eastern university pursuant to theoretical chemistry. This was the era of Nobel Laureates Francis Crick and James Watson. Model building led to their discovery of the double helix of DNA.

Theoretical chemistry was opening up as a career track. Unfortunately, my wife had our third child, and the stipend was not sufficient to carry us financially. The graduate curriculum appeared too challenging to allow time for an outside job. What to do? A semester postponement of the fellowship was granted.

It found me studying Chemical & Engineering News for sales jobs. I landed one with Nalco Chemical Company and was shipped off to Indiana after a month of technical training but no sales training. Only by accident, I discovered I had a faculty for reading people leading to success in sales.

Trained as a cognitive thinker, I found I could intuitively gauge buyers' moods and sense their readiness to buy. I also discovered I had the "killer instinct" for closing sales. Once buyer and seller were on the same page, I didn't hesitate to close the deal. Success followed, along with promotions, ultimately finding me working around the world.

It was in South Africa I had my epiphany. The world I had been programmed to see didn't bear out in reality. I resigned with no certainty as to my future. Returning to the United States, I bought a home in Florida. For the next two years, I lived on my savings, reading, writing and thinking, finding little clarity or direction for the exercise.

Where I had once lacked the courage to resist my da's wishes, I was now my own man but with a wife and four small children. Nearly broke instead of acquiring a job, I used the G.I. Bill and went back to the university full-time. I hoped to find answers there. I found none. I discovered instead that the university was the mirror image of the corporate world I had left. Professors were like sycophant managers with little power, except the grade, an amazing appetite for pettiness and gossip, and an aptitude for passive aggressive complaining, which was usually directed at the students.

OUR SECRET GARDEN

Most middle managers are equally powerless, but they have performance appraisal to hold workers in check, which is not unlike the grading system of professors, making them virtually identical caricatures of the each other.

Middle managers tend to get in the way of work with meaningless meetings the same way professors get in the way of learning with fractious practices such as nitpicking and promulgating personal and political biases, and subjective grading.

Middle managers are mainly echo chambers to authority no matter how irrelevant, while professors tend to rely on ancient notes failing to be active students of their own disciplines.

Lethargy comes to mine, but that would be misleading. Middle managers and professors are not happy campers. They are not doing what they would prefer to be doing. I seldom came across a professor or manager with a passion for the job. How do they punish? Professors become obsessive with ritual, while managers become obsessive with policy. The security of professors is based on tenure. The security of managers is based on seniority.

Doing is one thing; thinking is another. Balance and harmony come when what we think and do have consistency and synchronicity with what we are.

No one is absolutely good or evil, brilliant or stupid, competent or incompetent, secure or insecure, successful or unsuccessful, but a combination. If we ignore our susceptibility to evil, stupidity, incompetence, insecurity or failure, anyone of us can be cut down in an instant. Management guru Peter Drucker concludes, *"People of great strengths have great weaknesses."* Being alert to what we are can be powerful medicine for the soul. We must be eternally vigilant, self-aware and self-accepting of ourselves as we are in order to promote self-confident thinking.

Former president Richard Nixon broke in to the dean's office to see his grades at Duke University where he was an honors law student and was caught. He had all "A's," and finished third in his class. The Watergate break-in a quarter century later was orchestrated on his watch. He was ahead in the polls but wanted to ensure his reelection. He had to know if the polls were correct! He was reelected in a landslide, but was driven out of office in humiliation for the cover-up. The same snake that bit him at Duke bit him again in the White House.

Know this: we cannot erase who we are. It is what makes us human. If aware of our weaknesses, we can gingerly step around them without having them throw us off stride. It was why I could read people. My weaknesses and I were friends. Most of us can read strength in others. Isn't that interesting? But we can't read weakness. Why is that? Is it because we fail to recognize weakness in ourselves?

Success comes largely from accepting rather than denying our weaknesses. This may mean avoiding certain people, places and things because they magnify our weaknesses. If strength is what we do well, then weakness is where we need help. If these are known and balanced, you are less likely to be thrown off stride. We are then able to self-correct and adjust. Insecurity dogged President Nixon like a shroud. He never got a handle on it. When you are a stranger to yourself, brilliance can never make suitable purchase.

It is no accident the most powerful and successful people have enormous weaknesses as well as strengths. Life experience gives birth to both. It is the nature of life that it is a struggle between our angels and demons to the end. It helps, therefore, to have a sense of humor about our strangeness.

WHEN RETREAT IS THE BEST POLICY

Prudence is companion to alertness. You cannot be afraid to back away and take a "time out." This is especially true when internal stress and strain build up against accelerating and unanticipated external demands. Retreat can be a brave and prudent strategy.

To stay the course could actually eat away your spirit and poison your resolve to prevail. Society forgives us when we are physically ill. It is ambivalent when we are emotionally weary. This is sad because our sick culture has made it difficult to stay well.

After South Africa, I took a "time out" that became a two-year sabbatical. Was it necessary? The answer is, "yes!" Had I not taken it I don't think I would be writing these words. Others reminded me that I had a family to support, that it was not morally correct or ethically responsible for me to leave my well-paying job and promising career. I appreciated their sincerity, but their sentiments did not influence me.

I was a sick puppy, and knew if I didn't take a break and get my head on straight my life might spiral down into embarrassing disaster. We can sense our fall from grace if we stay alert. Society and our programming is telling us to stay the course. Our subconscious is bombarding our senses telling us to take a "time out!" Prudence is telling us to follow our subconscious.

Physically, I appeared quite healthy. No one could see what was increasingly obvious to me. I was heading for a nervous breakdown. Composed on the outside, tall, straight and smiling, I was a wreck on the inside, fatigued, disillusioned, depressed and demoralized.

South Africa was 180 degrees out of phase with who and what

I thought I was. Nothing made sense to me. I was programmed to respond positively to superiors, direct reports and the troops. This now left a bad taste in my mouth. The lie I was living weighed heavily on my heart. My mind started to think what a relief it would be to die and escape all this. My life had no meaning. It was inconsequential. I was a personal failure and a financial success.

So, in 1969, I took a "time out." Did I ask anyone for advice? No. My Chicago boss, while in London invited me to fly up from Johannesburg for an afternoon chat, a time consuming distance of thousands of miles, to what end, I asked myself. I found the request ludicrous, cabling: "Cannot come. Too busy. I resign." Around trip of 12,000 miles for a chat was simply a power move and I was fresh out of patience with the power game. Have I regretted that action? No. Have I ever been as successful? Not financially, but intellectually, yes. Would I do it again? Yes.

Confident Thinking is not driven by arbitrary standards of morality, but by a pragmatic appreciation of our fragile construction as a person. The only sin I understand is waste and I was wasting away. Confident thinking requires unraveling the multiple layers of our conditioning from early development on to discover our often neglected center, where our moral compass resides, which is our self-reliance system to personal freedom.

Society's arbitrary standards are spirit killers, and one of the greatest spirit killers is society's capricious definition of success.

Jean Paul Sartre as quoted in *"Sartre & Psychology"* (1994) gives us some perspective on this:

> *"A man can always make something out of what is made of him. This is the limit I would today accord to freedom: the small movement which makes of a totally conditioned social being someone who does not rend back completely what his condition has given... Society makes it very difficult for the average person to question the meaning of life and the value of role-playing. We are not here concerned with the obvious benefits that we derive from society. The issue is the ease in which present society can alter human consciousness and role-playing so that it seems natural to do what is clearly wrong... to buy security at any price and to believe that this purchase is*

reasonable."

Sartre (1905-1980) died before the intensity of this programming was manifested, but all the signs were already apparent.

If your success makes little sense to you, it is time to examine your programming. Don't confuse this with escaping your conditioning. That is impossible. Yet once you recognize and accept your programming, you can decide what works for you and what does not, and act accordingly. Reconsider some of the things you have been told to believe, to value, to consider important, to be true. Don't be surprised if many haven't survived the test of time.

Sometimes people say unflattering things about us. Our first reaction is to be hurt or angry, but do they hold a grain of truth? If they do, they provide us with a better insight into ourselves. Remember this: most people have only a vague notion of themselves. They see themselves more clearly when they are giving you advice for they are basically talking to themselves without knowing it.

Should they say, "Come back into the fold, and behave as we do!" Since you are not "they," and they are not you, you could say politely, "Thank you, but no thanks."

Recognize that no one can truly hurt you except yourself. You are fully capable of self-destruction, but equally capable of self-realization. Others can talk about you, sabotage you, even blackball you, but they cannot derail you from being your own best friend unless you capitulate to their whims and betray yourself.

Whatever their motivation, fear and envy are likely to be common factors. People are afraid to know themselves. Consequently, they may resent the confident thinking individuals. Knowing yourself is not enough, you must also accept yourself as you are, which leads to the corollary of accepting others as you find them. Our definitions of success may differ, but with *Confident Thinking*, however it is defined, it brings closure.

CONFIDENT THINKING
CREATIVE STAGE FOUR

EXPECT TO BE CONFIDENT
EXPECT PEOPLE TO LISTEN TO YOU
CONFIDENCE IS A
PSYCHOLOGICAL MINDSET

Everything without tells the individual that he is nothing; everything within persuades him that he is everything.

—**Xavier Doudan**, French Author

ONE MAN'S CUP IS ANOTHER MAN'S SAUCER

I**IF WE AGREE** success is ambiguous, then expectations are likewise ambivalent. This is not as depressing as it sounds. There is fluidity as we move from chaos to order with several bumps along the way. It is called "life."

Success often finds the present suspended as we dream about the weekend, of a special coming event, of a holiday in the future.

These are coping mechanisms to deal with the drudgery of the present that we must endure. Yet, the present is all we ever have. The clock is ticking and precious moments are fleeing.

As German philosopher Martin Heidegger puts it, *"As soon as we are born, we are old enough to die."* There is not a moment to waste but we waste them nonetheless. We have to have something to look forward to, we tell ourselves, to cope with the hours, the days, the weeks, the months, and the years. We go to school for twelve, sixteen or even twenty or more years to acquire professional credentials, and then, when we arrive, *"nothing is as good as it seems beforehand,"* as English novelist George Eliot puts it.

Why is that? A forty-year career can disappear like a puff of smoke. Nine years of college training or more may be a distant past, but while enduring them they can feel as if they will never end.

One obvious reason is that we are obsessed with *chronological time,* when the only time of consequence is *psychological time.*

In chronological time we put off doing what we think we should as long as possible. We call it procrastination.

With psychological time, we choose to act immediately.

That is the fallacy of chronological time. We are always going to do it tomorrow. We are addicted to painless action, or one-step-at-a-time correction. It seldom works because commitment and involvement must be total. They cannot be total unless the psychological commitment is genuine. This applies to dieting, smoking, drinking, taking drugs, leaving an abusive relationship, going back to school, getting a new job, changing careers, or a myriad of other pending requirements from getting a new set of tires for your car to having a complete physical.

As hard as it is for us to accept where we are right now, it is where we have chosen to be.

We can blame everyone under the sun but the fact remains that we have allowed someone to prevent us from making a choice, a psychological commitment, hoping that things would work out, when we know they won't, hoping that the job will improve, when we know it is unlikely, hoping that our mate will grow up, when we know the evidence is not encouraging, hoping if we loan money to an addictive sibling one more time, he or she will turn the corner and mend his or her ways, when we know their history suggests otherwise. Why do we hold such hope? We believe time heals, which is a great cliché, when time only puts off the inevitable. Personal enslavement is the mantra of chronological one-step-at-a-time.

Let us now look at false expectations and self-deceit, first in discussing the *"Fisher Model of Conflict Resolution,"* then *"Patterns of Expectations,"* and finally, the *"Triangle of Confident Thinking."*

THE WISDOM OF DR. MARIA MONTESSORI

We send and receive mixed messages every day, not only to others but to ourselves as well. We tell people one thing, think another, with them hearing a third. We hear what we want to hear and build our expectations on what often turns out never to have been said.

We believe people will change when we fail to accept them as they are in the first place. People can change, but rarely do. It is because change requires making choices now, when they would prefer to put it off until later, and later seldom comes. Dr. Maria Montessori believed in the early development of the child, seeing a strong correlation between a child's personality at seven-years-of-age with what it will be for the rest of that person's life.

Each of us spends a lifetime dealing with our early programming. This is programmed into us when we are most vulnerable. It is not only what is said, but also what we, absorb and process in our early years.

No one is spared an albatross being placed around one's proverbial neck. One prominent scientist, Richard Dawkins, a confirmed atheist, has written a book, *"The God Delusion"* (2006). A celebrated rationalist, he shows an indifference to epistemology. In debunking all religions as "blind faith," his words indicate he lives by the faith of reason, which we know is finite. As much as science knows and has found out, there is much more that it does not know, and will never know. Some people call this "God." I sense that Dawkins self-assuredness is the little boy speaking as the scientist who thinks he is an unimpeachable rationalist when his absolutism gives him away. There is no escape from self-blindness that takes residence in those first impressionistic years.

We play psychological games with each other and with ourselves. We verbalize promises we never intend to keep, as similar promises are verbalized to us. Trust is often built on this flimsy skeleton collapsing into a pile of disappointments. Many of us write books to see if we have an audience of like-minded souls. Rest assured, the more emphatic we are the less certain we are; the more we believe everything is a case of either/or the more likely it is neither.

There is a perverse consistency in the psychological driven dreamlike notion of expectations. People aren't made of bricks, mortar and cement, but strangely enough, of expectations coached in ephemeral language.

The problem with expectations is not having them. The problem is with the focus on outcomes and not on process. Dawkins is not wrong to state his case with passion. It is with the wrapping of his argument in reason thinking science is the end all of everything and that religion has no place in the matter. It was Einstein who said, "Science without religion is lame, religion without science is blind." We are a spiritual and material being. Dialogue is preferred to blind faith of any designation.

College students often see the degree once earned the end of the arduous learning process when it is only the beginning, which incidentally is the meaning of "commencement." Life feeds off of the joy, sorrow, disappointment, ecstasy, success and failure all in the course of life's journey. College is an opportunity to be immersed in the world of ideas and ride on the shoulders of giants. It can be that magic touchstone when ideas start to make sense and come together. But if students thought professors were tough, college is a walk in the park compared to bosses on the job. College is a time when adult-children are given permission to remain in suspended adolescence. Sadly, this pull is so strong many never make the transition into adulthood remaining in the grips of arrested development and learned helplessness throughout their careers.

James R. Fisher, Jr., PhD.

PSYCHOLOGICAL FORCES WITHIN INTERPERSONAL RELATIONS

Fisher Model of Conflict and Stress Resolution©™

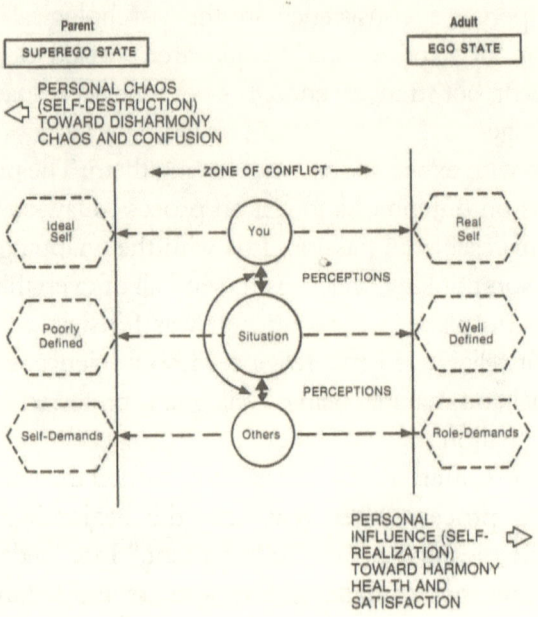

When you deal with others, you must ask yourself, "Who is speaking? "That is what I asked myself with Dawkins' declaration that God is a delusion. He has every right to say that and I have every right to differ with him.

Now, "who is speaking," not only applies to the person sharing his views, but also to "who is listening" in terms of his reaction to such views.

This brings us to the nature of what I call "the ideal self" and "the real self."

How we interpret and react to what we hear is predetermined largely by how we define the information, more directly, how we define the situation in terms of our "ideal self" and "real self." They are both valid parts of each of us.

Taking this one step further, acting on our minds will be two further dimensions of this process, and that is "self-demands" and "role demands."

Once it is clear that our reaction to a given situation is with either our "ideal self" or "real self," then it follows that either our "self-demands" or "role demands" are on display.

There are two pressures acting on us at all times, the "real self" and the "ideal self."

The "real self" is how we actually are, warts and all, a side we show when we think nobody is watching.

If we accept our "real self," chances are we won't get all bent out of shape when someone penetrates our facade. There is then a good chance we will define our situation clearly and act on it appropriately.

Once we start to think on our own, once we get beyond the support system of our family, and process information in the light of experience, that voice in the back of our head that was our parents is now quiet. It is still there but we have grown beyond that voice and have developed our own. We have discovered our authentic self. We cannot have an authentic identity until we are acquainted and comfortable with our "real self" as our friend.

Only we can establish identity consistent with our nature. No one else can do that for us. This gives birth to the "adult ego state," or the "real self." Thus we have the emotional maturity to see the situation as it actually is, not as it should be. We are ready to deal with each situation in terms of its real demands, which might be labeled "role demands."

The "ideal self" is how we have been programmed to behave. It is a combination of the "critical parent" (how we are supposed to be) and "nurturing parent" (forgiving us for our transgressions) that were programmed into us long ago, and which we have never managed to outgrow. Either our "critical parent" or our "nurturing parent" demonstrates its influence on us when it surfaces as we address our own children, or as we relate to our friends

The "ideal self" is the "superego state" or "moral self." It is the judgmental self that owns everyone's problems seeing the situation in terms of black and white, never gray, expecting the situation to behave, as it should, not as it is or will. Guilt and self-loathing are common with this state because the person cannot forgive himself for not being perfect, or the ego ideal. A parent in such a state could never admit to his child that he was far from perfect when he was young, or that he committed some of the same dumb things he is now scolding his child for doing.

Historians, as well as Freud, claim the perfectionist mania of Leonardo da Vinci may have contributed to his failure to often complete tasks (see Sigmund Freud's *"Leonardo da Vinci,"* 1916). It was a way to presage his brilliance "as if only" the work had been completed. Take the incomplete masterpiece Mona Lisa for example.

The "ideal self" denies its shortcomings and therefore is crippled by them. It is common with the *passive-receptive personality* to be emotionally dependent on others to make choices for him, to give him advice, and take control. He wants someone to blame if things go wrong. By abdicating responsibility, he sees himself as blameless when he fails or missteps.

"Self-demands" are prominent if we are needy. The needy person needs attention, approval, to appear to be somebody, to have others available to protect their fragile ego, and act as a sounding board for all their woes. Such a person needs to make a good impression, needs people to know how important he is; needs to be associated with people of prominence, needs to name drop, needs to attend a prestigious university, needs to be included in everything, and needs constant reassurance.

"Self-demands" find it impossible for the person to listen, as he is only interested in what is important to him and what he thinks. He can be easily offended with the slightest criticism, but thinks nothing of criticizing others. He is a rumormonger, a gossip, and tends to be passive aggressive, maliciously obedient, and obsessive compulsive.

"Role demands" focus on the situation. "Role demands" constantly change. They differ when listening to a friend, completing a work assignment, or providing emotional support to a loved one. The person who has a firm grip on "role demands" shows an easy grace and self-confidence as he changes from one demand to another never confusing the demands of the situation. He is not the center of the focus, the demands of the situation are. He brings the best out in others because he pays attention. He actively listens. This does not mean he allows others to set up straw men only to be bowled over. For example, he would not let a problem drinker get off the hook by hiding in "his disease." He is not a patsy for his or anyone else's excesses.

To better understand the difference between these two demands in terms of confident thinking, there is a simple checklist: With "self-demands, "it is evident that you need to protect your fragile ego; you need to let people know how important you are; how experienced and skilled you are; and how lucky they are to be working with you; you need to identify with people who are "somebody"; you are inclined to drop names of important people, to brag about your children as an implicit means of self-absorption; you need others to share your personal biases toward everybody and everything. If others don't fall in line with your thinking, they are classified as stupid in belittling stereotypes.

With "role demands," you perceive the situation in light of its specific demands. You demonstrate confidence and caring. For this, you earn group trust. You see a synergistic connection between individual and group needs. You have no inclination to compare and compete, to divide and conquer, or put one individual or group against another. You are kind, considerate, consistent, fair and respectful, but also firm. You treat everyone alike with dignity, while holding behavior to a high standard, according to the demands of the situation. You are no pushover. You display confident thinking without badgering others with it. Others feel better for being in your company. You know life is not fair, but that is not relevant. You are not an apologist. Nor are you sidetracked with self-esteem issues. Esteem, like everything else, has to be earned; to earn it we must do something. The cart will go nowhere if it is in front of the horse. The idea of "feel good" applies to "self-demands," and not "role demands." You expect your life and work to be judged critically, but fairly, and you expect you won't always see eye-to-eye with your bosses. So, it is no surprise that others don't always see eye-to-eye with you. You know life is not divided into semesters where you can bone up for exams, but a series of daily pop quizzes. Success comes when preparation meets opportunity. There is no luck involved as everyone gets a report card every day. The key to "role demands" is readiness. Consequently, if a person is obsessed with his "ideal self" and "self-demands," the situation will be poorly defined and misinterpreted. It is the blindness of old logic, a fraction that always seeks its integer.

Reason will not convince such a person to think otherwise. It is "the system" that is against him, and he will have it no other way. He is the victim. It is not his fault. He did nothing wrong. That may be true, but even truer is that he most likely did nothing right. He is an emotional cripple heading toward personal chaos, self-destruction, and if not corrected, toward constant conflict with others.

Since the confident thinker will be comfortable with his "real self" and "role demands," he will define the situation accurately. He will not attempt to avoid the consequences of his actions, but will face them. He will nip problems in the bud before they explode out of control.

For this attention, his personal security will be enhanced, his professional influence solidified, and his aspirations on the road to self-realization. This is not to imply that for every step forward there is not a step back, or that surprise and failure do not occur on occasion. It means he is ready for the most stressful situation. Even when everything is not going well, he is guided by *adaptive tension* that gets him through the difficulty. He is not paralyzed by *maladaptive tension.*

This is because he embraces his fears rather than runs from them, accepts the challenges at hand and deals with them the best that he can. At the end of the day, he is satisfied and has no regrets because he did the best that he could with what he had to work. The body and mind as one have amazing resilience when this is the mindset.

"Role demands" will also be demonstrated in helping others define their situation not by rhetoric or preaching, but by showing them the way. Self-confidence is contagious. Helping others to adjust to what they can do rather than what they can't do is a coaching function.

There is a natural dynamic in the "zone of conflict." It is the tension between the "real self" and "ideal self," and "self-demands" and "role demands." This determines whether the situation is clearly or poorly defined.

The drama of mounting anger is first rehearsed in our heads, often unbeknown to us, before it explodes between us and someone else.

If only we were more self-aware, when social pressure starts to build, we could take a deep breath, count to three, excuse ourselves, go somewhere private, take out a handkerchief and clean our glasses, or any number of things to bring our pressure gauge down to where we could react without embarrassment. Too often we "pop off." This is a form of rage. This was the case with actor, Mel Gibson, a deeply religious zealot, director of the acclaimed film, *The Passion of the Christ* (2004), when he was stopped for erratic driving. He resisted arrest, and went into a hysterical tirade against Jews, police and society, inconsistent with what he professed to be his "real self." Gibson insisted this was an aberration, and simply the harangue of a "wild ass drunk."

Freud would not agree. He would say he had real issues between his "ideal self" and "real self," as well as between his "self-demands" and "role demands," and that the persona he attempted to project of the devout Roman Catholic was loaded with conflict and inconsistency, and that all this repressed tension had to eventually surface. Unfortunately, when such rage finally surfaces, it is almost always ill timed.

Before you pass judgment on Mr. Gibson, know that part of us has little interest in our own best interests; and part of us has little regard whether our actions are destructive or constructive. The angels and demons of our nature are always active and likely to surface the more we confine ourselves to high stress situations with little down time.

The Fisher Model of Conflict Resolution©™ is never static, never one-dimensional, and can be accelerated or retarded by the clash of emotional temperaments. While we are at war within ourselves, this same conflict goes on within others as well. Consequently, a given situation can be perceived in multiple ways. This complexity can be mind-boggling but it need not be.

SEQUENTIAL CHRONOLOGY TO COOPERATION©™

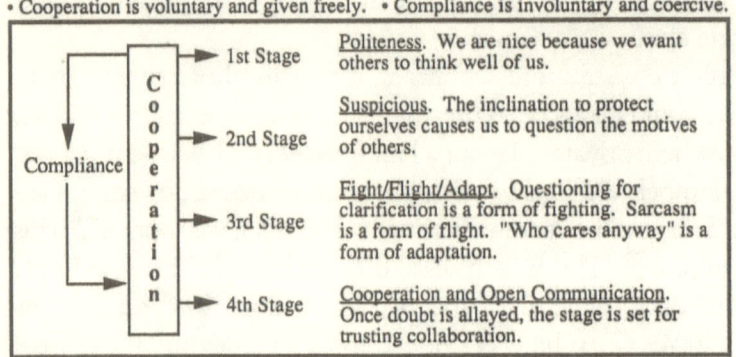

• Cooperation is voluntary and given freely.   • Compliance is involuntary and coercive.

Compliance / Cooperation	1st Stage	Politeness. We are nice because we want others to think well of us.
	2nd Stage	Suspicious. The inclination to protect ourselves causes us to question the motives of others.
	3rd Stage	Fight/Flight/Adapt. Questioning for clarification is a form of fighting. Sarcasm is a form of flight. "Who cares anyway" is a form of adaptation.
	4th Stage	Cooperation and Open Communication. Once doubt is allayed, the stage is set for trusting collaboration.

Fisher Sequential Chronology of Interpersonal Interaction.

Suspicion is a healthy filter to observe and screen out the wheat from the chaff of what is presented. Suspicion is also a good check off in examining the world within. Not only is self-denial bad for the soul, it is bad for the pocketbook.

A scam can work only on someone who is self-ignorant and believes you can get something for nothing; that there is such a thing as plain luck; that a perfect stranger wants to double or triple your money if you'll accompany him to your bank; or another stranger convinces you that you should be in Hollywood.

The "ideal self" can be fooled, but not the "real self."

"Self-demands" want us to believe the impossible is possible, but "role demands" smell something fishy from the start. Don't try to fool a fooler because he knows the territory well, and deals with it every day.

Someone tells you, "You're a genius. "The "ideal self" says, "Yes, I am, aren't I?" Then, you repeat to yourself the litany of all you have done to justify this sobriquet. But the "real self" steps to the fore and says, "Get serious, wooden head, if he only knew he'd be of another mind."

The struggle we go through "inside" our head to experience clarity "outside" is ongoing. What goes on within goes on as well between us in interpersonal interactions.

You can separate the two for discussion purposes but you cannot separate them in real experience. The way we treat ourselves has much to do with how we treat others.

My brother-in-law, Bill Waddell, grew up in a small farm community, graduated from high school, worked nearly fifty years in a factory, claims he has never read a book, but teaches me more about emotional self-reliance every time I am with him. He is the model for what is discussed here. He has a contentment that Walt Whitman wrote magnificently about in *"Leaves of Grass"* (1855). The irony is Whitman had little capacity for self-contentment in his own life.

This brings me to the "sequential chronology of interpersonal interaction." This model describes why there is so much wasted effort in enterprise, so much mistrust between partners in marriage and in business, so much contentiousness between students and faculty, politicians and the electorate, and as I have already implied so much distrust and self-deceit within us.

Conflict is natural to us individually and collectively, within us and between us. The problem is conflict avoidance only deepens conflict, as the avoidance of confrontation makes matters even worse.

How many siblings haven't spoken to each other for years because of conflict avoidance? How many children avoid their parents for unresolved issues that have been magnified over time? Yet, if these issues had been confronted initially, they would have been long ago resolved.

James R. Fisher, Jr., PhD.

Conflict is not bad. Managed conflict is the glue that holds us together as partners, a family, a company, a country, and a society. In fact, managed conflict is what holds a team to its purpose. We don't have to love each other, or even like each other to cooperate, but we do have to respect and trust each other, and be upfront about issues we have with each other for the management of conflict to work to our purpose.

The problem is we are impatient with the process of interpersonal interaction. We want to avoid troubling conflict and embarrassing confrontation in order to get on with the exchange. When we avoid conflict, we may call what we get "cooperation," but it is only "compliance." We must take responsibility for the wall between us by confronting it, and fighting through it. Only through confrontation is cooperation possible.

Cooperation is given freely, openly, and voluntarily, whereas compliance is a mechanism of forced demands conditional to a desired action. A great deception is the belief that incentives transcend this distinction. They do not. Nor do pay raises boost morale and improve performance. Efforts to bypass conflict management only increase the level of the demands.

If there is not self-evident justification between what is given and what is received, the strategy is counterproductive.

In the 1970s companies attempted to boost productivity in the face of emerging international competition. Traditional American markets for manufactured goods were shrinking. Companies commenced to give workers everything but the kitchen sink in hopes of reversing the trend. It backfired. Workers went from management dependent to counter dependent on the company for their total well-being. Entitlement programs skyrocketed into the trillions of dollars. Today this represents an additional cost of $1,500 for every automobile that comes off the assembly line of bankrupt General Motors. GM is the rule and not the exception in this faulty strategy.

Likewise, failure to be confrontational has found employees protesting infrequently and violently rather than frequently and politely. The same scenario can be put on a personal basis. Who doesn't have someone in their family who abuses alcohol, drugs, has a problem gambling, lying, stealing, cheating, or smokes to the point of ruining their health and those around them? I would imagine precious few.

Yet, when these people get into trouble with the law, relatives or friends bail them out and think they are doing them a favor, "after all, its family!"

This develops a codependency that has been written about widely. The person in question doesn't get better, but worse, and everyone suffers for this.

People who have their act together frequently fail to see the harm they do when they attempt to carry someone else's burden. They are strong because they suffered the consequences of their actions and expected no one to pick them up when they were down. For them to deny that role to a friend or sibling when they mess up is to weaken them and their resolve, and diminish them as a person.

We can only remake ourselves. We can create a climate for others but they must make the choices and suffer the consequences of those choices. They are neither our choices to make nor our consequences to suffer, only theirs.

This brings us to the mechanism of sequential interpersonal interaction. You cannot choose how another person is to behave any more than you can demand that person cooperate. Cooperation is voluntary and freely given, while compliance is involuntarily and coercively given.

Each of us has his own individual space. When someone violates that space, we are confrontational, take exception and adapt, or retreat into submission. Under the circumstances, cooperation is only possible with confrontation. Otherwise, our behavior registers as compliance.

The **_First Stage_** in interpersonal contact is the "politeness stage." We want others to think well of us. There is nothing expected of us other than to be civil. We feel no threat to our person or possible injury to our delicate psyche. Our social conscience is on display and the mask we wear reflects our geniality.

The **Second Stage** is the "suspicious stage." The natural inclination is to protect ourselves from the unknown, therefore to question the motives of others. We feel the situation more than we perceive it. Cognitively this translates into questions in our mind: where is he coming from; what does he expect of me; why is he being especially nice, or especially cold; what credentials does he have to be so self-assured? Why? Why? Why? This natural filter is a protective mechanism that is as natural to us as breathing. We would do well to listen. As Emerson said, "What you say speaks so loudly I cannot hear you." He was referring to this stage.

The **Third Stage** is the "fight, flight, adapt, submit, or surrender stage." This is when interpersonal relationships become complicated.

We are conditioned from our earliest memory to respect authority figures, to look for answers in books and from others, and to make light of what experience tells us. Yet our experience may contradict this programming.

We also are conditioned to be polite, obedient, respectful, patient, punctual, passive, non-confrontational, conforming, and quiet: to be seen and not heard. This programming was as much a function of the academic curriculum as reading, writing and arithmetic in grammar school during the past century. It still is.

Such conditioning worked well when we were an Industrial Society and in the Machine Age. Then, information and decisions were made from the top down as speed and timeliness were of little consequence.

Now, we are in the Information Age in a Service Economy where conforming behavior is a curse to the necessary innovation and initiative that is required at the level of consequences, or where work occurs.

It doesn't bode well for the individual or his association if he cannot lead; if he cannot take charge and act responsibly as the situation demands. He who hesitates is not only lost but may be out of a job as market intelligence is constantly in motion and the window of opportunity closes nearly as soon as it opens. If decision makers fail to have this information, it could be because those possessing it act with malicious obedience and withhold it or attempt to spread disinformation to sabotage operations.

In the past century, four in every five workers were conforming, and mainly passively aggressive and management dependent (See *"Six Silent Killers"* 1998). At mid-twentieth century, 80 percent of these workers were blue-collar or unskilled to semiskilled laborers. This number is now reduced to less than 20 percent with the majority of workers professionally educated at universities and colleges. Compliance didn't hurt the work process at midcentury because workers acted mainly as machine parts that were interchangeable and therefore replaceable.

That has all changed, as workers today are primarily knowledge workers with the most critical information in their possession. Answers today are more likely in the trenches than in Mahogany Row. With the advent of the computer, and its blinding acceleration in sophistication, mechanized intelligence at the point of consequences has superseded management and managers with a whole new set of challenges.

Cooperation is now necessary not only because of the changing complexity of the market place but also because of the changing complexion of work and workers. Now, four in every five workers arc college trained with credentials equal to or superior to those to whom they report.

Position power has had to accede to knowledge power. If position power is reluctant to share power with knowledge workers in a timely fashion, the consequences could be dire. It is why the "fight" is so critical in the *Third Stage*. Fight is questioning for understanding, clarification, and resolution of misgivings so that trust might be established. Since we are not programmed to be confrontational, fight often comes out as sarcasm, or obliquely in rolling of the eyes or other nonverbal ways. This should be picked up and explored because it is significant and could be consequential.

That is why the old formula of "corporate speak" is inappropriate:

"Listen carefully, don't ask question, just listen, what I have to say is important to you, don't interrupt, I am a busy man, and time is money. "That sentiment kills the spirit, chases minds away from the assembly, and defeats any chance of cooperation.

No longer is it prudent to talk at people, if it ever was, but to engage in dialogue, only dialogue has any chance to bridge the chasm between trust and distrust.

If those in charge insist on the old ways, then the troops will likely adapt, submit and surrender. This retreat from confrontation and managed conflict severely diminishes the chances of cooperation. Activity then, largely by default, becomes compliance. Compliance abandons the possibility of consensus, and may gravitate to a mindset of passive dependence. Workers bring their bodies to work but leave their hearts and minds at home.

The **Fourth Stage** is the "cooperation, communication, and collaboration stage."

Once doubt is allayed, and trust is established, the individual is ready to give himself to the relationship freely.

Typically, anxious to have the interaction reach fruition, an attempt is made to go from the **First** to the **Fourth Stage**, skipping the **Second** and **Third Stage** altogether.

Old school thinking interprets any challenge to authority the personification of disrespect, and it will have none of that! The problem with such thinking is that it yields to "self-demands" instead of "role demands." The latter are required to get everyone on board on the same page and off on the same dime. This calls for cooperation, not compliance.

Quite commonly, misguided "self-demands" drive a wedge between leaders and doers because these strategists don't see doers as thinkers, and so go forward strategizing with blinders on, or "ready, fire, aim!" Like it or not, the computerized world of mechanized thinkers today can derail a project without as much as a fairly well.

If the individual is comfortable with his "real self" and is guided by "role demands," it follows that he is likely to be confrontational in the sense of making certain that he perceives the situation correctly consistent with its situational demands. His "fight stage" may find him asking provocative questions. For this, he must not be labeled a "trouble maker," but be seen for what he is doing, exploring his suspicions. Conversely, if it is necessary for him to impress others with his "ideal self" fronting with "self demands," then he is not sincere and his aim is disruption. Others realize this, so he can be ignored.

As soon as someone is allowed to disrupt proceedings, there is little chance the situation will move to cooperation. This can be handled adequately if the person in charge exposes the insincerity of the disrupter.

The paradox is when those in charge are driven by "self-demands" the inclination is to treat some people harshly and others sympathetically. This behavior fosters dissension and discord between the leader and doers.

The "ideal self," given this display, is inclined to choose like-minded people for key positions. This magnifies individual to group weakness status and penalizes the organization with forward inertia.

EGO STATE ON DISPLAY

If the tendency is to be anxious about how we look and are treated, it is probable we will vacillate between the "parent ego state" and the "child ego state." We will suffer from the idealization of how we are supposed to be seen and treated compared to how others actually see and appreciate us.

Emotional dependence and immaturity are aspects of the adolescent child in the adult body, more worried about being hurt than being effective.

To give you some sense of this, consider the:

VOICE TONE

The "parent ego state "would be condescending and judgmental. The "child ego state" would be full of feeling and pleading. The "adult ego state" would demonstrate concern.

WORDS USED

The "parent ego state": *"Do you know to whom you're speaking?"* The "child ego state": *"You are disgusting!"* The "adult ego state": *"It is obvious you're upset, want to talk about it?"*

POSTURE

The "parent ego state" is likely to be very erect. The "child ego state" slouching. The "adult ego state" attentive with eye contact.

FACIAL EXPRESSIONS

The "parent ego state" wears a frown. The "child ego state" shows quivering lips. The "adult ego state" displays alert eyes.

BODY POSTURE

The "parent ego state" has hands on hips with a look of defiance. The "child ego state shows the "wringing of the hands with downcast eyes. The "adult ego state" is learning forward to pay closer attention.

If obsessed with how others see us, it is quite possible to become fixated with a victim's complex looking for evidence of persecution. This is moving in the direction of the "ideal self" and "self-demands," the direction of personal chaos, confusion and self-destruction. Happiness is created. It is not found in another person or in an occasional. It is impossible in this climate to generate cooperation, or promote competence.

On the other hand, if we see ourselves as we really are, and accept our status with humor, we will not become flustered when the unexpected occurs. We will be in touch with our "real self" and be guided by "role demands" and able to define the situation clearly.

With this mature and emotional self-reliant mindset, we will be disinclined to be judgmental, but equally averse to owning other people's problems. We will have a firm grip on our powers feeling no need to punish others with our expertise but be inclined to assist them in improving theirs. Others will like to be in our company because without a word being spoken we make them feel good about themselves.

With this disposition, our aspirations and expectations are likely to be compatible as well as real, creating a climate for self-realization.

THE FOUR KEYS WE ALL SHARE

The dynamic of this "conflict model" goes on every day and every instant of every day in our daily lives. The conflict between the "ideal self" and "real self" and between "role demands" and "self-demands" goes on within us and between us. It determines how situations are likely to be defined. The same dynamic goes on within the job, between family members, friends, and in other social situations. There is no escape from the danger of being hurt, misunderstood, criticized, or the possibility of losing focus.

If the forces within the individual and the situation are in a healthy state, the person will have little trouble balancing self-demands and role demands. On the other hand, if the individual's behavior is erratic, conflict is inevitable. The more mature the individual, which means the more ready to cope with conflicting situations, the more confident thinking the individual is likely to be.

What a difference confidence makes when your *personal system* (values, beliefs, interests, expectations and perceptions) is working towards a purposeful goal. Likewise, when the forces within you are in balance with external demands, you can function at a high level. Conversely, when these forces are in conflict, you cannot function well at all.

We all share four important keys:

- *We all love ourselves.* We are born egotists, and our fragile egos will do about anything to self-protect, which means relationships are bound to be difficult;

- *We are more interested in ourselves than in anyone else.* This finds us turning the conversation around to how we think and feel and what we value;

- *Without exception, every person you meet wants to feel important.* Treat people with respect no matter what their station in life, and respect will return to you tenfold; and

- *We crave the approval of others so that we may in turn approve of ourselves.* The hardest person to make friends with is ourselves, as well as the hardest person to love. If we can accept ourselves as we are, anything is possible.

Everyone suffers this handicap to a greater or lesser degree. Kindest given brings the light of kindness out in others.

PATTERNS OF EXPECTATIONS

Examining the quality of our expectations allows our human nature to fall into the semblance of some accord. Everyone has hopes and dreams. They stimulate us into action. Some are immediate, others delayed, some realistic, others fanciful. We have expectations because we want to improve. It is our nature to wonder how we are doing; how we are looking; and if we are making satisfactory progress.

There are four aspects or patterns of expectations, which are on display when motivated. Our expectations are:

- Real and attainable,

- Cohesive and not in conflict,

- Flexible and adaptable to our changing circumstances, and

- Self-generating.

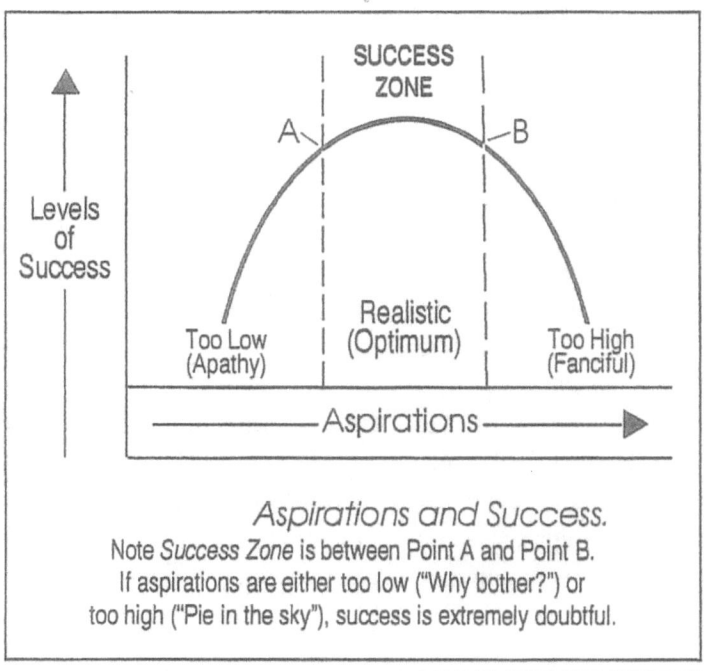

Aspirations and Success.
Note *Success Zone* is between Point A and Point B.
If aspirations are either too low ("Why bother?") or
too high ("Pie in the sky"), success is extremely doubtful.

To be achievable, our expectations must be consistent with our ability and the opportunities afforded us by circumstances. That means we must know, accept, and show a tolerance for ourselves as we are. Without this self-awareness, the tendency is to aim too high or too low, or fail to aim at all.

A cohesive pattern of expectations means that the pieces are related and support each other and are not in conflict. You can't expect to realize a college education if you also must be partying all the time. The building blocks are in place when suitable choices are made, sacrifices accepted, and purpose is clearly understood.

Life is full of surprises. A person must be flexible to demands and adaptable to consequences. Continuing the college analogy, let us say your health breaks down and you're not able to work a part time job and still carry a full course load. So, you take only a couple of academic courses and project your graduation a semester or two later than expected.

Note that the "Success Zone" is between Point A and Point B. If aspirations are either too low ("Why bother?") or too high ("Pie in the sky") success is doubtful.

You don't seek a goal. You create the architecture for the achieving the goal and then you pursue it. Goal generating is derived from self-generation.

David McClelland in *"The Achieving Society"* (1961) takes a page out of chemistry by proposing a motivation theory called "expectancy valence motivation." The idea of this theory is that we don't make progress in smooth linear progressions, but in static eruptions, which are human dramas. A small success encourages us to pursue a slightly more challenging goal, and so on.

There is no static or safe period in individual development. Once the individual attempts to play it safe, growth stops and the person starts to vegetate. Motivation is lost as well as competence as confident thinking lapses into apathy. Confidence and competence is self-generating. With expectations as with everything else, struggle is the name of the game. Get used to it.

There is a man I know who hated school and went into the army. In the army, he found a knack for organization and a skill for strategy. He worked to qualify for officers' training school. Once he was commissioned, he found he needed a broader understanding of the nuances of group behavior. So, he went back to school, while continuing his army career. First, he acquired his high school diploma. Then, he worked his way to a degree in psychology. Ultimately, he earned a master's degree in the discipline. He then retired from the army a colonel, and immediately became active in community services, in which he is now involved. Some might say he was lucky, but luck had nothing to do with it. He was proving the theory of *"expectancy valence motivation."*

Whenever the colonel encountered resistance, he embraced it, and was buoyed up by it to heighten his expectations. He had to "let go" of himself, trusting that his intrinsic self would suffice to give him control of ever changing and more challenging situations.

Growth and development are the payoff when expectations are fed with pain, risk, struggle and dedication. The colonel embraced his resistance to self-consciousness, giving him permission to have a psychological edge when each new challenge came along.

It is counterintuitive to suggest we embrace our fear, that we embrace failure, and that we think with our heart rather than our head when it comes to our career. We know that throughout time many failures preceded great successes of such men as Lincoln, Einstein, Edison and many others. They learned from failure. They energize to learn what their failures had to teach them. They understood the "Triangle of Growth," which simply is that most learning takes place when we are on the "Plateau of Failure," and not during moments in our lives when our careers are soaring. Einstein put it best, "It's not that I'm so smart; it's just that I stay with problems longer."

So, expectations bring the individual down-to-earth and face-to-face with what he is and isn't, and sometimes this face off can be derailing when it shouldn't be. Failure wasn't derailing for these great men. It need not be for us. We need only recalibrate our "Success Zone" to create a trajectory consistent with our interests, needs and energy. They were not paralyzed when they encountered failure, but took "time out" to reassess where they were and where they were going.

TRIANGLE OF REAL GROWTH AND DEVELOPMENT©™

The Power of an Open Mind

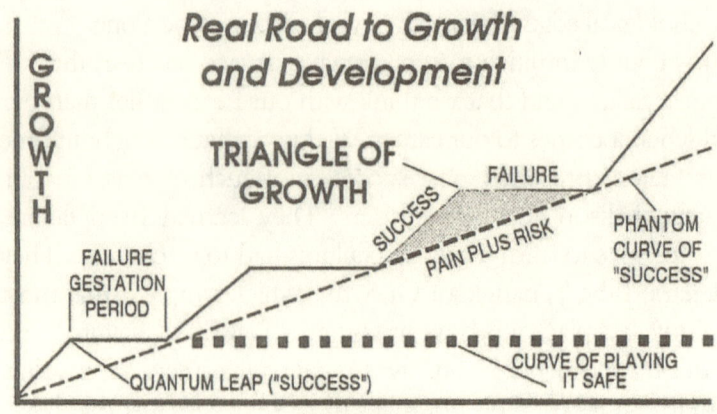

- ✳ Growth is not in linear increments, but in strategic leaps
- ✳ Gestation period is period of real learning
- ✳ Gestation period is time of trauma, retrenchment,
     assimilation of failure; a time when the learner
       Please Self Mentality:
         ✓ Is not concerned about letting the group down
         ✓ Does not have to appear smart
         ✓ Is open to taking risks and enduring pain
- ✳ Quantum leaps are periods of success,
     but of little real learning

The Triangle of Confident Thinking could also be called "teaching smart people how to learn." We have developed a surreal culture in which the only risk or pain involved is vicariously watching some reality show on television. In life, too many want to reach their fanciful goal by doing everything possible to avoid risk, pain, struggle, or indeed, failure. Paradoxically, success is only found in risking failure, never in safely seeking success.

Failure is not something to avoid but to embrace. Success is realized by embracing resistance to struggle by enduring the pain and risk that expectations demand. That means you neither shoot too high nor too low but in the optimal range of your ability and experience.

The mistake many smart people make is that they consider learning simply problem solving. The problems we solve are usually the problems we create with our thinking in the first place. To get beyond this, it is necessary to think differently on purpose, and to realize that progress is not a smooth linear curve, but a stuttered one.

The Power of an Open Mind

You don't wake up one morning and say, "I'm going to be a psychologist," and expect all your ducks to fall immediately into place and your star to soar to its appointed orbit. That is a phantom curve to success. It will never happen.

Instead, you can expect to experience many bumps along the way, which I call "plateaus of failure." These bumps could be anything: personal problems, trouble with professors (or bosses), difficulty managing your course load (or job), financial reversals, health problems, losing a scholarship (or promotion), or a sinking grade point (or being demoted). Whatever these perturbations, they are crying out for you to pay attention!

The failure plateau is a gestation period where real learning takes place. Your expectations are reevaluated, as well as your commitment and goal. You are forced to reassess where you are versus where you expected to be.

One of the interesting aspects of failure is that you are given quite a wide berth, as friends disappear, as if thinking failure is catching. This means you are spared the need to "please others." It also means you don't have to appear smart. Nor do you have to pretend everything is fine. You are in a position to take risks and endure pain. You are ready to grow and develop.

Contrast this with when you are swimming in success and possibilities couldn't be brighter, chances are your inclination to reflection is nil. When your career is soaring in a quantum leap to a new level of success, little real learning is taking place.

Learning resides in the failure plateau. It is then that we confront our reality and ourselves. This is a reassessment period. Processing knowledge gained and obstacles encountered produces invaluable insights. It is chemistry of being in its naked splendor. We have no choice but to look at ourselves in the mirror stripped of all pretense.

All growth requires gestation periods of failure to realize success. This is yours. So, the triangle of *Confident Thinking* has a rising success slope followed by a failure plateau with a base in which pain and risk take place, leading to the next burst of rising success, and so on, ad infinitum. You need never stop growing.

That is one reason why learning is so explosive when we are young. When young, we are not intimidated by failure. We are not afraid to make a fool of ourselves. Failure is not even relevant to us. Indeed, the young are open to diverse experiences taking risks without a thought to the possibility of getting hurt or looking stupid. It is why young people have a facility for learning foreign languages whereas adults resist this challenge because of possible embarrassment.

Our aversion to physical pain appears to level off at an early age, whereas our aversion for psychological pain never seems to crest. This is important to note.

Since the pain we experience, as we grow older becomes more associated with psychological pain, we tend to go to great lengths to avoid it, staying in a job we hate, a relationship that is destructive, or a mindset that is self-alienating.

Likewise, we are reluctant to take on a more demanding project because the element of failure is in the back of our mind. Self-protection has formed a cage around our existence. It is as if success is a static form and a frigid substance. Because of past hurts or failures, we are fenced in and confined to self-imprisonment. This finds us avoiding certain relationships, economic opportunities, intellectual challenges, and other life experiences.

Confident Thinking involves embracing failure to realize success; and that success, itself, is a process and not a product. We learn little from success, which is the outcome itself, but a great deal from failure, which involves the process.

Nor will looking in the mirror and repeating a mantra do the trick: "I am confident, I should be confident, I will be confident."

Confident Thinking comes in the same manner that growth and development come, that is, in strategic leaps.

We become a more confident thinker as we come to grips with new information, learn how to handle its complexities and then employ it as a tool to benefit others.

We are learning to understand ourselves better independent of others. This gestation period is a time of trauma, retrenchment, assimilation of past failures and successes, a time of learning. It is not concerned with letting others down. It is not concerned with appearing smart. It is however open to taking risks and enduring psychological pain.

The quantum leap will likely be a surprise, not something you can predict with accuracy. It is a time when expectations and life experience are in concert and you are moving forward no longer getting in your own way.

CONFIDENT THINKING
CREATIVE STAGE FIVE

RECOGNIZE THE IMPORTANCE OF OTHERS BECOME OTHER-PEOPLE DIRECTED ENABLE OTHERS TO BE SUCCESSFUL

"It is one of the most beautiful compensations of this life that no man can sincerely try to help another without helping himself."

—Shakespeare

THE TWISTED TIMBER OF MAN

E NABLING PEOPLE TO be all that they could be does not mean you become self-absorbed in the well-being of others. That is their responsibility. It means creating a climate that brings out the authentic self of others by being facilitative to that purpose within reason. It means helping others to help themselves. You may have skills in that regard of which you are not aware.

Take Dr. Donald Farr, a former NASA scientist. He has more physical maladies than most people—broken spine, eye disease, and diabetes—yet he finds time to teach, work as a volunteer to Operation Gratitude (for American military personnel stationed abroad), to keep up with his discipline so as to mentor graduate students, to maintain an e-mail network of several hundred collating and dispersing these messages daily to interested parties, and much more. Now, 80, he hasn't slowed down. Dr. Farr says he enjoys helping people, and must "keep on, keep'n on." He personifies the wisdom of the Shakespearean quote.

It starts by being empathic, progresses to enabling others to find their own center, and finally evolves to observing them lifting themselves out of their difficulty, whatever it may be. Sometimes all that is needed is someone to listen.

Without our moral compass, we cannot find our way. When our center is misplaced, we need help in finding it again. Don't expect the person needing the help to embrace support with open arms. Often we are that person. So, when we help someone else, we are helping ourselves as well.

People who need help may be resistant. Don't be discouraged by this stance. It is created to protect their fragile ego. It is hard to ask for help. Observing others, noting inconsistencies or departures from the norm, are telltale signs help is needed.

Don't expect their facade to collapse once you smile with reassurance. When we are hurting, emotions are flooding the gates and we can hardly see much less think clearly.

Experience teaches us two things: (1) a sick soul has a steep curve to climb to collect itself out of the pit of its own hell; and (2) hate and self-pity are family to such a mindset.

You are asking another to abandon his morass when being messed up is what he knows best and is more akin to him than anything else. Even if it happens to be hate, this has kept him upright and functioning even if self-destructively.

It is a long and torturous road from self-destruction to self-realization. A person must get inside his hate, not intellectually, but emotionally, to discover what feeds this hate, and why.

Irrationally, but nevertheless true, hate has become a comfort to him. Nor is it enough to show hate is causing the problem. To suggest hate is wasteful and degrading will not move him. He must want to eliminate the disturbance. He would prefer his situation to change without any work on his part. That of course is not possible.

If I am not conflicting, he thinks, I will be at peace. He wants to avoid this hatred not embrace it, to retreat into sleep or take some medication to dull the disturbance. This only aggravates the problem. Life is conflict. To avoid conflict, to attempt find solace and security in isolation is quite irrational. Life is the constant cacophony of disturbance. The best medicine is to get inside the disturbance and manage the conflict. This takes work. Any disturbance, including hatred, can be controlled once it is understood. It will not disappear. Since it is part of him, the aim should be to bring it to the surface so he can see through his deception.

If a person wants to discover why he hates, he must first understand what he loves. If he has no capacity to love then hate is not his problem, apathy is.

Complicating the matter further the thinking that formed the hate must be understood to control the problem. The origin of hate is often self-contempt, which is projected on to others for satisfaction. There is a good chance he is not aware of this mechanism or how it has poisoned his life. He believes everyone thinks as he does when quite the contrary is true. His inward insecurity makes it impossible for him to accept others as he finds them or himself as he is.

Consequently, he has a low tolerance for people of difference, people with differing points of view, people who don't share his biases, indeed, for people in general. By this peculiar circumstance, agitated as he is, he makes other people's problems his. He takes ownership of them allowing their actions, which he cannot control, to constantly frustrate him. He resents them for this obsession, which turns to hate. He cannot solve their problems because he is outside them, resenting them all the more for this fact. In exasperation, he thinks, why doesn't the world behave, as it should, as I wish it would?

Once he gets inside his hate to see it for what it is, and why it is so disturbing; once he realizes that the origin of this disturbance is his failure to be self-accepting, not as he thinks he should be, but as he actually is, then a change starts to take place. He finds himself increasingly tolerant of others as he finds them. He has discovered his moral compass, reset it on "tolerance," and is finding his way back to being comfortable with the twisted timber of his soul.

As soon as this tough customer of the self is won over, he cannot do enough for others.

It is a heady thing to contemplate. A person can go from apathetic confusion to energetic collaboration with others once love is discovered. His hate has simply been turned inside out. Love was always there only hidden by hate. Love is buried in the most hateful because hate is the other side of love. We cannot be all loving without a modicum of hate, or all hateful without a modicum of love. It would not be human.

There are positive things to hate as well as positive things to love. To hate abuse of others or violence are good thing. When love is not balanced with an appreciation of hate, it becomes a weapon used against us. We see this in extreme holy causes and passionate crusades. This can happen, has happened and is happening today and so it will be considered in this next segment.

THE IMPORTANT EARLY YEARS OF LIFE

Being social animals, we cannot survive without each other. Physical and nurturing care is essential from the moment we come into this world. Dr. Maria Montessori (1870-1952) captured its essence when she declared a child is essentially formed by the time it reaches its seventh birthday. Her reference was to the conditioning process, which takes this amorphous mass that is the child, pliable, formless, impressionistic and defenseless, and shapes it into a personality and person. It is this early programming that will determine to a large measure how we will view the world for rest of our lives.

These significant first seven years are the reasons why children grow up with such different attitudes, aptitudes, dispositions, and behaviors. It behooves those who have the privilege of early nurturing care not only to be aware of this somber responsibility but how lasting their influence. Crippled souls are a product of corrupting early experience.

The Roman Catholic Church of Ireland and Germany is currently under siege for physical, psychological and sexual abuse of children in the care of priests and nuns some fifty or more years ago. A middle-aged man in Germany, who was sexually abused repeatedly by his pastor when he was a boy, put it bluntly, "My pastor murdered my soul."

Incredibly, these offending priests and nuns were not disciplined, not turned over to the authorities, but transferred to other institutions where the offensive behavior was repeated. Words of cover up were associated with the leadership of former Pope Benedict XVI, who was Cardinal Joseph Ratzinger before in Germany. God only knows how many lives have been ruined for placing Church politics above the Church's mission.

There is no reparation for this damage as every adult who was abused as a child holds that wounded child forever in his heart.

We learn to be evil. We are not born evil. But evil can be found where we least expect it, and therefore we are all vulnerable to it.

People telegraph disturbances. We see this in *attention deficit disorders,* in restless behavior, in displays of profane language, in inappropriate dress, in massive body tattoos, and in singular belligerence. Such people are making a statement: Pay attention, world, I am somebody!

The world has never gotten used to the fact that 80 percent of what and who we are represents nearly a match with everyone else in the world. Yet, we compare and compete as if we are truly different only to magnify the 20 percent difference that might actually exist.

When I was a boy about seven, an Irish uncle said to me one day, "Jimmy, you need the clothes on your back, a roof over your head, three square meals a day, and if you have that you're in company with the richest men in the world." He was of course right but he wasn't apparently aware, nor was I that fifty percent of the world's population failed to enjoy that luxury. I've carried that somber reality into the autumn of my years.

My uncle provided me with the wisdom of insecurity, which is the best form of Confident Thinking. When you have that, no man can corrupt you with the promise of financial or other gain.

Even with proper nurturing, we can lose that advantage. Studies indicate that when a child first starts to develop his personality, away from the nurturing care of his parents, peers exert inordinate pressure on him to comply with certain deviancies in order to belong. Gangs are notorious for using this strategy.

Middle class parents once thought their children were exempt from such pressures, that only the lower classes were plagued with such deviancies. They were wrong. In fact in the recent past, middle class children have been instigators of deviant behavior. They have used their wits to flaunt the law, and then play on their parents' embarrassment once discovered to promote a cover up.

Judith Rich Harris writes perceptively about this problem in *"The Nurture Assumption"* (1998) demonstrating the incredible influence of peers. She writes:

> *"Peer pressure is less a push to confirm than a desire to participate in experiences that are seen as relevant, or potentially relevant, to group identity. Teenagers seldom need to be pushed to conform to the norms of their groups; that got settled a long time ago, in childhood."*

This has spiraled into a collapsing moral center in which parents preach one thing and practice another, and consequently, unwittingly have fashioned an army of cynical children that haunts society today. Gang behavior is rampant across the American landscape at all socioeconomic levels. Children seemingly are losing both the capacity for and interest in being individuals, settling instead for merely belonging as true believers with a herd mentality to the antics of others.

DICHOTOMY OF BELONGING

A rather unusual experience put this in perspective. I was on a consulting trip and being held over at the airport in Cincinnati because of bad weather. Paul Brown and the NFL Cincinnati Bengal football team were there as well. Earlier in the day, my client had told me a story about Coach Brown. He had attended a rookie training camp, and asked the coach, "How in the world do you decide who makes it and who doesn't?" Brown smiled. "I don't. They do."

Then he stretched out his hand and pointed to the players on the field. "See those guys over there?" A group was diligently working drills. "They're all going to make it." Then he pointed to a group shooting the breeze around the Gatorade cooler. "They're not." Coach Brown, a good-looking man, with an Irish tilt to his hat, only smiled when I walked over and asked him to confirm this story.

Winners hang together and so do losers. I suspect winners were doing as much as they could to make the most of the opportunity, while losers felt it was a rookie camp and they need not showcase their talent. They were wrong. Coach Brown was known as a disciplinarian who valued character as much as athleticism.

Another client, an ex-con, after serving his time at Florida's maximum-security prison in Raeford, came to me with a proposition. He wanted me to write a book about his life. I never did, but his situation did have relevance to this discussion. He seemed a nice young man. I had to wonder how he had gone wrong. Why did he associate with such losers? He looked at me as if I were dense, "Don't you know," he said, "They were the only ones who would accept me."

Here was a man who had been reared by a mother who was a prostitute and an alcoholic. Often there was no food in the house, only booze, with him and his little brother having little to eat for days. His mother would bring men home, and if he and his little brother made any noise the men would beat on them until they were quiet.

One time, a drunken regular looked for them as soon as he came into the house. He hid his little brother in the pantry, where the man never looked. He believes that saved his little brother's life. He was not so fortunate. He was beaten unconscious and left for dead. He was six-years-old. Neighbors called the police and he was taken to the hospital and his brother put in foster care. After a month's stay in the hospital, he ended up in a foster home but separated from his brother.

When I met him, he was a mountain of a man about six-one and weighed more than 350 pounds and appeared as solid as a rock. He had the incongruity of kind eyes with the hint of repressed terror suggesting how a trapped wild animal might look if cornered.

He confirmed my suspicions by saying, "I got myself in a terrible mess the first time the police came for me by going berserk." Indeed, I learned he threw nine policemen around as if they were confetti, injuring three seriously when they tried to subdue him. This and subsequent encounters ended with him being sentenced to prison at Raeford.

Was he a bad man? No. Was he a good man? In many ways, yes. He rebuilt his life, married a much older woman who became a surrogate mother. He had one daughter with her, and became foster parent to several children, whom he raised with loving care. He became religious in prison, joined the Masonic Lodge, and found satisfaction in that association. He was a heavy equipment operator working on highway construction and made a decent living for his family. He died in his fifties of a heart attack.

For every one like him who escapes the stigma of the ex-con, the wonder is how many do not?

The jury is out on why we are so cruel to each other, and why we do such terrible things to each other. Equilibrium collapses when the expected collides with the unexpected. Fear flickers in the hidden recesses of the eye of all animals, humans included, as survival kicks in leading often to self-destructive behavior. Panic is enemy to good sense. Envy is the poisonous venom of fear. And religious fanaticism can possess undeveloped minds and wreak havoc.

111

This is being written in the era of "international terrorism." We see society in a state of hysteria since Islam fanatics have declared jihad (holy war) on Euro-American countries.

On April 15, 2013, during Patriot's Day, and the running of the Boston Marathon, two immigrant Muslim brothers, 26 and 19, born in the Chechen region of Russia, set off two small pot pressure cooker bombs in the crowd, killing three and wounding one hundred and seventy, several losing limbs.

The Twin Towers in New York City were totally destroyed on September 11, 2001 when jihad terrorists took control of two commercial jet airliners using them as suicide missiles. How could this happen? How could people behave like this?

The answer may be in the study of laboratory animals. Rodents when subjected to overcrowded conditions began to kill each other; turkeys when spooked trample each other to death. It happens in a crowded building when someone yells, "Fire!" Rogue nations and groups can and often do act like trapped animals.

DICHOTOMY OF FEAR

It would be nice if Confident Thinking could bypass the subject of fear, to disregard the subject of death, destruction and terror altogether as it relates to human beings who turn themselves into suicide missiles, but that is not possible.

Ordinary people are receptive to the promise of eternal bliss when their life on earth is literally hell. Those who have little to lose can be persuaded that paradise awaits them on the other side. We want to describe them as ignorant and contemptible, but it took training and brains for those that flew commercial jet liners into the Twin Towers and the Pentagon. Then there are those two Chechen young men who launched their own private war of terror on the innocent, but to satisfy what? What could drive men to that ultimate fate? The short answer is only they know, but chances are the dichotomy of fear was at play.

Fear can exist only in relation to something else not in isolation. We cannot be afraid of something we do not know. Therefore, we cannot be afraid of death. Fear is in relation to the known. Death is not known. I know life, so I can be afraid of life, not death. If life is hell, something I know, life may be made to be something I desire to escape. Jihad hides behind religion, but could it be simply the fear of life, itself?

Many might question the suggestion that we are afraid to live but not to die. Think a moment. We think we are afraid of death, but our fear may be that life is too exasperating, too unpredictable, too demanding, and too terribly unfair.

We crave association, a sense of belonging, a sense of identity with something bigger and more important than ourselves, some cause, something, and we find others equally lost and attracted to the same set of true beliefs that puts the burden of our turmoil on others, say Euro-American countries that seem to have it all, and therefore they are our natural enemy. Alas, we have found a cause to die for!

This distorted version of Islam became the litmus test of the Islam fanaticism of the late Osama Bin Laden. It has succeeded against incredible odds because it retches up world fear to the point that nations become paralyzed with an obsession with security at the expense of their freedoms. Thus Western society that prides itself on its enlightenment is reduced to irrational panic. The jihadists have used their fear of life against the West to trigger theirs. Few seem to see the absurdity of this.

We may think our fear arises from our conscience, but our conditioning forms our conscience, so conscience is still the result of the known. So, what do we know?

We know what is programmed into us to know. Knowledge is having ideas, opinions about things, having a sense of continuity in relation to the known, and no more. Ideas are memories, the result of experience, which is in response to problems. Therefore, I am afraid of the known, which means I am afraid of losing friends, losing things, running out of ideas. I am afraid of discovering what I am, afraid of being alone, afraid of being at a loss, afraid of pain, which might come into being when I am nothing and have nothing.

From this, you should be able to see how the terrorists work their magic on little boys and little girls who become suicide bombers by programming them practically from birth to not be afraid of the unknown, which is death, which cannot be feared because it cannot be known. It would be very unfortunate if we chose to believe that jihadists were very different than we are.

These human death machines have been programmed to believe they will be eternally happy in paradise for their sacrifice. We don't have to make much of a leap of faith to recognize that St. Paul had a similar message. Christianity, as he perceived it, promotes the idea that this life is only preparation for the eternal bliss of heaven, where the last shall be first and the first last.

It can be argued that Jihad programming is another version of Christian martyrdom once famous in early Christian history. For those who would scoff at this, martyrdom was once considered the ultimate sign of holiness, and promise of heavenly paradise. It was part of my Roman Catholic education.

DICHOTOMY OF COMPLEXITY

There are two limiting conditions in our cranial cellular congress to cope with reality. The brain capacity to process information is finite, and the machinery with which to do it is not a conscious unity. When the space requirements of problems fit the network there, things go well. When they don't, things go to pot.

Source: *Have Fun at Work* (1988), William L. Livingston

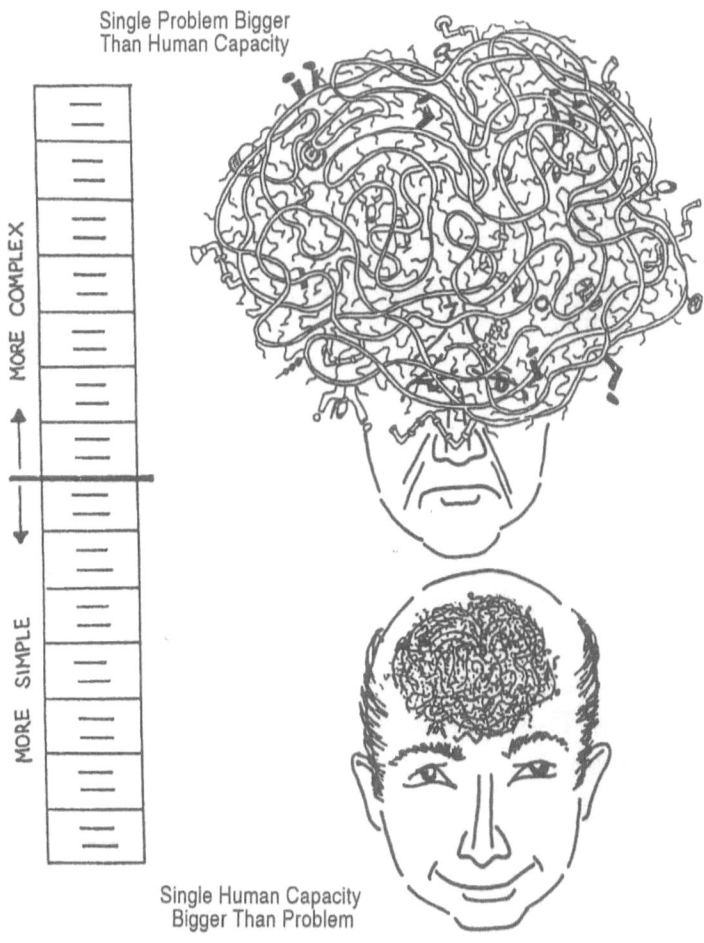

Finite Individual Coping Limits

FIRST AND LAST FREEDOM

Our world is getting much smaller. Stephen Hawking, who occupies the chair in physics at Cambridge once held by Isaac Newton, insists that we must colonize other planets because he can envision the human calamity of over crowdedness. We are already experiencing it between the haves and have-nots among nations. It seeds terrorism.

Novelist and essayist Aldous Huxley has written:

> *"Man is an amphibian who lives simultaneously in two worlds, the given and the homemade, the world of matter, life and the world of symbols. In our thinking we make use of a great variety of symbol-systems—linguistic, mathematical, pictorial, musical, ritualistic. Without such symbol-systems we should have no art, no science, no law, no philosophy, not so much as the rudiments of civilization: in other words, we should be animals."*

To understand the misery and confusion that exist within ourselves, and in the world, we must first find clarity within ourselves, and that clarity comes about through Confident Thinking. This clarity is our first and last freedom. It cannot be exchanged with another. Clarity is not the result of verbal dexterity, but of intense self-awareness, and self-acceptance.

This is not the outcome of the mere cultivation of the intellect, nor is it conformity to patterns or conditioning no matter how refined. It comes with the self-knowledge that there is no preordained place to go, no refuge from the fact that much of life is aimless. Yet we have to take aim at something while trying to sustain the illusion we are not lost.

We operate mainly on automatic pilot, aimless, but not seeming to know we are. Therefore, without understanding ourselves, we have no freedom, no basis for thought. Without self-knowledge, what we think is so is not only not always true, but is second hand information, and not ours at all. This is so because our system of upbringing is based upon what to think, not on how to think, to operate without our own roadmap. These Confident Thinking ten stages are designed to provide that roadmap.

Meanwhile, we have a situation in which television, electronics, and speed-of-sound travel have made us a global community.

At the same time, crushing humanity seems to be increasing across the globe beyond its capacity to manage this explosion. When aware of the crush of the crowd, when thinking clearly and acting wisely are crucial, many of us are in a state of paranoia bordering on panic.

We have electronic surveillance of our every move and have willingly sacrificed our freedom for security. Not only are there no secrets anymore, there is no privacy. The idea of freedom, which is the foundation of the United States, is disappearing as freedom's support system collapses.

America has gone from the "Lighthouse on the Hill and Beacon of Hope to the World" to being enmeshed in its own troubles. The world, on the other hand, has taken America's material success as an index and measure of its own.

We see this in emerging technological progress of Communist China and Democratic India. Shanghai has become a modern city with workers building skyscrapers, being paid only enough to keep body and soul together, but not their promised wages. We see India emerging into a technological power while 80 percent of its people are far removed from this sophistication.

The world as it emulates the United States has become a well-dressed man hiding decay inside the suit. You step outside the major cities of emerging Third World countries and you encounter pervasive neglect and poverty. The United States doesn't escape this comparison.

In the United States, the venerable middle class is shrinking:

- In 1982, there were 42 billionaires; in 2005, there were 474;

- In 1981, there were 20,444 millionaires; in 2003, there were 181, 282.

- In 1982, there were 1,858,000 with incomes of about $250,000; in 2004, there were nearly 6 million with this income.

Meanwhile, those below the poverty line are also increasing so that the vibrant American middle class, once representing some 55 percent of all households is now around 40 percent and falling. The United States has a burgeoning upper class and a rapidly increasing underclass with a disappearing middle class.

No society can be an effective foil to violence, chaos, and social upheaval without a significant middle class, that is, without a majority of the people sufficiently educated, economically prosperous and spiritually committed to support a vibrant society. If not, infrastructure implosion is a certainty. It happened to Rome.

We have seen in Africa the aftershock of post colonialism of new nations on that great continent. Africa is bleeding human misery. South Africa, which avoided civil war after the fall of apartheid, has mass unemployment, murder on the rampage in major metropolitan areas, and Bantu-on-Bantu crime that never occurred during the draconian rule of the Afrikaner government.

Colonial warp finds a good share of diverse African peoples forced to climb out of adolescent *passive-receptivity*. After centuries of repressive subservience, they are expected to behave as if self-governance was part of their heritage. Tiny European nations such as Portugal and Belgium, as well as Great Britain, plundered this continent and these indigenous peoples, ripped away the fabric of their cultures stole their precious natural resources with impunity, and subjugated the natives to Western religion and tradition, while denying these selfsame people the continuing practice of their respective cultures.

Joseph Conrad captured this clash of cultures in *"Heart of Darkness"* (1902) as Europeans journeyed into the blackest heart of the Belgian Congo. The story shows how Western idealism exposed to the savage violence among the natives and the crushing heat of the jungle was no match for them. Mr. Kurtz, the powerful and enlightened manager of the Inner Station of the Belgian Congo, sets out to change the natives into a civilized people only to be changed into an evil atavistic savage.

Conrad's journey is a symbolic one into the blackness central to the heart and soul of man, a journey deep into primeval passion, superstition and lust. He shows those from the West, who hope to bring light into the darkness, are doomed to be swallowed by that darkness and evil they hope to penetrate.

The nightmare of today's Africa is the legacy of yesterday's European colonialism. The vacuum of despair here often has the face of AIDS. Three quarters of all the deaths from AIDS in the world are from Africa with tens of thousands dying every month. This is a monument to past neglect and hopelessness. African national independence spread across the continent in the late twentieth century. Africans were left mainly to fend for themselves without the tools and programming for nation building, without the infrastructure or educated workforce, without the industry and commerce. Where was Europe when Africa most needed her?

Africans were expected to make the transition to self-governance without a vibrant middle class, adequate commerce, and a viable infrastructure, without seasoned leadership and without an established national agenda, or the will or the way to make it happen.

For hundreds of years, these Africans were used and abused and treated as fodder for the will of European ivory hunters and captors. This has left scars and open wounds to be exploited by their own people, people educated in the West and in Western ways, people who used divisive tactics and mercenary authority to rule.

African leaders have often treated their own people worse than the colonialists. I lived in South Africa during the era of apartheid. While the Bantu are taking hold of governance uncertainly, I applaud the fact that they are free of the yoke of European and Afrikaner dominance. If we are our brother's keeper, then there is a lot of making up that must be done.

Someone once said that there is only one religion but it has a thousand faces. If you look beyond the dogma or doctrine of Hinduism, Confucianism, Shintoism, Buddhism, Islamism, Judaism, and Christianity, to name only a few, you see how true this is. Respect for another is basic to all religions. They have kept the world reasonably stable but they are losing their grip in spiritual influence. This seems to have been magnified with the explosive growth and disruption of social norms after World War II.

Drunk with the power of toys supplied by technology, we have not yet awakened from our hangover to perceive the damage done to others and ourselves for the "cut and control" tranquilized drive towards empty "progress."

Along with this indulgent dance, we have weapons of mass destruction, and rumors of WMDs in the hands of rogue nations. This complexity and finality of these weapons is too much for us to get our heads around. This gives those in power the psychological edge to do, as they will.

During the George Bush administration (2000-2008), we had the good twins of Dick Cheney and Donald Rumsfeld that resembled in so many frightening ways the evil twins of Joseph Goebbels and Hermann Goring of Nazi Germany of WWII in the use of psychological warfare.

As vice president and secretary of defense, respectively, they used propaganda and patriotism as their trump cards on our national psyche. It took the 2006 Democratic sweep of Congress at mid-term elections to dislodge this dynamic dual from the scene. The damage, however, was already done with the preemptive invasion of Iraq and the war in Afghanistan.

Now, we are in a pesky recession that lingers on after the 2007-2008 subprime meltdown, the malfeasance of Wall Street, the collapse of General Motors and Chrysler, which required government bailouts to survive. President Barak Obama, the first United States African American president, is now in his second term and still has to deal with a recalcitrant Congress, mainly led by "Tea Party" Republicans.

Nazism rose out of Germany's humiliating surrender at Versailles, France after WWI and the mythical pride of Germans being an Aryan Master Race. Obama led us out of Iraq and plans to have us out of Afghanistan in 2014. He is an intellectual and a perfect foil to those who think one race superior to another.

Few question the sobriquet of the United States as "the lone superpower." Yet the US didn't look too super after the Katrina disaster, the stalemate in Afghanistan, the hasty withdrawal from Iraq, or the handling of economic collapse of 2007-2008.

Nor today does the US look quite super when nearly half of American students fail to finish high school, the middle class is shrinking, the infrastructure is in sad shape, obesity is on the rise, corporate and government corruption continues unabated years after the subprime meltdown. Meanwhile, Fannie Mae and Freddie Mac are still hurting as are Citigroup, AIG and the Big Three automakers. And there are no failsafe guidelines to avoid another debacle.

As this is being written, the Dow Jones Industrials have soared above 16,000, while tiny North Korea is saber rattling threatening to launch nuclear missiles against South Korea, Japan and the United States Island of Guam. You can never take your first and last freedom for granted.

Psychologist James Hillman in *"A Terrible Love of War"* (2004) sees war or rumors of war normalized as an everyday affair. War gives soldiers and victims a profound sense of prestige. War fosters an impossible collection of opposites: murder and soldierly comradeship, torture and religious conviction, destruction and patriotism, annihilation and immortal glory. People dead to life find war exhilarating, lifting them out of their stupor and despair. Death is preferred to life. With life, you cannot hide from fear.

Even ants behave better than humans as E. 0. Wilson shows in *"Naturalist"* (1994):

"When an ant dies, and if it has not been crushed or torn apart, it simply crumples up and lies still. Although its posture and inactivity are abnormal, nest mates continue to walk by it as though nothing has happened. Two or three day's pass before recognition dawns, and then it is through the smell of decomposition. Responding to the order, a nest mate picks the corpse up, carries it out of the nest, and dumps it on a nearby refuse pile."

Possibly, Hilton's terrible love of war is why renegade Islamic groups behave as they do. Suicide bombers take on the guise of the heroes in a time without heroes convinced that a better life awaits them in paradise. Insanity as sanity is the prime mover in the "love of war."

This is as true of advanced as of primitive societies, as true of the East as the West, the North as the South. Suicide bombers are a sad reality, but crimes against humanity take many forms. Take the incarceration without rights of prisoners in Guantanamo Bay. Fear is the only justification, fear of what they might do if given their freedom. This fear is palpable and people everywhere understand it as they have the same trepidations. Fear was the confection that guided the good twins as it did the bad twins, and fear is always the province of the unknown or the unknowable.

Fear has shown its face in Iraq and Afghanistan where young men and women with guns have been known to commit atrocities common to war, behavior uncommon to their nature. Nearly a quarter of returning American veterans suffer Post Traumatic Stress Disorder (PTSD), many attempt suicide. You place anyone in harm's way where fear is his only companion and terrible things are bound to happen.

Fear is the driving force in the economics of plenty. It has taken the life out of death, and put death into life as these young men and women know only too well. By our national over striving to impose our system on Afghanistan and Iraq we have lost our confidence as a people. We expected to be able to stabilize their system when we cannot seem to stabilize our own.

Afghanistan and Iraq, among other Middle Eastern countries, reflect the gamesmanship played on their turf by the West since WWI and after WWII. It is madness for one culture to impose its idiosyncratic ways on another to demonstrate its superiority and expect no pushback. Afghanistan and Iraq reflect the way colonial Americans reacted to colonial Great Britain, and unhappily, we fail to see the resemblance. We had a great Civil War between the North and the South that nearly destroyed us as a nation. Would we have wanted interference in that war? I think not.

We have this problem of failing to see our villainous ways,

choosing instead to see our intentions as always noble, our thoughts always above board, always altruistic, as if we have answers to everyone's dilemma when we seem unable to solve our own.

We are a nation not prepared to accept ourselves, as we are, much less to be students of other nations as they are. How can tolerance be possible when some are seen as "jungle bunnies" and others as "lords of welfare"? How can we come to understand that by the accident of our birth and circumstance, ethnicity and gender are who and what we are? We are a nation that is overweight, undereducated, unsophisticated, grasping for straws while waving the American flag as if that changes everything.

These are some things that come to mind for us to live in peace with each other:

- We must learn to understand each other, not from the perspective of our own experience but from that of theirs.

- It means looking at others through their eyes and not ours.

- It means having some understanding of their history and culture and what is especially meaningful to them in that context.
- It means having some familiarity with their struggles and triumphs, tragedies and challenges, and how these came to define them.

- It means being acquainted with their leadership, both fanatical and moderate in governance and religion, and how this has influenced them as a people.

- It means seeing them in the light of today and what they are struggling for, and why.

- It means knowing others as much as possible as they know themselves.

What you are likely to find out is that most people prefer to live in their own culture and be left alone, to enjoy the comfort of the family, to work in their chosen ways, and to live in peace with the trappings of their provincial life and culture without restrictions or interference.

We are not, by nature, a people in general, but persons in particular. Much as we are alike, tolerance and acceptance does not preclude us preferring our own.

When collateral damage of civilian population is considered a necessary cost of warfare, insanity rules. In Viet Nam, when a commander says, "I had to destroy the village to save it," insanity rules. Insanity and inanity has a common human face. When al Qaeda destroyed the Twin Towers to make a statement, taking 3,000 lives, insanity rules. When the US invades Afghanistan, a country run by warlords that previously humiliated the Soviet Union, insanity rules. When the US invades Iraq, a sovereign nation run by a dictator under the contrived justification of its having WMDs, insanity rules.

When the US withholds humanitarian aid from the democratically elected Hamas government in Palestine, because it has been designated a terrorist organization, insanity rules. When the US conducts a "war on terror" and spends hundreds of billions of dollars on a war with no defined enemy and no ultimate victory, insanity rules. When the heart and soul and will of a country remain flabby because of self-indulgent, insanity rules.

The Confident Thinker has to step back and sift through all the information that bombards his senses to see what makes sense and what does not. This calls for deprogramming himself of old conditioning. It is only through creative understanding that there can be a world in which insanity no longer rules.

We should not look to media to do it for us, nor government, nor the church, nor our neighbors, nor our bosses, nor our family. The answers are not in *Time* or *Newsweek*, not in *Foreign Affairs*, *The London Times*, *The New York Review*, *The London Review*, *The National Review*, *The New York Times* or *The Washington Post*, not on network and cable television news, not on the *PBS News Hour with*

Mark Shields and David Brooks, not in the plethora of tabloids with insider gossip that glut the counters of supermarket checkouts, not from pundits, think tanks or Ivy League dons, but from processing experience that might include talking to a Pakistani service station neighbor or Thai barber, Vietnamese grocer, Indian bookseller, Iranian dry cleaner, or hundreds of others who connect us to a common world and to life.

This is not easy for a nation that adores celebrity, worships youth, plans never to grow up or grow old, that spends more for plastic surgery than the *Gross Domestic Product* of many African nations, and plies its innovative nature to all manner of escapism. When there is no place for reality, "nowhere land" becomes home.

Talking can be a tricky business for even when we speak the same language we seldom say what we mean, or mean what we say. We must get past the words to know how other people feel. The heart reads people better than the head. Someone who talks like you, dresses like you, spouts a litany of similar biases, can sway your head, but not your heart if it has your attention. The heart recognizes the counterfeit.

To learn where another person is coming from, you need to listen, not to lecture. The less you fill the void with your noise the more apt you are to learn. This means fighting the inclination to be judgmental. The critical parent oozes from our subconscious not necessarily from our lips. If you think critically of another, chances are that person will feel it. Remember, when helping others help themselves, it is not all about you.

On a wider scale, it is difficult to be empathetic about the plight of another when you are worried about losing your $800,000 home. Your kitchen is likely to cost more than a tent city of one hundred refugees in Darfur. You cannot change this picture, but you can put aside your xenophobic biases about immigrants, legal and otherwise, who are your convenience store workers, gas station operators, taxi drivers, short order cooks, dishwashers, fruit pickers, house cleaners, beautician shop sweepers, computer installers, and neighbors. Xenophobia doesn't do anyone any good.

The United States of America is an idea, and the idea is in trouble. It is not a place or a space. It is an idea. It is a thought that has survived for a little over two hundred years, and it can die if others are considered less important than ourselves. If that should happen, with apologies to T S. Eliot, the idea will die not with a bang but a whimper.

We, who live in relative peace and plenty with the freedom to exercise our minds, and keep our bodies and souls in harmony, have difficulty seeing our connection to the emaciated child covered in flies and dying in Darfur, while its young mother already shriveled up and old at thirty attempts to feed the child from a dried up breast.

Dr. Maria Montessori talks of having a child for seven years. Much as we may desire to shed the yoke of those first years, the paradox is we tend to replicate the good, the bad, and the ugly of that early childhood experience as adults. Likewise, decades of cruel and inhuman treatment of Africans by colonialists have established the colonial mindset. We see this reemerging as African on African violence has led to the slaughter of hundreds of thousands of the innocent. As some adults have managed to outgrow their faulty indoctrination in due course, so also will Africans.

If you believe we are our brother's keeper, there will be no comfort falling back on bromides and rationalizations. Ultimately, belief in the importance of others is not a zero sum game, where some are important or acceptable and others are not. Acceptance is a question of tolerance, and tolerance means you help others as best you can, but you never own the other person's problem. You do what you can as we have seen in the case of Dr. Donald Fan and his many activities. There are tens of thousands like him across the United States. Alexis de Tocqueville in *"Democracy in America"* (1834) declared that voluntarism gave Americans a distinct identity. That caring has led to America's prominence in the world.

CONFIDENT THINKING
CREATIVE STAGE SIX

START LIKING YOURSELF
THE MORE YOU LIKE YOURSELF
THE MORE GENEROUS YOU ARE
LIKE YOURSELF AND YOU HAVE
NO TIME FOR HATRED

"To have a friend you must be a friend starting with yourself."

James R. Fisher, Jr., *The Taboo Against Being Your Own Best Friend*

THE TRADEOFF WITH DESPAIR

NOVELIST ROBERT GODDARD writes in *"Borrowed Time"* (2006):

As I've grown older, I've learned to analyze my own behavior as well as other people's. I've come to understand that just as every mood is temporary, so is every triumph and every disappointment. It isn't much of a consolation, but it's an effective antidote to despair. One day, I suppose, it'll make even death seem an acceptable tradeoff with reality."

Who is the most difficult person to accept? It is ourselves as we are. Another word for "accept" is that we "like" ourselves. Why is this so difficult? Murray Kempton wrote in the *"New York Review"* (1995):

"The Almighty is presumed to pass His judgments and dole out His penalties to individuals, which allows us to suppose that nations are spared painful sessions with *the Recording Angel. But if ours is ever so summoned, we may suppose that the inquiry into its cardinal sins might begin with the question: 'And why, America, did you, in your arrogance, teach so many of your children to hate themselves?'*"

Kempton was referring to four-time United States Olympic Gold Medal winner in both the springboard dive (1984, 1988) and platform dive (1984, 1988), Greg Louganis. The Olympic Champion happens to be gay. He found his life turned inside out once his sexuality was made public. Some can roll with the punches of social abuse once secrets of their lives are revealed, but most of us cannot. Self-loathing enters. This was the case with Robert Goddard's fictional hero. It was also the case with this great athlete.

In June 1993, The Reader's Digest published my article, which opened with "To have a friend you must be a friend starting with yourself." The volume of reprint requests prompted me to write, *"The Taboo Against Being Your Own Best Friend"* (1996) where I wrote:

"We are all authors of our own footprints in the sand, heroes of the novels inscribed in our hearts. Everyone's life, without exception, is sacred, unique, scripted high drama, played out before an audience of one, with but one actor on stage. The sooner we realize this the more quickly we overcome the bondage of loneliness and find true friendship with ourselves."

You would think society would want to affirm this, to create a climate in which our uniqueness would flourish. It does quite the opposite.

OUT THERE, THE WALL

Few of us would disagree that we are in a competitive society. In fact, we take pride in being such a society, but is that beneficial? I submit that many of us are unhappy campers. If we were happy, escapism wouldn't be such a big business; nor would we be so hard on ourselves.

We also live in a conforming society. It is so pervasive that many of us don't realize our parents and teachers failed to perform the essential function that even the lowest animal carries out with complete ease.

They failed to initiate us into appropriate interaction with the wider world.

They failed to teach us how to engage and live with others of difference.

They taught us only how to behave.

Behavior without the inner richness of choice and the inner sense of contentment is bound to be superficial and driven by ever accelerating external demands. We are now in the Information Age with ubiquitous cyberspace changing our lives in ways we still do not comprehend. But we do know one thing. We have become compulsively voyeuristic and at a distance from each other, except electronically. We have gone from a robotic to mechanized trance with the assembling line being replaced by diagnostic systems, algorithms and computer-driven data paradigms counter dependent to some hand held somnambulistic electronic device.

What is worse, we as parents and teachers have repeated this by our ambivalent approach to sex and sex education for our children. At a distance sex is fine. We can take it or leave it, but up close and personal we are surprised for the trouble.

U.S. Representative Mark Foley of Florida was forced to resign from the US Congress throwing the mid-term 2006 elections into turmoil. For years, he has been writing sexually explicit emails to teenage pages. This salacious practice, which was known and tolerated, came to be treated as if only just learned. The hypocrisy doesn't stop there.

Turns out that the Reverend Anthony Mercieca, now in his 70s, admits to fondling the nude Foley in saunas in the 1960s when Foley was not yet a teenager. Self-righteously, the archdiocese spokesperson said, "Such behavior is morally reprehensible, canonically criminal and inexcusable." All this is true, but why does it happen so often, and why do its victims repeat it on others?

We are a violent society. Sociologist Philip Slater writes in *"The Pursuit of Loneliness"* (1970):

> *Americans have always been a people with marked genocidal proclivities: our systematic extermination of the Indians, the casual killing of American blacks during and after slavery, and our indifference to dropping an atomic bomb on a large civilian populace—we are, after all, the only people ever to have used such a weapon—reflect on this attitude."*

The one emotion that gives us a sense of being alive is our anger. And we are an angry society. Anger evolves from two roots:

- Reaction to feeling dominated or entrapped with no ready escape.
- Frustration when we feel entitled and don't get our way.

The latter is a more productive anger. It can be converted into some form of assertiveness or independence. Our anger in any form was intolerable to our parents and teachers. It signified, and still does, a certain spirit, a kind of assertion of self, indeed, a kind of life of its own, perhaps a vitality, that challenges ownership. Anger takes imagination and imagination is not too healthy in the present conformist climate.

Control is simply another name for ownership. So, this anger that is so natural to us must be stifled. We must give preschoolers Ritalin to calm them down and make them behave. Once the regimen of the drugstore becomes the gauge to controlling natural emotions, it must be continued throughout life so that we behave as toys that can be switched on or off as the case may be. For anger, like our sex drive, must be controlled at all cost. Unfortunately, the more draconian the control the more out-of-control the behavior.

"Out there is the wall," the technological world, which, by definition is a skeptical world, a cold world. At the wall, belief is replaced by cynicism, faith by doubt, hope by despair, and a sense of belonging by a pervasive fear of intimacy. The gap between man and machine has widened. According to David Brooks, Steven Jobs cleverly camouflaged this gap by making Apple products feel like colorful nonthreatening artifacts.

Most societal violence is against someone we know. Divorce can be violent. More than 50 percent of marriages end in divorce and 40 percent of new mothers are purposely having babies out of wedlock. Many consider husbands a lifestyle impediment or another child to raise.

Stealing is a violent act against property. Industry loses tens of billions of dollars from employee theft. Tens of billions more are lost to employee substance abuse. This causes absenteeism, violence on the job, poor performance, and mounting traffic fatalities. Then there is violence against trust by insider trading, junk bond fraud, Ponzi schemes, and other sophisticated scams most notable in the recent economic meltdown. Another form of violence against trust is the admission by 80 percent of high school honor students to regular cheating on examinations.

We are not happy campers. We have lost our moral compass and our way. We have replaced it with a CD-ROM, iPod, iPhone, BlackBerry, downloading copyrighted material with impunity. Primitives were never so lost to themselves.

DEALING WITH THE WALL

Our approach to life is a result of early training and response to situations. Role demands and self-demands surface early on as does the "ideal self" and "real self." We are programmed to be self-critical rather than self-accepting. Small wonder we are driven by denial and self-deceit.

The self-critical approach is fed by comparing and competing. Little Johnny is compared to little Sally, and they are compared to their parent's friends' kids, and then to what pundits and critics on television say little Johnny and little Sally should be able to do, until the whole matter gets out of hand and little Johnny and little Sally escape into their fantasy worlds, as they quickly tire of being told they should be as bright, athletic, attractive, accomplished, and perfect as other kids their age.

Comparing and competing, at every level, make for a powerful "no win" situation. Just as two snowflakes are not the same no two individuals are the same. Each is unique. Each can have a fulfilling life by discovering what is unique to them. To imitate duplicate replicate what others have done, psychiatrists Willard and Marguerite Beecher say in *"Beyond Success and Failure"* (1966) is to be *"humanly dead. Competition produces zombies! Nonentities!"*

There is no reason for us to be down on ourselves, especially since we can be none other. These psychiatrists find competition is the chief obstacle to self-reliance and maturity. They reason competition enslaves and degrades the mind, and is one of the most destructive forms of psychological dependence. Kahlil Gibran in *"The Prophet"* (1972) reminds parents:

> *"Your children are not your children. They are the sons and daughters of Life's longing for itself. They come through you but not from you, and though they are with you yet they belong not to you."*

It is a monumental struggle for the youth of today to make the transition to the adult they are expected to be. They must abandon the adolescent mindset of seeing themselves always falling short of the mark and embrace their fears to become confident thinking adults.

Our youth will attempt to solve adult problems with a child's evasive tricks. The shortest distance between the problem and solution is a realistic assessment, not a cover up or denial of the facts. On the other hand, the adolescent adult takes certain pleasure in projecting the blame or in denying the problem. Schadenfreude, pleasure obtained from the troubles of others, is a manifestation of this childish behavior and an example of self-hatred.

Surely, being competitive makes it difficult to know and accept ourselves as we are, and therefore nearly impossible to like ourselves. What is the first reaction when you strike out playing baseball, fail a test, lose a job, have an automobile accident?

Most would say it forces them to pause and assess, not in a positive sense, but in terms of disappointment, self-disgust and the realization of letting others down. Lost in this is the individual, you! Every failure is a wake-up call, not something bad at all, but a chance to get your corporate head on straight. Yes, each of us is the CEO of our destiny, and failure is a reminder that a course correction may be advisable.

Too often self-contempt takes on the face of the victim. "It was not my fault!" For healing to occur, however, it must be accepted as being just that "your fault!" Acknowledging the fact is key to the mind as healer instead of as slayer.

It is uncommon for us in our culture to take failure or unexpected circumstances in stride. Life has been built around certainty, predictability, security, and control, all of which are anathema to surprise, failure, loss, or disappointment. Yet, all of these are part of life and living. Failure is the learning plateau but too often is seen as the plateau of humiliation.

We have been programmed to be competitors. Competitors are programmed to win, to be in control, on top of things, to succeed, to keep failure at bay and therefore defeat beyond mention. Unfortunately, life is more about failure than success. It is the reason it is a learning experience. The mean batting average of major league baseball player over a century, according to the late paleontologist Stephen Jay Gould, a fanatical baseball statistician (*"Full House"* 1996) is.250, which means more than seven out of ten times baseball players failed to hit safely.

Eventually, if obsessed with winning, a person will be afraid to take chances, afraid to grow. He will instead become dull, imitative, mediocre, burned-out, stereotyped, devoid of initiative, imagination and spontaneity. Competition will have killed his spirit. The enemy of his enemy will be himself.

Why are we such a competitive society? The short answer is

that we have a narrow gauge to measure excellence, and that narrow gauge is not based upon the individual competing against his unique self but comparing that individual with others in terms of skill, talent, brilliance, athleticism, beauty, culture, sophistication, and achievement. We have a mania for heroes, and heroes must appear beyond belief or like gods.

Competition leads to copycatting. Pressed to the extreme copycatting can make us so inauthentic as to become a caricature of ourselves. Copycatting has managed to produce a new category of people, celebrities, and persons with no defining talent other than their celebrity.

We have the journalistic polemicist Ann Coulter on the right of the political spectrum and Michael Moore on the left. They rant cruel and tasteless nonsense shedding little light on current issues of public concern, playing on the deep darkness of divisive self-hatred. To be credible they have the figment of truth in their cobweb of lies. They don't wish to inform or promote rational discussion and accord. They mean to amuse by exploiting the discordant stereotypes of a self-hating public. Glenn Beck and Rush Limbaugh are anointed knights of this charade with many copiers too numerous to mention.

Competition breeds fear. Fear breeds comparison. No matter how healthy, wealthy and wise you are there is always someone more so. Competition breeds greed. You are never successful or powerful enough. You always believe you should be more. There is no time to relax, to hang loose, or to go with the flow. The mantra: no pain no gain is a drum roll. You must urge yourself on; never content to be the person you actually are, minting yourself into alchemist's gold, or something you're not or could never be. So, you perfect your outsides without time to attend to your insides. Self-hatred makes certain the two sides will never be in harmony, always in conflict.

The perfectionist is a manifestation of self-hate, the increasingly frightened competitor who always must win to be secure chasing security like it was the Holy Grail. The perfectionist has played a game with his mind believing perfection embodies truth.

Implicit in this truth is to be above criticism by those less perfect. The perfectionist is constantly comparing, calibrating his advantage, fearing it is in jeopardy. You know him by his fault finding and belittling of others. No one is ever good enough in his critical eye, while, paradoxically, unable to see his own fault lines, and therefore easy to exploit.

There are two kinds of people, creative people and self-haters. Self-haters hate because they compare, fear and compete. Creative people are lovers of life and take pleasure in activities for their own sake. Self-haters are competitive and tie their minds in knots, as they must win be it in love or war. Creative people find work is love made visible. Love does not need an object. Love is in the doing. There is no room in love for fear.

DEALING WITH ANXIETY

Next to competition being a sickness of the soul, there is the matter of aloneness and loneliness. They are not the same.

Aloneness, or "al one-ness" is the basis of our greatest strength. It is a holistic view of life. If we don't enjoy our own company, how can we ever feel fulfilled and enjoy the company of others?

Loneliness is a sign of our greatest weakness. We need connection to others and are dependent on them to think and behave properly. We dare not rely on ourselves. Life becomes a second hand experience guided by someone else's information.

Aloneness is a mark of maturity. Loneliness is a mark of immaturity. Robert Putnam writes in "Time" magazine (July 3, 2006):

> *"Americans are more socially isolated today than we were barely two decades ago. The latest evidences of that comes from a topflight team of sociologists who, after comparing national surveys in 1985-2004, report a one-third drop in the number of people with whom the average American can discuss important matters."*

135

Putnam, author of *"Bowling Alone"* (2000), assumes from this that Americans are getting "lonelier." The good professor falls into the trap of the United States of Anxiety. He suggests the cure for loneliness is "more community involvement, spending more time with family and friends, work in a family-friendly workplace and have a picnic or two," and then adds the clincher, "it could just save your life." If it were only so simple.

The problem with this is that loneliness will not be cured with a confection of involvement. Yes, it will create a more conducive climate for homeostasis. Loneliness, however, is the state of emptiness that is felt when a crippling dependency takes possession of the spirit and the person feels never more alone than with others.

Obviously, communal involvement has merit, and having a close family connection cannot be faulted, but they are not panaceas for loneliness. Nor will family-friendly workplaces necessarily be reinforcing. The typical high tech workplace for the past quarter century more resembles a playpen than a workplace, and it hasn't reduced anxiety on the job.

The dependent person has not learned how to enjoy his own company. He must have a personal trainer for exercise, constant noise from the moment he rises until he goes to bed. He needs someone to continually reassure him he is okay, someone who can amuse, divert, distract, and define for him what he is and what he should be doing. Loneliness is the complete inability to face the world alone.

The lonely person most fears a quiet mind. He would be intimidated by the quiet of nature. This quiet would force him back on himself placing him in the company of that friend inside that he so desperately seeks outside. In short, the dependent person needs and seeks a baby sitter. He has not trained himself to invent activity of his own, to create, design, build and make meaningful and sustaining discoveries in the world in which he lives.

Gore Vidal once said, "To be interesting, you must be interested." You cannot be interested if you are always looking for stimulation outside yourself, always seeking the hand of someone else to lead you to something interesting. When a person finds no one will provide such stimulation, will not make him the center of their attention, deep and abiding loneliness may set in, to be followed by boredom and then despair.

This appears to be the culture of our times. Kempton's words ring loud: "And why, America, did you, in your arrogance, teach so many of your children to hate themselves?"

Putnam is right about lonely people when he says they are unable to establish enduring relationships. Lonely people also tend to be nonproductive and shallow, while others find them boring and inconsequential and avoid them. They are needy. The needy person demands so much and gives back so little. As a result, lonely people are thrown back on themselves. This reinforces their loneliness.

Programmed from birth to lack self-reliance, the situation is unlikely to change. Failure is self-reliance's good teacher. Failure avoided erases learning from experience. This in turn can lead to loneliness. You are never alone doing something you love. The problem of lonely people is they never go to the trouble to find such love.

Aloneness, on the other hand, is the mirth of hearing our inner voice because we have somehow managed to steer clear of the clatter of outside noise.

We don't have to have the television on as soon as we rise in the morning, conning ourselves into the conviction we have to know what is going on in the world and the latest weather report. We don't have to have the car radio on listening to talking heads spewing their nonsense as we make our way to work. We don't have to rush to the cafeteria to have a coffee and chatter away with others with the current gossip. We don't have to have a cell phone in our ear as we eat lunch alone, go shopping, are waiting to see our doctor in the waiting room, or for the light to change at the stoplight.

These compulsive nervous tics of behavior have become so routine as to belie the madness they epitomize, which is the terror of being alone for only a moment!

Nor do we have to repeat the same action in reverse as we

go home at night, having the television on again until we retire without a single moment in the entire day free of noise. We have not had a chance to ponder the beauty of being alive.

The mature individual has learned to shut his mind off from this conflicting noise to listen to the music of his inner world. With aloneness, we finally "let go" of desire to compete, to possess, to dominate, to exploit, to manipulate, or to retreat into childhood fantasies. We are ready to hear what is going on within, to listen to that inner voice that alone belongs to us that waits so patiently to be heard.

Krishnamurti puts it succinctly in *"You Are The World"* (1972):

> *"In oneself lies the whole world, and if you know how to look and learn, then the door is there and the key is in your hand. Nobody on earth can give you either that key or the door to open, except yourself."*

DEALING WITH OUR PROGRAMMING

If this is so, why are we so blind to the fact? It goes back to our programming. The creative destruction of progress is civilization's most important product, and we have been made into machines to desire, distort, improve, modify, discard and change the outside world finding little contentment within ourselves as we are. As a result stress often becomes distress, and distress leads to several major types of illness: cardiovascular disease, cancer, arthritis, and respiratory diseases. Of course, we help these along by having an improper diet, smoking and drinking to excess, becoming workaholics, getting too little exercise and sleep, and becoming chronic worriers. We try to compensate for this dilatory behavior with a retinue of drugs.

Kenneth R. Pelletier in *"Mind as Healer Mind as Slayer"* (1977) claims we can take a holistic approach to preventing these stress disorders, but it is not easy:

> *"Personality factors as they relate to illness are an exciting area of research, since the opportunities for*

prevention are so dramatic. For the most part, people are more sensitive to their own subtle psychological states than they are to minute shifts in neurophysiological functioning. Thought it is cult for people to alter their lifelong behavior patterns, behavior is clearly more amendable to voluntary change than are elevated levels of adrenal corticoids in the blood. For this reason, if behavior can be truly shown to have a direct causal relationship to disease the potential for prevention is enormous."

Pelletier is going on about distress when he is referring to stress disorders. As Hans Selye shows in *"Stress Without Distress"* (1974), *"Stress is the spice of life."* Without stress, we would be vegetables or dead. When we say someone is "under stress," we mean they are under excessive distress.

The stressed out person feels there is "not enough time," or is "overwhelmed with too many decisions to make," or that there is "no way he can stay within the budget," or that there is "no chance of meeting schedule."

Then there are problems on the home front with a son or daughter "out of control," or the wife or husband "on a senseless spending spree." These can cause distress, and that is when we look for some crutch such as drinking and smoking which only aggravates the stress level. Add to this the accelerating complexity of life, and you can see why a "time out" or "step back," or, indeed, a "total retreat" may be the best medicine of all.

Technology is the god of the machine. There isn't an institution that doesn't deaden if not kill our spirit because of the constant cacophony of this machine. We must have a cell phone in our ear, laptop on our knee, an iPad, iPod, iPhone or BlackBerry in our hand to ensure we are electronically connected to that umbilical machine and to the ubiquitous world of cyberspace. There is no place or time for our inner world.

Self-acceptance suggests contentment with "what is" which is anathema to progress. With self-acceptance, there is a fullness of the spirit, which knows no feeling of want or poverty. We are never alone when we are "al one ness." Loneliness is the empty world of constant seeking of outside reassurance. It is the need for change for change's sake. Nothing can be left to resonate on its own.

Modern Man's intelligence and sense of urgency created the modern world so that he could afford to relax and enjoy the magnificent civilization he had created, only to find it impossible to escape the old sense of urgency.

Modern Man is like the man Colin Wilson refers to in *"Access to Inner Worlds"* (1983). This man we find living out on his lawn in a tent, while building a magnificent house. Once completed, he absent-mindedly continues to live in the tent and leaves the house empty. That is precisely what modern man has done. He has created a climate to relax but has never found the time. Indeed, he runs faster and faster. This is not a recent development.

Budd Schulberg captured this frightening mania in *"What Makes Sammy Run"* (1941) over a half century ago. It is the story of Sammy Glick who fought his way from New York's lower East Side, over the necks and bodies of his friends and mistresses to the top of the heap in Hollywood, and he could never stop running. It was a novel about twentieth century man but fits twenty-first century man to a tee, who is afraid to stop to find out where he is for fear he will be lost in the race for good.

We are in perpetual motion like the man who has been driving all day, and who keeps waking up at night, imagining himself still behind the wheel. We are part of the lonely crowd in transition from a national to a global status slipping into the insidious habit of anxiety, tension, over-alertness, and always being "on," craving connection to fill a void that only exists because we are afraid to stop. Today the hysteria is for the "global village," which is an empty abstraction without meaning. When it comes down to the reality of life, everything is local. A global community cannot exist because to love everyone is to love no one or anything.

Some reading this may declare that they take care of themselves physically, earn a living, build a business or profession, manage a family and otherwise conduct themselves with success in public and private affairs, so what is this about self-acceptance anyway?

You don't necessarily have to accept yourself to prove functional, but you do have to accept yourself to understand when change is advisable. With self-contempt you can become hateful, cynical, alcoholic, tyrannical, depressed, psychotic, neurotic, and an emotional burden to others. With self-acceptance you learn how to be emotionally self-reliant with the maturity of the adult to make decisions in your own best interest. Unfortunately, with self-contempt, you are likely to be suspended in terminal self-indulgent adolescent mired in distress and learned helplessness.

Should this be the case, it is not totally your fault. We have been programmed to be *passive-receptive* and controllable so that we behave predictably.

We are constantly bombarded with commercials, not just of products to purchase, but ideas and lifestyles to adopt. Television news is a commercial, sermons in church are commercials, and now we have bloggers and Facebook. The Internet fills the airwaves with attitudinal commercials. What is Fox News, Glenn Beck, Rush Limbaugh, Howard Stern, et al, but commercials?

Commercials of animated giants stare down at us like the terrifying eye of F Scott Fitzgerald's billboard in *"The Great Gatsby"* (1925) as we drive to and from work. Newspaper and magazines are little more than commercials. The constant cacophony of commercials finds us emotionally dependent and subliminally reactive to neuron bombardment, when we have a need now for creativity, spontaneity, initiative, innovation and discretionary maturity.

We are creatures of culture. We are also creatures of structure. Culture and structure are wrong for the times. What is required is deprogramming and reprogramming to a culture and structure more in tune with the times. This cannot be accomplished by aesthetic change. It must be a radical transformation. This is the daunting challenge.

The pioneering spirit has eroded over the last century to find us today only imitators of that spirit. We are what we do, not part of the time, but all of the time. And what we do is a blueprint of who we are.

If you have comfort in numbers, social scientists estimate that only about 10 percent of the American population is emotional self-reliant and mature. It prompted Daniel Goleman to write *"Emotional Intelligence: Why It Can Matter More Than IQ"* (1997). Goleman's book is an effort to improve emotional self-reliance by alerting people to the importance of passion, and how passion acknowledged and utilized can lead to fulfillment.

Passion is a gift of the self-accepting mind. Such a mind is self-trusting which is a gauge of emotional self-reliance. We don't need someone to look over our shoulder for us to do the right thing. We are not kind and considerate to please others with our virtue. We don't do the best possible job because it will mean a good performance appraisal and segue to a raise. We do it because we can. With emotional self-reliance, initiative is as natural as being in competition with others is not. We do all these things because we have a passion to create a better world. It is not necessary to be found out. It is enough to know within ourselves that we are making a difference.

DEALING WITH DEPENDENCE

Systematic distrust and emotional immaturity are common to a top heavy managed society such as our own. Even with all the electronic means of controlling workers, we are still structured as if we need a supervisor or manager for every twelve workers to get the job done. Middle management hangs on when it has no practical role. Reluctance to acknowledge this is a little like what happened to is a little like the railroad. Literally for years, after trains converted from coal-fired boilers to diesel locomotive engines, there was a coal handler in the engineer's cabin.

One reason many parents send their children to private schools at a cost in the five figures per year is because there is a teacher for a score of students or less. We don't trust students to do the work assigned nor do we trust workers to complete their jobs.

Once it was the weary eye of a person standing over us. Now it is as likely the ubiquitous electronic eye of a hidden camera, or electronic sensing device monitoring our computers. Managed society has implanted psychological self-loathing on its people with the result that creative pursuit and spontaneity are as rare as the appearance of Halley's Comet.

Workers and students are programmed to be dependent. Consequently, top-heavy management and teacher-dependent learning are considered doctrinaire despite spectacular technological innovations.

To be fair, electronics have resulted in a healthy Gross Domestic Product. Nonetheless, US markets continue to shrink for manu-factured goods, the trade deficit soars, while student performance fails to keep pace with other advanced societies despite the US investing more in education per student than any other nation.

When told what to do and precisely how it should be done, there is little learning and even less creativity. Intellectual rigor mortis sets in without creativity or initiative in the process. This was the case while America slept, a score of years following WWII, when the global marketplace roared into action strip-ping away American markets. Digitized panic followed.

Young people and seasoned workers were now expected to be automatically "born again" in the new religion of self-management, initiative, self-discipline, and emotional maturity, shedding their dependency, without losing a beat.

Instead, students and workers dissolved into feelings of inadequacy, insecurity, falling apart and out of control, and predictably, looking for someone to rescue them.

Since South East Asia , Japan and South Korea, have taken markets away from automakers and other manufacturers, there has been a push in industry for individual initiative, in education for "no child left behind," and in society in general to become increasingly innovative. The problem thus far is that it has proven wishful thinking. It is a utopian dream to rally such expectations without sacrifice or radical change. Painless, rhetorical and cosmetic change amount to no change at all. And now there are India and China to contend with as well.

By mid-twenty-first century, China may be the number one economy in the world. It is that country's intention, but the United States need not lose its dominance if it rekindles the spirit that made it great in the first place, which is the promotion of the common good.

That said, our cultural programming has never solved the problem of emotional self-reliance. Nothing in our culture has prepared the individual to know how to stand-alone. The paradox is that a person cannot truly work together with others until he first is able to stand-alone.

As each year passes, more and more children are sent off to school with only a degree of emotional self-reliance. It is a habit of our culture to do more and more for our children and to expect less and less of them.

Later, when these same children are of an adult age, they are inclined to act as if obedient or disobedient twelve-year-olds suspended in terminal adolescence either management dependent or counter dependent on the company to take care of them.

When a crisis comes up and it is not in their job description, they don't report it or take charge of the situation. Instead, they echo the sentiment: "Not my job!" To imagine them self-responsible, is absurd.

PROMOTING SELF-AWARENESS

In this cultural climate, accepting ourselves as we are is difficult if not impossible. First, we are programmed not to be comfortable with who and what we are apart from others. Second, we have never been programmed to seize the "day!" We live in the past or pine away the time dreaming of the future. Our programming has failed to make us comfortable "being" what we are, persistently pressuring us into "becoming" what we are not.

As a result, we take little comfort in the journey but are obsessed with the end. Few students enjoy what they are doing now, at any level. Education is treated as a right, not the privilege that it is. The same can be said of workers. A job is a privilege, not a right. Both are looking to the future, failing to find joy in what they are doing now! Since the *Great Recession of 2008*, there are 2 million fewer jobs than before the downturn, largely because of "smart machines." Workers are put on notice, no one owes them a job, develop new skills or join the unemployment cue.

Against this reality, workers are looking forward to having a bigger job increasing their pay, and to eventually retiring no longer having to work. For students, they can't wait to get to the next grade level, to acquire their college degree, and put their education behind them. For both, it is as if work and education leave a terrible taste in like a medicine that "they have to take."

The whole focus is "getting out!" and not "being in!" It is as if life doesn't start until it is nearly over.

Life is a bore a burden a mind-numbing experience. So, whom do they blame? Students blame teachers. Workers blame bosses or the company. No one stops to realize blame is irrelevant. Blame is not even a factor. It is life that is being treated contemptuously, and they don't seem to get it.

Students drop out of school because it is boring. Workers retreat into substance abuse or dog it on the job because they are fed up. Notice boredom is always someone else's fault, never the fault of the bored. They think life is entertainment and they want to be entertained, not educated, certainly not employed to provide value-added skills.

The problem with this mindset is that there is no past and no tomorrow, there is only today. Since that is too heavy a problem to contemplate, they retreat into ubiquitous noise. There is violence here, violation of good sense.

Life is "being," and "being" is now. There is nothing to achieve, nothing to get, nothing to prove, nowhere to go, no "Big Brother" checking on us, no head higher than our own. "Being" is all about reality. It is about right now. It is all about us! "Becoming" is:

- Wishful thinking and the illusion of progress;
- Ambition and recognition without paying the price;
- Neediness on steroids;
- Dependence on the approval of others without self-approval;
- Feeling emotionally empty and bankrupt;
- Searching for rewards on the lottery treadmill;
- Hoping for a better existence without the courage to create it;
- Abdicating the responsibility of living now;
- Living on the edge for the ultimate thrill.

How many times have we heard people say they hate what they are doing but they have a plan and when the plan comes to fruition everything will fall into place? When you ask them about the plan, chances are it has little to do with what they are now doing, or what they are trained to do.

To prevent being self-hating and to find our way to liking ourselves, we must become involved in self-knowing. There is a three-stage process to assist you in this regard:

SELF-AWARENESS

Awareness is seeing yourself as you actually are, warts and all, comfortable in that knowledge. You have your secrets and they need not be known to anyone else, but must be appreciated by you. They are the touchstones of your character as you have encountered and dealt with life. They are the possible missteps you have made that assist you in better understanding yourself. They are life as you have stumbled upon it. No attempt should be made to evaluate why you are the way you are, or why you did the things you did. They are you, and they are not good or bad, but only life knowing itself. Self-awareness is to see yourself as clearly as your mind allows.

SELF-ACCEPTANCE

What you are you must accept unconditionally because it is the way you are. Acceptance is another word for "liking yourself as you are." Many factors and circumstances occur in life to make you as you find yourself. There is no point in becoming judgmental, or blaming parents or circumstances for your predicament, whatever it is. You accept what you find and allow yourself to be tolerant, understanding and forgiving in that acceptance. It will provide you with an amazing insight not only into your own character, but also into the character of every other person you meet. When you refuse to hide from yourself, others cannot hide what and who they are from you. The con must go elsewhere to ply its trade.

SELF-ASSERTION

Once you see yourself clearly and accept what you see dispassionately, you can continue to act as you are or you can choose to change, whatever serves your best interests. It is a matter of choice. Self-assertion is the "action step." You no longer reflect or attempt to intellectualize your predicament, but are ready to act upon what you find. You have a strong sense of pleasing yourself, which is not selfish but a matter of self-preservation. It is best reflected in not experiencing difficulty saying "no" when it is the optimum response to the situation. You will not carry other people's baggage because you will not own their problems. They may not realize this but you are doing them a favor because carrying someone else's burden only makes them weaker, not stronger.

This three-stage process leads to emotional self-reliance, and maturity. You are your own person thinking confidently because you see yourself on the main stage of your own life and not in the wing waiting for someone else to mouth your lines or call you out to perform.

DEFINING FRIENDSHIP

Whenever we define friendship, it is always about someone else. It is assumed we are natural friends to ourselves. If this were so, we would be more generous of spirit towards ourselves and therefore towards others. Jean de La Fontaine (1621-1695) captures the essence:

> *"Friendship is the shadow of the evening, which strengthens with the setting sun of life."*

Friendship is a maturing process strengthened by the ordeal of life. Pioneering psychiatrist Alfred Adler (1870-1937) points out that friendship is indeed a shadow thing with so much that is unconscious in our consciousness and so much that is conscious in our unconsciousness that it is useless to separate ourselves from friendship. If we cannot be friend to ourselves, then to whom can we be friend? So often we seek friends to exploit to our advantage right down to taking the shirt off their backs. To such people a friend is someone who would not resist exploitation. Often the one exploited with such thinking is the person himself.

I have a son-in-law who is constantly exploited by such friends: he gives them work and they don't complete; he loans them cars and trucks and they take them to be their own; he goes into partnership with them and gives them generous shares of the business with little investment, and then they don't hold up the terms of their agreements. Obviously, he is as guilty as they are and shows little friendship with himself, indeed, little self-acceptance or liking of himself.

Most relationships we call friendships are nothing more than mutual-advantage or mutual-exploitations, pacts, something-for-something, which dissolve as soon as the element of mutual advantage disappears on either side.

I have seen this particular scene repeated again and again. We tend to drift apart when it is no longer emotionally or physically profitable to know each other. The problem with ourselves is that we cannot do that, or if we do we are self-estranged, spinning in a terrible cycle of confusion, adrift in constantly becoming, never being, and therefore never arriving, anywhere.

Real friends are those who accept us as we are, not as we should be. Real friends like us for who we are not what we are. Friendship is limited first by our ability to be a friend to ourselves, comfortable in our own skin, with a tolerance for others as we find them. Friendship makes no demands. "It is," that is, it is a condition of fullness that flows from everything we do and over everything we are. Like rain, it falls impartially on all our peccadilloes and virtues. It demands nothing for itself and allows everything to fulfill itself in its own way and time. Friendship is without a need to control others or to withhold itself. It lives and it lets others live.

Being a friend to yourself means you live in the main house and not in a tent on the lawn as in Colin Wilson's story of "Access to Inner World." It also puts you in charge, on center stage, and author of all your own deeds. Remember, the two amazing gifts that one receives who accepts (likes) himself as he is: the incredible talent of reading people accurately, and the ability to say "no!"

When people constantly fool us, and we cannot find the capacity to say "no," we have the problem of addiction. Yes, I said addiction. Addiction is not limited to substance abuse. It is an addiction when we constantly choose our friends unwisely; evade the demands of everyday life; have a ready alibi for not facing what is demanded of us; and choose to be self-hating because then we don't have to confront the image of ourselves as we are.

Confident Thinking demands living and working in an association that is reinforcing and therefore is in harmony with ourselves as we are. It is an environment that is self-friendly where we are the host of life and not the guest, where we are in the driver's seat and not a passenger to someone else's destiny, and where we have a moral center with a working compass.

James R. Fisher, Jr., PhD.

CONFIDENT THINKING
CREATIVE STAGE SEVEN

DESIRE TO CREATE SOMETHING
GOOD FOR OTHERS
SEE THE LIFE FORCE IN
ALL THAT YOU DO
STRIVE TO ENHANCE THE QUALITY
OF LIFE FOR EVERYONE YOU TOUCH!

A man may be outwardly successful all his life long, and die hollow and worthless as a puffball; and he may be externally defeated all his lift long, and die in the royalty of a kingdom established within him. A man's true estate of power and riches is to be in himself not in his dwelling, or position, or external relations, but in his own essential character. That is the realm in which he is to live, if he is to live as a good man.

—Henry Ward Beecher (1813 —1887), American Clergyman Brother of Harriet Beecher Stowe, author of Uncle Tom's Cabin (1852)

THE PROBLEM WITH GOODNESS

WHEN IT COMES to Confident Thinking in terms of creating something good, we must first define "goodness," and then take on that most ambiguous expression of all, "the quality of life."

Novelist George Eliot (born Mary Ann Evans, 1819 —1880) wrote under a pseudonym because women in her day were not accepted as creative artists. She captures the sense of goodness here:

> *"By desiring what is perfectly good, even when we do not quite know what it is, and cannot do what we would, we are part of the divine power against evil, widening the skirts of light and making the struggle with darkness narrower."*

Complement to this is the more muscular definition of American theologian Tryon Edwards (1809-1894):

> *"To be good, we must do good; and by doing good we take a sure means of being good, as the use and exercise of the muscles increase their power."*

Goodness, then, is your vital connection within the fabric of being. Ralph Waldo Emerson (1803-1882) states it metaphorically: "Your good nature is stronger than tomahawks." Goodness, then, is a constant war against darkness, but the question is what darkness, and whose darkness? Is it the darkness of ignorance of nature and the universe, or of the human soul? Or is it both?

Goodness is idealistic and action dependent on both the physical and spiritual plane. Science has focused its creativity mainly on the physical plane at the neglect of the spiritual, whereas most of us are likely to create something good for others by our actions in the social and psychological sphere. C. S. Lewis in *"Mere Christianity"* (1952) clarifies language:

> *"We don't use the words begetting or begotten much in*

> *modern English, but everyone still knows what they mean.*
> *To beget is to become the father GI; to create is to make.*
> *And the difference is this. When you beget, you beget*
> *something of the same kind as yourself. But when you make,*
> *you make something of a different kind from yourself"*

Therefore, initially, creating something good is derivative of good sense out of a positive character that makes allowances for failure, and is energized by judgment and candor, especially candor. The Confident Thinker is not afraid to see the darkness in his own soul but instead is willing to work through it to create new light.

That brings us to the expression "quality of life." Never has there been greater disparity between the quality and inequality of life than at the present time.

"Quality of life" is not only a matter of the rich becoming richer and the poor poorer, which is widening, but the distance between what is construed to be good and evil is surprisingly narrowing. I'm not referring to conventional evil, but the malevolence we do to each other and ourselves by our addictive lifestyles. Such evil has taken on a kind of normalcy. We do it because we can. Consequently, few appear interested and less seem able to address the monumental gap between good sense and sound behavior except rhetorically. Consequently, the "good life" has gotten a bad name.

While 80 percent of the world's wealth is controlled by 20 percent of the world's population, while 80 percent struggle in deprivation to make do with 20 percent of the world's resources, despicable waste and self-indulgence has become meter of the times. If this were not bad enough, the minority, which controls a majority of the planet's natural resources, has failed to find happiness or bliss, or, indeed, even satisfaction in its materialism. On the contrary, it would seem that materialism without the complement of spiritualism gives credence to the charge that we collectively personify the "Wicked Witch of the West."

Writing of the French Revolution and the *"Reign of Terror,"*

Charles Dickens (1812-1870) opened *"A Tale of Two Cities"* (1859) with these familiar lines:

> *"It was the best of times, it was the worst of times, it was the age of wisdom, it was the age of foolishness, it was the epoch of belief, it was the epoch of incredulity, it was the season of Light, it was the season of Darkness..."*

Dickens could have been describing our times. Unfortunately, we can describe our dilemma but we cannot seem to find the will or the way to deal with it.

Edward de Bono writes in *"Parallel Thinking"* (1995):

> *"Our thinking habits and our education has placed all the emphasis on analysis and judgment. There has been no emphasis placed on design and creativity. Yet the present day problems of the world are crying out for those skills."*

He notes that critical thinking captivates us, which is dealing with what is already known, while we are seemingly averse to creative thinking, or what is not known but could be found out.

Creative thinking is conceptual, nonlinear, systemic, provocative, and contradictory, or the geography of the unknown. We have the pieces of the puzzle, but we don't have the box top picture to which to refer. As much as we love to solve puzzles, we don't like the handicap. We are technology dependent and won't attempt to explore the darkness without this picture. At the very least, if provoked to do so, we demand night vision goggles.

We have little intuitive confidence that we can find our way forward by embracing the darkness of the soul. Critical thinking is afraid of such darkness. Fear melts into confidence by embracing this darkness. So, as the human spirit becomes more lost in this eerie fog, the will to take action diminishes. Explanations become ends in themselves.

The scientific community has a point. Throughout the ages, philosophers and most learned theologians have fallen prey to the error of identifying their purely verbal constructions as facts, or even the more enormous error of imagining their symbols more real than what they stand for. It was St. Paul who said, "Only the spirit gives life; the letter kills." Yet, we take this creative man at his word. It is worthy to note the Buddha never preached the truth. He saw that you had to realize it within yourself.

Critical thinking is searching for the solution. We are a solution driven society looking for problems to attach to our plethora of solutions. Our solutions in describing our problems reveal the full extent of what perplexes us. In our feverish quest for answers, solutions expose the full nature of our problems rather than resolving the issues at hand. In that sense, solutions have value if they were only seen in such terms.

Creative thinking designs and constructs a way forward, not to solve the dilemma but to improve the situation through control. Creative thinking understands problems are never solved, at best only controlled, and control is always temporary because change is constant.

It is the conceit of Western man to be preoccupied with "final solutions." There are no such things. "Western thinking is failing," de Bono continues, "because its complacent arrogance prevents it from seeing the extent of its failure."

This failure, he argues, is because Western thinking is not designed to deal with a changing world. It has proven inadequate to deal with change because it does not offer creative, but only temporary and flawed actions forward. It has a mania "to solve problems" now and for good. Therefore, the problems critical thinking solves are the problems it creates, repeatedly.

The nuclear arms race has now resulted in a colossal problem of nuclear waste disposal; global warming is given faint attention as the East now attempts to out-West the West in technological progress and modernization. So-called "rogue nations" want the bomb, complicating the waste disposal problem even more should they only acquire "the bomb" but never use it. The bomb is the product of a toxic mind built on fear.

Why not more attention to fusion than fission or to solar energy;

why progress at any cost? Fear, the darkness of the human soul, consumes while critical thinking remains slave to change without embracing it. Meanwhile, aspiring candidates for nuclear weapons widens, while nations with nuclear arsenals seem impotent to discourage such developments. It isn't a pretty picture.

There are exceptions to this mania. Denmark, for instance, is well on its way to be independent of petroleum through creative solutions, greening initiatives, and a populace willing to bite the bullet and radically change its lifestyle. Hopefully, this will inspire others to sacrifice and pursue a similar course.

With all the wonderful tools as toys modern society has created to promote "quality of life," man has been in the main on a century long self-destructive terror.

Tens of millions were slaughtered in conventional warfare in the last century. Now, in a new iteration of terror, there is the possibility of a nuclear holocaust. We have seen that anyone can be a suicide bomber in such places as Iraq, Afghanistan, India, Israel, or Indonesia, and now the backpack bomb attack at the Boston Marathon in April 2013 by the Tsarnaev brothers. Imagine if such fanatics had dirty nuclear bombs strapped to them.

If this were not enough, the governments of Sudan, Somalia, and the Democratic Republic of the Congo, Nigeria and Zimbabwe have seen much bloodshed and the displacement of tens of thousands, which has often led to mass starvation. As horrendous as these tragedies, the conflicts in Darfur, Cote d'Ivoire, Somalia, Nigeria, and northern Uganda continue only to be outstripped by the devastating death rate of HIV/AIDS infected Africans. Now, since 2011, the Syrian Civil War finds more than 100,000 deaths, most civilians, and nearly 200,000 Syrian refugees now in Lebanon and Jordan. The innocent are always the most to suffer in such senseless conflicts.

These calamities rise out of material and human deprivation, while Western man's self-destructive lifestyle continues unabated in the midst of plenty. On the other hand, as impressive as China's progress, hundreds of millions of Chinese peasants have not been brought to the banquet table. This is China's greatest challenge. If

China fails to find a solution to this majority, calamity and even revolution may be in its future.

CREATIVITY IN A CHANGING WORLD

While modernity celebrates its accomplishments, goodness has often been on holiday in a homeless mind.

The greatest challenge to creativity is finding the key to behaving in peace, harmony and mutual support of each other. Creative humanism starts with those nations with the most. This means abdicating self-indulgent lifestyles by behaving more responsibly and caringly.

Once the role of religion was to spread light in this darkness and guide the human soul to find its way forward to goodness and light, but no more. It would appear religion has lost its way in the past century or so. Now God is confined to pomp and circumstance, ritual and rites of passage, or jihads. Long-established religions are currently more absorbed in image protection and self-promotion, and as a consequence, less a deciding, defining factor in normal daily life. We saw this with the Roman Catholic Church and how it handled the sexual abuse scandals of the church's priests.

Why is it that Buddhism is the only religion that has never gone to war or resorted to violence in order to spread its message? Could it be because Buddhism recognizes only the god that everyone has latent inside? Understanding its creed means slowly waking up to that inner god. True, there have been isolated incidents when Buddhist monks have become defensive, and mounted acts of aggression. Does this, however, rise to a Buddhist Holy War?

Materialism engulfs the planet and materialism has nothing to do with leadership. Machiavelli notwithstanding, sustained leadership has always been grounded in spirituality, and this is missing today, everywhere. Modern surrogates to religion, the social sciences, have only compounded the problem with their doublespeak and suspect research, mainly, because they are critical thinkers, obsessed with what they know, and not creative thinkers, explorers in the no man's land of the unknown and perhaps the unknowable.

Psychiatry has failed, psychology has failed, anthropology has failed, sociology has failed, and all the social and behavioral sciences have failed because their attention has been on description rather than action. Most of what they tell us we already know, and that is the problem. We need to find a way out, not more solipsistic explanations why we have dug ourselves so deeply in this rut. Listen to your priest or minister or rabbi and you will hear an echo of these disciplines with a common mantra.

These disciplines are concerned with the values that arise from the "truth," but what is truth? Christianity has its truth, Judaism its truth, Islam its truth, and are they not the same truth? Can there be a cafeteria menu of truths? Religions may be in decline but the old habit of formulating creeds and imposing beliefs in some dogma persists even among atheists. The strange idolatrous overestimation of words and symbols, emblems and totems continues unchecked.

Have you ever noticed how you behave when you are lost? Panic sets in and you feel you have to do something, you need to act. The United States Air Force Academy teaches its students survival strategies, having them imagine their plane goes down in the desert and they have lost communication with the outside world. The strategy proposed is not to act, but to conserve energy, and to map out a way to make it easier to be found while adapting to the situation using their training; in other words, to think outside the box.

We are lost our moral compass and our way. We need a map, a strategy, and a way to find our way back to safety. Instead, panic has set in, and we're going in all directions at once and getting nowhere, certainly nowhere close to safety. Parents once provided a map. Religion once provided a map. But the maps they provide have proven unreliable. Instead, we maintain the illusion that we are not lost.

It is time we embrace the unknown, think differently on purpose, and turn our passive nature into an active response to the situation of being lost. An active response doesn't mean action for action's sake. It means to assess the situation and to think laterally as Edward de Bono proposes. That could begin with recreating the moment allowing the mind to become quiet and envisioning how we got to where we are, right now, even if it is in the middle of the desert, allowing the mind to work for us rather than against us.

The disruption of WWII and its explosive economic aftermath changed our culture radically with the maps from parents and the church no longer credible guides to the new generation of children.

For the past seventy years we have been living without our moral compass or reliable maps. The evidence is apparent in our chasing every fad under the sun, or escaping into deadly addictions, while being blown away by an increasingly technology dependence, while giving the impression that we are not lost at all. It puts me in mind of the subconscious dread that K experiences in the Franz Kafka novel, *"The Castle"* (1986). K sets off to report for duty at the castle, but as he walks towards the castle it seems farther and farther away.

Social sciences search for understanding of man's plight with statistical correlations rather than designing means to alleviate suffering. Action! They operate from ivory towers not from the trenches of the sick and weary. Action! They can be found as consultants in the boardrooms of corpocracy, not on the line. Action! They conduct studies of penal institutions rather than developing strategies to civilize and rehabilitate the deviant and lost. Action!

Likewise, modern medicine and pharmacology seek to discover cures for AIDS and other lifestyle diseases, which is honorable. Yet, they play a complicit role with the critical thinking of social science when they fail to think outside the box. Behavior causes this dreaded disease, the diseases of poverty, of lost hope, of unemployment, of corruption, and always, neglect. Why not focus creatively on these sources of the dilemma?

It is no longer a matter of discovering "what is" the problem, but of designing a way forward out of the problem, not with a drug, not with a strategy, not with a master plan, not with the commitment of billions by philanthropists, not with fund raising concerts, but with a reliable map that gets beyond the bells and whistles of self-congratulation and deals with our lost spiritual momentum.

A better miracle than feeding the hungry with loaves of bread and baskets of fish would be to teach people how to produce grain, bake bread, fish, and turn their own natural resources into income for themselves, not riches for their colonial masters. The irony is that some of the riches deposits of natural resources are mainly located in Third World countries in South America and Africa, where the indigenous peoples of those countries rarely benefit from the fruits of their garden of paradise. Why is that?

It may be a matter of creating new bold counterintuitive ideas directly opposed to conventional logic rather than repeating the standard ones. The rich people in these third world countries have the power, and they are not likely to relinquish it.

Many African leaders have never gotten past their deep-seated hatred of colonial repression. It still rankles these indigenous peoples although only the shadow of colonialism still exists.

Robert Mugabe of Zimbabwe came to power in 1980 when the white regime collapsed and the country was liberated from the Ian Smith regime. Smith had previously proclaimed unilateral independence from Great Britain in order to maintain minority rule of Rhodesia, as it was then known.

We in the West have made Mugabe a caricature of a one-dimensional man reducing him to a terrible and recalcitrant despot of this poor country. There is some truth to this, but it leaves out his fight for majority rule, his years in prison, and his attempt, once in power to involve white farmers in open discussions on land sharing and land reform.

For his efforts to involve whites, he was always met with silence. Eventually, he annexed the land with negative results and equally negative international press. His methods have often been harsh and draconian as the country has sunk deeper into poverty. It is clear white Rhodesians in particular and the West in general have not wanted him to succeed. Collectively, they have confirmed his conviction that the roots of colonialism run deep and need to be cut away again and again. The West has imposed economic sanctions driving the country into deeper depression and opening the opportunity for the East, especially China to step into the void.

The West manages by commission and omission to combine, its magnanimity with intractable ideology to misapply its good intentions.

Take the AIDS epidemic. It is not a moral issue. It is a public health issue. A way forward is possible only if there is a softening of hard-edged thinking and condescending morality.

Bless the *Doctors Without Borders*, bless the volunteers in the most deprived circumstances, bless the missionaries who quietly educate and train, bless the UN workers who have found life's purpose, bless Bill Gates and his foundation, bless Bono and his work with the UN to forgive the debt of Third World Countries, bless the journalists who attempt to reveal the source of African carnage, bless actors like George Clooney and his father who have attempted to bring attention to the suffering in Africa, mainly in Darfur, bless former president George W. Bush for his quiet initiative of $18 billion dollars to see that the anti-retroviral drug for AIDS was available to some 1.3 million Africans to combat this disease, bless these and all the others that are the exception to this charge. The map that guides them is love of humanity.

These people are the heroes of our times, and the hope of our collective future. They understand the challenge of creativity in a changing world where you do what is possible and leave idealism at home.

They are like George Eliot's definition of goodness, showing in action a desire for what is perfectly good without knowing clearly what it is. They are not waiting for the perfect moment or quintessential paradigm. They are a very small army of hope creating good.

PROBLEM WITH CRITICAL THINKING IN
THE AGE OF INFORMATION

The focus of critical thinking is on identifying, evaluating, describing, and then assessing the problem with hard logic. A set of objectives, a process to correct the problem, including monitoring and evaluating results, then looking backwards to how these results compare with previous interventions. This is Machine Age thinking.

The horse is already out of the barn when it comes to the "right time" for action.

Much of modern science is conducted without a single human being directly involved. Individuals are relegated to statistical numbers. Science is most comfortable in this impersonal world. Individuals are often coded in a stratified random sample to ensure statistical significance, or reduced to genomes or DNA verification.

Psychometrics or the measuring of people is an art form treated like a religion. Can you imagine being told you are limited in potential because you have only an average IQ?

James Watson, the co-discoverer of the double helix of DNA, admits to having an "average IQ," Imagine if he had said, "I'm not bright enough for science." Einstein scoffed at the idea that he was a genius:

> *"With fame I became more and more stupid, which of course, is a very common phenomenon. There is far too great a disproportion between what one is and what others think one is."*

Watson like Einstein was obsessively curious. Read his book, *"The Double Helix"* (1968) and you'll get a sense of this.

It is the antiseptic nature of the modern scientific method that is the new dogma, and unquestioned for its relevance. There is little room in this canon for subjectivity, or value analysis because objectivity does not permit such contamination. Nor is there a place for human provocation or contradiction. If the results cannot be replicated, they do not exist. They are spurious.

161

Dependent and independent variables have no room for discursive data. There is a mania for "control of data," for "value free" analysis, and consequently, too frequently valueless in the end when it comes to the spuriousness of human behavior.

Science gets the results expected in linear terms with elemental verification. One of the odd things about science is that it infrequently publishes experiments that fail, when failure reported is often the riches learning experience.

Human behavior vacillates between deprivation on one front and lifestyle excess on the other. Between these poles, the AIDS epidemic continues to spread unabated while more people die every day from overeating, overdrinking, smoking, and various forms of drug and lifestyle addictions, as well as from senseless brutality, suicide, patricide and homicide.

Local television nightly news of any metropolitan area is likely to open with a litany of carnage among ordinary citizens in the last twenty-four hours. Is this schadenfreude? Does this drive people on the psychological edge to such crimes? No one knows because mayhem and murder are good television news.

The Drug War has become a tragic comedy. It has failed because law-abiding citizens do drugs. In the sanctuary of their fine homes, and their clubby relationship with law enforcement, they use illegal recreation drugs with impunity.

George Michael, the British singer, smoked a marijuana cigarette while being interviewed on the British television network ITV, claiming, *"This stuff keeps me sane and happy."* And then adding in a showy way, "I'd say it's a great drug, but obviously it's not very healthy. You can't afford to smoke it if you've got anything to do."

The diabetes epidemic continues for America's poorest because it lives on a high caloric diet of condiments not infrequently purchased at a premium price from fast food and convenient stores across the nation. Fast foods make up a good portion of school lunch programs. A 2006 study in Great Britain found three out of every four teenagers were too fat for military service. France, which has prided itself on its regiment of diet and discipline, is growing

McDonald fat.

Why has little been done to change this diet, or eating habits?

Cigarette smoking is the cause of the majority of lifestyle diseases such as heart disease, lung cancer, emphysema, and strokes. Yet, every day 5,000 American teenagers start up smoking cigarettes for the first time, a habit that has led to a meteoric rise in health care insurance costs for all Americans. What has been done about this problem except rhetorically? Nothing!

A CASE IN POINT

The Tampa Tribune columnist, Daniel Ruth, has written a series of articles (October 2006) on the anti-tobacco fiasco. Florida in 1997 settled with the tobacco industry for $14 billion. The state's legal "dream team" collected $3.2 billion in attorneys' fees, or $112,000 per hour according to the Cato Institute. Yet, the very reason for suing the tobacco industry, writes Ruth, "was to prevent youth smoking, which has been reduced to the Dollar Store equivalent of public policy." Funding for the state's Tobacco Control Program for this purpose was $70 million of this $14 billion in 1999, being since whittled down to nothing in 2003, and beyond. Tampa lawyer Steve Yerrid collected $200 million in attorney fees for his work on this settlement.

MEDICINE AS LIFESTYLE APOLOGIST

Obviously, while much is made of the breakthrough in genome research based on solving the riddle of DNA, little attention has been focused on understanding the DNA of man's soul. The soul directs behavior and the body follows its direction, not the other way around.

Freud, perhaps unintentionally, describes this in terms of the relationship of the "ego" (the adult) and the "id" (the child) in psychoanalytical terms, inviting us into the world where the horse is in charge (the "id") and the rider (the "ego") follows. He writes:

> *"The horse supplies the locomotive energy, while the rider has the privilege of deciding the goal and of guiding the powerful animal's movement... the not precisely situation of the rider being obliged to guide the horse along the path which it itself wants to go."*

What could better describe modern medicine and science as lifestyle apologists? The rider ends up in the direction that the horse already wants to go. Medicine doesn't lead but spends its special talent aided by the support of the government on research to combat lifestyle excesses of the self-indulgent. This makes a mockery of the concept of purpose and progress, independence and autonomy.

When science looks at man, it takes the easy roadmap and looks at the disease, not the person, not the cause, which is most likely inappropriate behavior. Man, the person, has become a magnificent toy to manipulate from the scientist to the entrepreneur with little apparent motive to find a way forward out of this trap. It is no accident that the greatest strides in modern medicine in the past 100 years have been made in public health, such as sanitation, potable drinking water, sewage treatment, pest control, slum rejuvenation, work standards and workplace conditions, industrial waste disposal monitoring, and so on.

Contrast this with the consumer oriented medical and pharmaceutical industry: the diet pill, smoker's patch, methadone for drug addicts, AIDS pills, heart disease pills, cholesterol pills, the birth control pill, headache remedies, Ritalin for ADD children, and so on. Senior citizens commonly take a regimen of 15 to 20 or more pills and think nothing of it. No one asks: What is going on here? Why so many pills? What other alternatives are there?

Christopher Lasch writes in *"The Culture of Narcissism: American Life in an Age of Diminishing Expectations"* (1978) that consumption has become therapy for an anxious age. Thirty- six years later it is far more anxious than he envisioned. He saw a flight from feeling and good sense, as well as a shattering of regenerating life. It was as if, "why bother!" Alarming as this explanation, his words changed nothing. He sold a few books; stunned the American populace with a mosquito bite that didn't change its cadence.

No real attempt has been made to change the mind of *modern man*. No one wants to penetrate the darkness of his soul. It is enough to have him lying on a couch, a specimen in a petri dish, or an algorithm to manipulate on a computer, and then objectively manage and measure these data as if correlations were verifiable causation.

The mind and behavior have been classified, categorized, defined, compartmentalized, and digitally mapped to satisfy curiosity, but not to take appropriate action. Action takes other more safe forms.

Modern kinesiology has made great strides in understanding the principles of mechanics and anatomy in relation to human movement. The lag is not in man's physicality; the lag is in his mentality. The Greeks once worshiped perfection of man's athleticism, but not at the expense of the cultivation of his mind. Today athleticism is mainly a spectator sport as is the exercise of the mind.

The confident thinker believes in a sound mind and sound body and not the development of one at the expense of the other. Nor does the confident thinker retreat to couch potato status glued to electronics in a bloated body with an empty room for a mind.

While only ten percent of Americans are emotionally self-reliant and mature, it would seem a healthy balance between mind and body would be even less so. Recent reports indicate Europeans are declining in the same direction and at nearly the same rate.

WHEN CREATIVE THINKING WAS IN VOGUE

One of the earliest creative thinkers was the English clergyman Roger Bacon (1220-1292), called the first scientist. He challenged the orthodoxy of the day, that is, the authority of the papacy and the immutable truth of Roman Catholic dogma.

Father Bacon advanced the understanding of optics, predicted everything from the horseless carriage to the telescope and stressed the importance of mathematics in science, and was long credited with the invention of gunpowder. His scientific writings were passionate attempts to warn the Church against suppressing the new science, and for it his works were banned.

Just as the Information Age created the Internet and changed our lives, the invention of the moveable type printing press by Johannes Gutenberg (1400-1468) dramatically changed the world. Printing led to books, books led to a reading public, which in turn led to translation into multiple languages, which then led to the creation of nations, and nation states, and which finally led to a new world economy and social order.

Printing also fueled The Protestant Reformation of Martin Luther (1483-1546), which spread like a prairie fire once ignited by his 95 theses of protest against the selling of indulgences by the Church.

Staggering change was in the air. Polish astronomer Nicolas Copernicus (1473-1543) came up with the mathematical proof that put the sun at the center of the solar system in which the earth was but one planet of several others orbiting around the sun. The implications were philosophically mind-boggling. It denied the ancient belief that the earth was the center of the universe befitting a creature made in the image of God. The work was published in the year of his death (1543) and so the Inquisition could not touch him. It did, however, disturb the lives of many brave and creative thinking men who followed.

Galileo (1564-1642) called the "first physicist" confirmed the work of Copernicus and was tried by *The Inquisition* and placed on house arrest for the rest of his life.

Giordano Bruno (1548-1600), a Dominican friar, and enthusiastic supporter of Copernicus, left his sanctuary in France to return to his native Italy to teach and lecture on science, only to be tried by *The Inquisition*, tortured and burned at the stake.

Johannes Kepler (1571-1630), called the *"Protestant Galileo,"* was attacked for his laws of planetary motion while his mother was tried as a witch (see "Kepler's Witch" by James A. Connor 2004).

In Church history from the time of Constantine when he declared Christianity the Roman Empire's religion (312 ad) until the high Middle Ages and the Renaissance (1260-1594) the clergy remained the intellectual power. So, it is not surprising that the clergy went beyond what was known (critical thinking) to explore what was not (creative thinking). Essentially amateurs, they introduced the scientific age under great physical and psychological duress.

And so creativity that is in the heart of every human being, discouraged for centuries, managed to breakthrough with a handful of courageous and curious men to see the light of day amidst the darkness.

FAST FORWARD TO THE PRESENT

Once again critical thinking is more in vogue today. Why is that? Certainly, there is no physical danger to thinking differently. The rudimentary tools that were available for Copernicus, Galileo and Kepler did not prevent them from making universe-shaking discoveries by abandoning the conventional.

Scientists today have laboratories, technicians, and every imaginable electronic tool to make millions and even billions of accurate calculations not available to these pioneers. Yet, while science continues to make significant breakthroughs in the subatomic to the cosmic universe, man's behavior as subject matter seems to be lost in the chase as if an imponderable conundrum. In a way it might take the same ingenuity and toolbox of imagination that was the lot of early scientists to make similar breakthroughs in the study of man. These early scientists were dreamers, as was Einstein. Dreaming is currently in short supply while frenetic data collection is not.

Medical science can do laser research, transplant organs, even engage in genetic cloning. To date, science hasn't been able to explain let alone isolate or analyze the 64 grams that expire from the body when a person dies. Nor has it been able to predict human behavior, much less control it.

Man's complexity has shattered man's confidence as much as Nietzsche's declaration, "God is dead!" Engineer and inventor

William L. Livingston puts it:

> *"When problems appear too complex, we ignore the fact and solve the problems we can."* Then he adds, *"When simple problem solving techniques are applied to complex matters, the original problem becomes more complex."*

We have seen this played out on the War on Drugs, Homeland Security's handling of the Katrina Hurricane, the War in Iraq and Afghanistan, the War on Poverty, the *"No Child Left Behind Program,"* and on and on. Einstein concurs with Livingston, noting, "No problem can be solved from the same consciousness that created it." Since critical thinking represents this same consciousness, we have ample evidence of this fact.

In a climate of too much affluence, too many toys and too soon old, the baby boomer generation knows only too well the words of John Milton:

> *"The mind is its own place, and in itself can make a heaven of hell, a hell of heaven."*

There are more than 80 million working baby boomers in America now between the ages of 50 and 65 who were toddlers during the Korean War and the great Communist "Red Scare." They were coming of age during the Vietnam War, and have endured the frantic Nuclear and Space Race, been shaken awake by the *Sexual Revolution,* the *Civil Rights and Women's Rights Movements,* and then lulled back to sleep with runaway economic prosperity into self-indulgent Viagra middle age seeking refuge in youth restoring consumer products.

Baby boomers at work became pyramid climbers going the extra mile to make an impression, and then getting a tummy tuck, nose job, breast enhancement or some other physical modification from plastic surgery to look as young as their children. Ever resilient and optimistic, they bought into the utopian American Dream and made it their reality. Now dogged and depressed by global competition with rumors their employers are talking merger or filing Chapter 11 bankruptcy, they wonder if they'll retire with a pension.

Nothing prepared baby boomers for September 11, 2001 and the al Qaeda attack on the Twin Towers in New York City using American commercial airlines as missiles with 3,000 dead in the horrible conflagration.

They did not expect problematic consequences for living beyond their means off credit card debt, buying homes they couldn't afford with subprime contracts, or driving tank like gas guzzling SUV's they couldn't afford. Nor did they expect to be haunted by an international economic meltdown and global recession that they were told they created. They were clueless because Baby Boomers never felt the pain of reality and therefore the consequences of their actions.

Meanwhile, baby boomer children are in the workforce but not defined by Iraq and Afghanistan, as these wars did not necessitate the burning of draft cards. There was no draft, and so there was no need for protest of these wars. They were safe. They have been swept away by the technological tsunami of cell phones, computers, iPods, iPhones, iPads and the Internet, by multiculturalism, the War on Terror, and if this were not enough, made to feel self-conscious about speaking only English and being Christian. They frantically attempt to gain purchase of something to hold them in place.

Children of baby boomers see their parents uncertain and confused, running scared on varicose veins and say, "Lighten up!" They, themselves, are just hanging out, going with the flow, having a good time while they can, and repeating the same sins as their parents only without the guilt. They have abandoned the race and abdicated the leadership role that their parents turned inside out, preferring to paint their bodies with tattoos, listen to tribal noise, take shortcuts, cheat, live for the moment, and treat their electronic tools as toys of distraction. Baby boomers were all about "me," their children all about nothing. They are as lost as their parents were, and without a reliable map, but they find this status, "cool."

Where creativity exists it is in technology with its ubiquitous electronic eye of surveillance. This has made self-trust, self-reliance, self-activation, and self-renewal difficult if not impossible.

Panic increases with every attempt to displace it. The more children of baby boomers are warned that this may be the beginning of the descent of the United States the more they turn to fast cars, fast boats, and a faster lifestyle into the great escape of constant noise.

Their collective psyche demands they be in relentless motion serenaded by this noise, the louder and more atonal the better.

Advertisers, always privy to societal madness, use public service announcements to alert young people to the danger of drugs. One of the most bizarre public service announcements is that of eggs frying on a skillet to show how drugs fry the brain. Panic sells. Advertisers know people don't want to think, but to be shocked into awareness, but awareness to do what; certainly not to give up their lifestyle. I can remember years ago when nearly everyone smoked cigarettes, and smokers laughed and called them "cancer sticks," but they didn't quit smoking, that is, until they couldn't walk across the room.

Can we find our way back to pastoral peace, to connection with the simple rhythms of life, to where love is possible, relationships real, where trust and hope are not just campaign slogans? Confident Thinking says we not only can but also that we must.

There is little doubt that the climate of the "big lie" of George Orwell's "1984" took hold after World War II and was ratcheted up into high gear in post modernity, where self-estrangement has sometimes taken on Faustian form. Nor can it be denied that Orwell's doublespeak is the language of our times, where war is peace and pain is pleasure and sorrow is happiness and insanity is sanity. Can we reverse this?

Again, *Confident Thinking* says a resounding "yes." All we have to do is decide to be kinder to ourselves and therefore by extension kinder to each other; to blend our natural spiritualism with our materialistic demands; to make every day the best day of our lives by touching someone with love, affection, and support.

This does not mean we carry other people's burdens but rather that we assist them in mounting that challenge. It is the only way to make them healthier, wealthier and wiser. We don't have to go to the other side of the world to do this. Indeed, it starts by making a self-intervention by improving our minds and paying attention to our bodies; shedding our reactive skin and becoming actively involved in our family, church, school, and community; making a difference believing we can make it so.

It is so easy to run away from our problems. More books are being published than ever before although fewer people are reading. The ranks of the affluent grow, but more people are dying of hunger and disease. Education is accessible to nearly everyone, yet illiteracy is greater than it was a century ago. More leisure time is available, but increasingly the void is filled with work. A city of any size can flood extensively from a single summer rain because cement, concrete, asphalt and crushed rock defy absorption.

Creativity is not in happy circumstance. We can change that. We are a social animal and meant to make connection, not separation, first with ourselves and then with others. Connection rises out of the soul from where it lives, and then projects a level of trust to make the world better.

In my experience, I have found little more than ten percent of the people I have dealt with to be what I would call self-reliant and mature. As discouraging as that assessment, even more alarming, I have not found ten percent of the people I have managed, taught or met to be creatively self-confident. Creativity and confidence is not a matter of dress, manner, elocution, diction, syntax, or the oozing of self-assurance. Nor is it a matter of credentials or socioeconomic status. Confidence comes from "within" as does creativity. Such individuals have a moral compass firmly in place, indicating where they are what they are about and where they are going.

CONFIDENT THINKING
CREATIVE STAGE EIGHT

LOOK AT PROBLEMS AS DOOR OPENERS
YOU AREA CHANGE AGENT
START THE CHANGE PROCESS
WITH YOURSELF

`Today is not yesterday. We ourselves change. How then, can our works and thoughts, if they are always to be the fittest, continue always the same? Change, indeed, is painful, yet ever needful; and if memory has its force and worth, so also has hope."

Thomas Carlyle (1795 —1881), English Historian/Philosopher

GREAT DILEMMA: OBSESSION WITH CONTROL

G OETHE WOULD ARGUE with Carlyle's assessment, as he preferred courage to hope. He saw hope as a great deceiver. We cannot hope our way out of our problems. We must display the courage to embrace them. Hope seduces its victims with promises so that they might lean on her, and not on themselves. Hope is that great bromide of wishful thinking: if only I stay the course long enough my luck will change. I will be extricated from my misery. Hope does have a rhetorical ring to it as President Barak Obama's bestselling book, "Audacity of Hope"

(2006) attests.

Hope entices us to postpone action in the present as if there were a miraculous future upon which to depend. The more we depend on hope the more we fear the present and the situation in which we find ourselves.

Remember when Pandora opened the box of evils, and war, pestilence, disease and famine poured out into the world? The greatest evil came out last, the great postpone, the tempter to abdication, the deathblow to initiative. Hope is fear of the present. So, we must husband our courage to rescue us from ourselves.

What is the one thing of which we seem most fixated? To be in control!

We all like to think we are working our own agenda, living our own lives, and on our own terms, but are we? A better case could be made that we are out-of-control, indeed, that no one or anything is under control. Everything appears in a state of flux.

This in no small way is due to our programming. We are a solution driven society that expects problems to be solved when they can only be controlled. We desire stability in the vortex of change, which is to deny its inevitability.

The world is changing. Technology is driving change. Populations are exploding. Values are changing. Developing nations are developing faster. Pollution is increasing. People are living longer. Nothing is ever as we might desire it to remain or to be.

We can pretend that this doesn't affect us that we can insulate ourselves from change, but that of course is impossible. Yet our conditioning, indeed, our thinking is designed for a stable society not an ever-changing one.

CONTROL AND FALLACY OF THE PROBLEM SOLVING

Our programming of course is failing, especially in our schools. The most egregious offenders find themselves marched off to the principal's office with a pink slip and a call home to the parents. Self-control is not in the mix. Conforming behavior is praised as the controlling norm. Teachers are exasperated unable to control students in their classes much less between classes. School has become a combat zone in which little learning takes place. Could it be because students are considered property and not persons?

The more we demand control of children the more they are inclined to be out-of-control. Kahlil Gibran in *"The Prophet"* (1972) reminds us why:

> *"You may strive to be like them, but seek not to make them like you. For life goes not backward nor tarries with yesterday. You are the bows from which your children as living arrows are sent forth. The archer sees the mark upon the path of the infinite, and He bends you with His might that His arrows may go swift and far. Let your bending in the archer's hand be for gladness. For even as He loves the arrow that flies, so He loves also the bow that is stable."*

Those inclined to put "a cork in the bottle" arbitrarily labeling children who deviate from the norm as "troublemakers," "disruptive influences," or candidates for Ritalin or some other mind-altering drug without considering them as developing human beings serve no useful purpose.

This reminds me of the School District of Washington, D.C. profiled across television on PBS News Hour and Frontline showing miscreant students marching off to the principal's office with a pink slip and a call home to the parents, or even more incredible showing a consultant interviewing (on television no less) a teacher and a principal about to be fired. Schools may need to be helped, but first they need to be rescued from these turnaround specialists who champion their roles while victimizing their clients.

There are quiet exceptions. Dr. Blondel Senior and his wife, Gloria comes to mind. More than thirty five years ago, they envisioned creating a safe haven for boys 12 to 16 years-of-age with learning disabilities suffering from ADD, ADHD, dyslexia and other learning and maladaptive behaviors.

They created The Advent Home, which is located in a Tennessee pastoral setting where these boys live, study and work applying Dr.

Senior's *Maturation Therapy®,* which is a totally drug free approach to healing. With their approach, students are fed a carefully regulated diet of nutritional food to combat the compulsive eating disorders many bring to the home.

The Advent Home is environmentally free of typical distractions where individual counselors can focus on each boy's needs. This methodology consists of three areas of personal progress: (1) foundation of growth; (2) foundation of self-regard; and (3) foundation of interpersonal skills.

The boys work the farm, study in state-of-the-arts classrooms and laboratories, organize play and recreation, develop skills in self-mastery and mastery of some discipline, but have limited television. In the process, they become self-responsible, more self-knowing, and self-aware, and grow in learning, maturity, thinking confidently with a sense of ownership of what they do. The Advent Home has an impressive record of how damaged youth can be restored to health and purpose, and productive lives.

That said the most sophisticated and seemingly intelligent of parents too often go along with short cut rehabilitation with an emphasis on drug therapy. This remedy can become a lifelong ritualistic drug dependency with these children never transitioning into adulthood. Pill popping of some kind becomes an axiomatic response to pain or discomfiture.

Forget about Thoreau and his declaration that we all march to our own drummer. Society insists on programming us to behave according to its arbitrary standards even if it means making us walking zombies.

It doesn't end there. An ADD or ADHD person can be stigmatized for hyperactivity or an attention deficit disorder. Imagine, a child starting school, a new person in the cocoon of life already with the label of a "problem child."

Parents kick start this downward spiral by feeding their children processed sugar products. This activates the hyperactive centers of the brain, finding the child bouncing off the walls. A change in diet could reduce this to more harmonious synapses with fresh fruit, vegetables and a high protein diet. Instead, parents continue to feed the sugar, give their child a pill, then the school gives him another pill, and then when he comes home from school, he is given yet another pill so that he will sleep without interrupting his parent's television watching, work on their laptops, or conversation with each other. Then we wonder why we have all become chemical junkies.

Addictions are nothing more than exaggerated habits, which hide the shallowness of our inner lives. It is apparent in adults with a lack of independence, self-sufficiency, and emotional self-reliance.

Parents unwittingly make their children the equivalent of animated spinning tops by a regimen of pills. Later, the pill is replaced or complemented by the cigarette, the cocktail, or an illicit recreational drug. As a child, the pill was the child's friend and company, now as an adult pill replacements are meant to ward off loneliness. Addictions are props and stress signals.

They crush initiative with the face of a needle, powder, or pill to put off the ravages of boredom, despair, uncertainty or the feeling of being lost. Addictions tell us more about who we are, about what we want to say to each other, and what we might be capable of doing were it not for the addiction.

What makes matters even more complicated, according to a published study in *Nature Neuroscience*, is that rats become addicted to junk food (potato chips, burgers, Cheetos, Twinkies, candy bars, etc.) in the same fashion that people become addictive to nicotine, cocaine and heroin. This indicates that the brain reacts similarly to junk food and drugs. Hyper-eating has become a cultural addiction leading to extreme obesity as people look for a buzz in food or the bliss point, not simply to satisfy hunger.

Psychiatrists have become unwittingly the front men for the pharmaceutical industry, as they attempt to drug ADD and ADHD maladies to death. It is as if our biochemical synapses are at war against us, and the only way to countermand their advantage is to wage a similar biochemical war against them.

This has a frightening resonance with how society attempts to solve its problems, that is, by attacking the symptoms. Lost in this is the individual child who is simply struggling at an early stage to get its insides and outsides adjusted to each other. For this to happen, the child requires tolerance, guidance, direction, a climate for growth and development, play and recreation, and the patience of fair, firm, consistent, gentle, and loving care. Caregiver would also be well to find the voice that has "no" in its vocabulary.

Jane doesn't need to be compared with Johnny, or Sally with Betty, or Fred with Oscar but rather to be shown how unique each is in one's own sense and yet common to each other in another. Thankfully, a child has remarkable resilience and can often triumph over lackadaisical care.

Later, I will share the case of William George Mosley who demonstrates just that. Mr. Mosley managed to get his insides and outsides to work together with little help from anyone save his grandmother, whom he was exposed to for only three years.

The child who has too much, too many, and too soon has more than might be thought with the child who has too little, too few, and too late. Both are handicapped. The spoiled child has handicapping of scale that fills the void with insatiable want while deprived child suffers insatiable need, or the positive and negative aspects of excess. *"Our desire,"* Freud says, *"is always in excess of our capacity to satisfy it."* With handicapping, we judge wants before we find out what needs are. To wit:

- Children are handicapped the moment the poison of comparison rocks their hearts. Suddenly, they are aware of being inadequate and vulnerable. The world comes to feel hostile, or at best unrewarding. The persistent feeling is one of being trapped. Feelings are not reasons nor does deprivation have a cause. It is the pain of emotional reliance. When children feel undervalued, then nearly anything goes.

- The abandoned child and the spoiled child are polar opposites that can come to resemble each other with indifferent parental stimulation. This occurs when children are seen but not heard.

Compulsive and erratic behavior follows.

- Affluent parents often indulge their children with the latest electronic innovation as babysitter. Indigent parents, not to be outdone, use television as their children's babysitter, allowing the colored pixels to dance off their children's eyeballs putting them in an equally merry electronic daze comparable to their affluent counterparts.

- Both approaches are equally hypnotic and chaotic. It is not uncommon to find a three-year-old child of affluence with its own cell phone, computer, iPod and MP3 player. It is equally likely that a family on welfare has cable television with a hundred channels for their children to cruise with the remote at their leisure massaging their delicate psyches with bizarre fantasy images.

- Parents of all socio-economic classes have a much easier time saying, "yes" to everything asked for than "no" to anything. Saying "no" would demand explanation, and parents seemingly have neither the time nor the inclination to communicate meaningfully with their children on their level.

- Children learn practically from birth the power of tears and advantage of screams or tantrum disruptions. If there is anything that fuels a child's anxiety, it is the lack of attention. A child soon learns that tears bring action and satisfaction.

- Children quickly discern the ambivalence between parental rhetoric and reality concerning do's and don'ts. Not yet able to read, the child can already gauge sincerity and consistency. While the mother fastens her little darling into her car seat, it won't be long before that child noticed mother hasn't fastened her seatbelt. A budding cynicism is on the verge of blossoming.

- Children fed breakfast cereal loaded with Fruity Loops instead of a breakfast of proteins and fresh fruit will soon repay the favor by behaving consistent with the diet.

Long before children find themselves in school, they have been introduced to doublespeak. This is the theme of Robert Smith's book, *"Where did you go? Out. What did you do? Nothing."* (1974). It is the rare parent who can master a child's dissembling language, penetrate its code and discourage such beating around the bush.

Dissembling is a cultural norm. Children sense this. Former President Harry S. Truman had no time for it. He had a plaque on his desk: *"The buck stops here!"* He wanted straight talk no embroidering. Straight talk identified his presidency, but straight talk has become an empty cliché. Grownups know this only too well. You never talk straight to the boss. When he asks how things are going, you answer "fine," when they are not. You don't want to the messenger who gets killed. You tell him what he wants to hear, as children do their parents. So, dissembling follows us from cradle to grave.

Solutions are aplenty but no one wants to tackle real problem straight on. They are too complex. But does this allow us to get on top of the situation? I don't think so. To control our problems we need to define them and then face them. This demands courage, which is in short supply.

The hardest part of a problem is defining it; the easiest part is the solution. Guess where we usually put the emphasis? On the solution of course. As Livingston puts it:

> *"Complexity has become a given. This finds us solving the problems we understand, whether or not they are the problems we actually face."*

He has developed a four system complex problem solving strategy: the technical system (toolbox), which is inseparable from the social system (relationships), and the purposeful system (the problem domain), which is mated to the control system (the solution domain). Problems, he insists, are never solved only controlled. What is counterintuitive about this strategy is that he has found problem domain is coherent and tidy while the solution domain is incoherent and riddled with contradictions.

We might argue that this is not true citing the venerated statistical correlation as proof. But correlations are just that, correlations, and often wide of the mark in terms of causation despite being replete with algorithms, pie charts, graphs and schematics.

Take Jeffrey Kluger's featured article in *Time* (July 10, 2006), *"How your siblings make you who you are."* Kluger's opens with the caption, *"The new science of siblings."* That should do it. Who is going to dispute scientific findings?

According to these data, parents, teachers, preachers, mentors and other authority figures are placed in secondary roles to siblings. It is another way of taking authority figures off the hook, "not their fault!" It is not the fault of authority figures that the world is a mess standing on its head with few mature adults on the scene.

Children have endured the prospects of being essentially their own parents through the 1970s, 1980s, 1990s, and into the 2000s, as both parents are likely to have full-time jobs. These parents don't expect ever to become old and so never have to grow up. They work hard and play hard verifying their eternal youth by zest and exuberance, while expecting their children to grow up straight and tall and true without any directional control or influence from them other than extravagant materialistic support.

It didn't happen in the 1970s, and it isn't happening now. It may make good copy to suggest that siblings carry the load of influence. If so, it is a matter of default not by design, while burying the problem once again (reference: Livingston's strategy).

We want so desperately to explain away the aberrancy of children, and to take society, especially parents off the hook, because the society we have created is a sick society and no one wants to tackle that complexity (translated: can of worms).

We have created little monsters at all levels of society, some of them running the country, and the only chance we have of correcting this problem is by installing a *Confident Thinking* problem solving governor in children at an early age where they make choices that are self-creating rather than self-destructive, where they are the masters of change rather than its slaves, and where they live in harmony with their internal clock and external environment, and don't try to burn the candle at both ends, and where they have confidence in the change process as change agents, not victims of change.

Children are our only hope. There is little hope of changing chronological adults suspended in terminal adolescence. There is no panacea to make them instantly mature, self-reliant and emotionally responsive problem solvers. If you have any doubts about this, read *"Six Silent Killers"* (1998). Counter dependent behavior is not only a management problem but also a societal one. You cannot "will" people into becoming creative problem solvers comfortable in taking risks when they have been programmed critical thinkers with conformist mentalities, and passive responsive attitudes stubbornly clinging to stability and predictability in a climate of constant unanticipated disruption.

THE PROBLEM WITH THE PROBLEM SOLVER, AND CODEPENDENCY

We have handicapped our culture in the problem solving.

There is no shortage of television gurus and authors who have all the answers without having the slightest knowledge of the persons whose problems they are attempting to solve, other than superficially, in the studio on national television of all places.

You cannot prescribe a cure for the loveless marriage, the drug addict, or the perennially unemployed worker by a three-minute session with some television crony in an hour-long Dr. Phil love fest of adoring fans. It is simply a praise of folly.

If truth were known, you can't do it with 3,000 hours if the relationship is one of passive engagement, looking for answers or attitude adjustments outside of one's own chaotic experience. We each have to do the heavy lifting ourselves.

If you don't have your ducks in a row, don't have a clear identity in terms of your "real self" versus your "ideal self," or have failed to come to terms with the difference between self-demands and role demands, any therapeutic exercise is one of futility because you will never come to define your problem, as it is actually being experienced. You will not be able to design an action plan forward without a map, the map that fits your profile and is created by you with the possible assistance of a therapist.

The more dependent we are on other-directed authority the more progressive the retreat into delusion and personal drift. The attraction to gurus is a closet desire for change without pain. Indeed, you want the option of blaming someone else should your life not turn up roses. It will not happen. No one can save you from yourself but yourself.

Melody Beattie has written a series of books such as *"Codependent No More"* (1987) and *"Beyond Codependency"* (1989), which have all the right words and ideas about getting beyond making the situation worse for the person you're trying to help, but does it work?

Perhaps the reader has had a needy family member or friend crippled by continual "help." What invariably develops is that the needy person comes to expect to be "bailed out" no matter how serious the fix or repeated the chronic contretemps. It is never the person's fault. The needy person knows your vulnerability, knows how to exploit your weaknesses with the precision of a surgeon with little risk, and even less sense of regret should you destroy your own health and security in the process. The needy have only sensitivity to their needs, never yours.

Once the pattern is established, it never changes. Gradually, the high crimes and misdemeanors of the needy person escalate until you are so emotionally and perhaps economically drained that you can hardly cope yourself. The phone can ring at any time of night or day and you are expected to be there for that needy person. Were the positions reversed, do you think the needy person would be there for you? If pigs could fly!

Here is the irony. If you refuse to play this game, you are exempted from being contacted by the needy person. The person doesn't waste time where help is not automatic, where there is no chance that tears, guilt, blackmail, or threat of suicide will work. Now why is that?

The needy person recognizes there are limits to his manipulative skills, and therefore employs them judiciously where success is assured. It is the same with the child. The child knows when and with whom to toss a tantrum or erupt in a crying jag.

Is such unresponsive behavior cruel? Heartless? The questions are not relevant as it puts the onus on the responder, not on the needy, not on the person who is on a self-destructive tear. A long time ago, if that person had been alone in the rag bone cellar of the heart, and had no one else to pick him up, he would have picked himself up and gone forward. He would have developed the rudiments of the problem solving. That is the nature of Life's instinct for survival. That has been denied the needy person. Therein lies the tragedy.

Let us for a moment switch from the needy to the helper. Why do so many of us get caught up in this irrevocable cycle of aiding and abetting codependency? French psychologist Serge Viderman claims it is due to our compulsive narcissism:

> *"The hell of the narcissist is the tyranny of his need for others."*

We feel helpless not to "help," and so we are pulled in. It takes two to play this codependency game. If you refuse to bite, if you won't be driven by narcissistic guilt, then the helpless needy person must and will move on to others.

This brings us to another point. Consciously or unconsciously we are all looking for the safety and security found with the father. It is the primary driver in religion. Even our institutions are symbolic surrogates for the father. We feel helpless and abandon without the father connection. Freud writes:

> *"The terrifying impression of helplessness in childhood aroused the need for protection, for protection through love,*

> *which was provided by the father, and the recognition that*
> *this helplessness lasts throughout life and made it necessary*
> *to cling to the existence of a father."*

Since Friedrich Nietzsche's *"God is dead,"* and George Orwell's *"Big Brother,"* the surrogate father appears, and reappears from false prophets to gurus, while helplessness continues unabated.

Freud has a special take on helplessness that could easily be misunderstood. He claims helplessness is the most important thing about us because it means we never feel complete and will strive without illusion. On the other hand, if we cannot bear helplessness we cannot bear real satisfaction. Helplessness, understood in this way, is far removed from codependency individually and counter dependency collectively.

"Learned helplessness" is the illusion that plagues the codependent and the counter dependent because the individuals or workers of this mindset are looking for someone else to carry their burden and thus escape inevitable incompleteness that is life itself.

Psychologist Mihaly Csikszentmihalyi chooses to look at this matter from a different perspective. He has made his reputation advocating, "going with the flow" *("Flow: The Psychology of Optimal Experience,"* 1990). The idea here is that flow is why a painter gets so absorbed in his canvas that he loses track of time; the musician disappears into the piece she's playing, the athlete plays with a broken bone unaware of the pain; while the chess player feels alone with his board when millions are watching his every move on television. They are all in an apparent state of ecstasy where everything comes together. They are "in the zone" with good neurotransmitters flooding their synapses.

Notice these people are emotionally committed "to doing something" to attain the illusion of "completeness," but still aware that even disciplined control has its normal disruptions and limitations. The Major League baseball pitcher, after a "perfect game," knows he is helpless to repeat it as much as he desires to. People "in the flow" enjoy Freud's satisfaction in the moment, but helpless to repeat it without a measure of failure along the way. Not to worry because they don't.

How did they get that way? Chances are it was not from reading a book. Chances are better that they followed their bliss triggered by seeing a painting, hearing a musician play a piece, watching a sports figure they admire perform, or following the exploits of a chess master, and saying, "I can do that!"

Then they embraced the steep learning curve of commitment ineluctably penciled with many failures and setbacks, but pressed on. That was the roadmap for Israeli-American violinist Itzhak Perlman. At the age of three, he heard a violin concerto on the radio and was hooked for life. He claims that his skill is a matter of three words, "practice, practice, and practice."

The satisfaction comes not from perfection but from acceptance of imperfection, that is, incompleteness, helplessly losing the self in the quest for completeness, knowing that he will die, like we all do, half finished, incomplete. Perlman, that three-year-old-violinist-to-be faced that first sense of helplessness, and decided to be undeterred. Freud writes:

> *"The original helplessness is the primal source of all moral motives."*

It is when our predisposition to contribute and to "do good" first manifests itself. Too often we see only the finished product, not the person who has had the courage to push the envelope of his inherent talent to the limits. Excellence takes hard work. Is that why so many avoid it? Only you can answer that question for yourself. Too often the inclination is to look for short-cuts to the good life to avoid sacrifice, pain, failure, or inconvenience, to deny our nascent helplessness, and therefore never to experience real satisfaction but only its synthetic forms.

Unfortunately, when you are at wits end and trying to grab something, anything, to make sense of a problematical situation, there is always another book to read or lecture to attend to ease the mind if not resolve the issue, or to take you off the hook.

Judith Rich Harris wrote a controversial book that gained wide attention, *"The Nurture Assumption: Why Children Turn Out The Way They Do"* (1998) with the subtitle, *"Parents Matter Less Than You Think and Peers Matter More."* Dr. Harris was taking on the debate between nature and nurture, and siding with the latter. As with the "Time" article weighing in on the influence of siblings, "the nurture assumption," again, is something of an apologist for parental abandonment. Harris writes:

> *"Now we live in complex times and two age groups are no longer enough; a person can be as big as an adult but not an adult. We've had to create new social categories to contain such people who were older than teenagers but who refused to identify themselves as adults ... they had their own category, though no ceremonies to mark the transitions. You entered it by leaving home to go to college or to join a roaming band; you left it upon reaching the upper boundary set by the members themselves. Never trust anyone over thirty, they said. They meant, anyone older is them."*

The draft board and the Vietnam War gave cause to form a loose nit group. There was no draft board for them to dodge for the Iraq War and the Afghanistan War and so they could ignore with impunity. But, alas, there was and still is their parents to blame for their contentiousness.

"The new science of siblings" and "the nurture assumption" is admittedly eye-catching declarations, but do they provide greater insight into the nature of self? My sense is that the "nurturing generation" is still locked into *passive receptivity*. Instead of looking for "door openers," it would seem the *"Occupy Wall Street"* crowd and the "Tea Party" movement profile angst at opposite ends of the same stratum as if suspended in terminal adolescence, as all we know about these two groups is what they are against.

GETTING BEYOND THE BLITZKRIEG SCHOOL

What makes problem solving so critical to Confident Thinking is that the person must first be aware that he has been programmed to think, believe, value and behave as he does. That programming was reasonably effective up to and through World War **II,** or during the first half of the twentieth century Change was at a tortoise pace, compared to the last several decades. Now change is off the charts. Nobody is in charge, which means we have to be our own change agents in the problem solving.

The newest generation, readers nine months and twenty-one-years-of-age, perhaps cannot imagine when African Americans were called Negroes and confined to isolated ghetto like neighborhoods in the North as well as the South. Women didn't smoke on the street. The stigma of shame was on any woman who had an abortion, which was illegal. Husbands could beat their wives, and often did, and nothing was made much about it. Few went to college and even fewer left their hometown to seek employment elsewhere. Executive pay was modest. If you wanted to have clout, you became an MD. There were millionaires but no billionaires. There was no television only radio, newspapers and magazines. Professional football was a minor sport compared to baseball. Jackie Robinson had just broken the color barrier in baseball. Divorce was frowned upon. There was no Little League or parent organized sports for kids. Youngsters made up their own play. Little kids looked up to older kids with respect. Students didn't talk back to teachers or step out of line. If they did, chances are they would be expelled, permanently. As a kid if you got into trouble with the law, you went to Reform School, no questions asked. During summer vacations, kids worked on the farm, did chores around the house, went to movies, the swimming pool, or hung out at the soda fountain. Movies were black and white. People dressed and spoke differently from one community to another, even in the same state, and quite differently in various regions across the country. People who sported tattoos were stereotyped as ex-cons, bikers, or ex-military. Most families, Negroes included, were two parent families. No one was self-conscious about being Christian or celebrating Christian Holy Days and Holy Seasons. Nor was anything made about calling pretty women "girls" or handsome men "boys." The best jobs for the working middle class were in manufacturing, especially in the automotive industry. Everybody had a job who wanted a job. There was no Women's Lib, no Civil Rights Movement, no boycotts of stores, or national protest movements. The A&P Supermarket and the National Tea were the food shopping stores of choice. Girls took most academic honors in high school and boys most academic honors in college. Being gay had nothing to do with sexual orientation. It was less than likely anyone in your family had ever flown in an airplane. Many Catholic boys became priests and many Catholic girls became nuns. Authors became instant celebrities such as Ernest Hemingway and William Faulkner as ordinary people read books and looked up to their creators. Nearly everyone tried smoking by the age of sixteen. Professors and students smoked in college classes, workers smoked on the job and in their offices, people smoked in movie theatres, in supermarkets, department stores, soda fountains, ballparks, nearly everywhere but church. There were no malls, but when they were built people smoked in them, as well. High school graduates were likely to marry and be parents by the time they were twenty with the mother at home and the father working outside the home. This is just a sample of how it was up to and immediately after WWII.

The programming since that war to the present has created a passive society with a reactive disposition. Three generations or nearly seventy years later, with wars in Iraq and Afghanistan few have been asked to participate and even fewer to make any sacrifice. Enter *"Blitzkrieg School of Problem Solving."* It solves problems with a vengeance. Unfortunately, they are problems only peripheral to the problems we face.

This school believes throwing money at education will solve illiteracy; finding a cure for AIDS will stem the epidemic; conducting massive layoffs and redundancy exercises will bring back corporate health; searching for miraculous cures for obesity, diabetes, and other lifestyle diseases will climax self-indulgence.

Cause and effect have become interchangeable synonyms. AIDS is an effect caused by ignorance, poverty, and lifestyle misfortunes, but promiscuity is targeted, which is like trying to capture the wind in our hands. Meanwhile, a search for the definitive AIDS virus antidote continues as the epidemic spreads.

When causes are addressed, results are dramatic. While modern medicine receives the accolades for improved mortality rates, lower birth defects, longevity and societal health, the credit more deservedly should go to public health. It all started with Edwin Chadwick (1801-1890), a statistically inclined British public servant, who launched an investigation in 1838 into the possible relationship between sanitary conditions and disease in five under privileged areas of London. For this pioneering work, public health education and public sanitation, safe drinking water, efficient control of waste removal, studies of soil and well contamination have virtually eliminated such dreaded diseases as cholera and other epidemics from modern cities.

Still, we remain in awe of medical science with its "CAT" scanners, x-ray, renal dialysis machines, cardiac pacemakers, and magnetic resonance imaging (MRI) machines that can identify nearly every bodily function.

It is clear "Nuclear Man" has gambled almost everything on a mechanistic quantitative approach to his physical and psychological well-being. The "heart of God" now resides in science. Translated: man can ravage his mind and body, and by extension his environment to wanton glee, and science will come to the rescue ultimately as superman. Stem cell research and cloning have captured the imagination, while medical science merrily makes organ transplants, as well as creating synthetic organs altogether. The benefits of this remarkable work are diminished when they represent forgiveness for an undisciplined existence.

What is paradoxical about science is that the cleaner the technology the more perplexing the ramifications. Take nuclear power. Nuclear energy has become the consensus source of cheap and clean fuel to rescue the planet from global pollution. Yet, nuclear waste cannot be destroyed. Meanwhile, barges roam the seas and byways of the world in the dead of night like vessels without a country looking for a safe haven to dump their dubious waste unbeknown to the living nearby. It happened on the Ivory Coast of Africa, as it always does, where the average citizen has the least awareness or clout and lives in suffocating poverty.

What are we to make of the *Chernobyl Nuclear Power Plant* meltdown in the Ukraine in 1986 or the earthquake and tsunami at the *Fukushima Nuclear Power Plant* in Japan in 2011? Both sites are now essentially ghost towns and will be so for many years to come. Where will the next nuclear shoe fall on the grid?

We like to think "big," but are crippled by thinking "poorly" small. Little things are killing the planet and us with them. Lifestyle excesses start with feeding sugar to babies giving them what they want rather than need, which continues through adulthood. What is a cigarette but a pacifier and candy substitute? This has become metaphor to our times, codependency from cradle to grave.

PROBLEM SOLVING WITHOUT CREATIVE THINKING

Creativity is apparently on holiday. Education focuses on grades rather than creative thinking. Creative thinking encourages students to embrace the unknown. Critical thinking reifies what is already known. The word "education" means to "to lead forth." Simply regurgitating information is not education.

What exactly are of SAT, ACT and GRE cram review courses for? If they are necessary for students wanting to qualify for the best colleges or graduate schools, what was the purpose of four years of high school? What are these examinations measuring? Certainly they are not measuring conceptual skills. Better yet, what did these test takers learn in school in their degree programs in preparation for these tests? Are schools that poor that the student has to have a cheat sheet to pass muster?

Since course work is largely regurgitation, I suspect once it is completed it is soon forgotten. This backdoor cram-exam preparation for qualification personifies a reactive society that never gets on top of its problems because its focus is always on effects.

In my day, students bragged about never taking a book home in all of high school. Today nearly every child has a backpack loaded with homework from preschool on. My wonder is it simply ritualistic practice with little to do with conceptual learning. If it is, it is doomed to spill over into adult life.

LEARNED HELPLESSNESS AND ITS CONSEQUENCES

Learned helplessness is educated into our society. It cripples the student when study demands initiative and passion. It cripples the worker when timely decisions are required at the level of consequences and he blames others for not allowing him to make them. This gives students and workers justification for practicing "learned helplessness" which is blame's sacred sanctuary.

The rhetoric may be "take the initiative" but the unwritten rule is draconian "compliance" to policies and procedures which have become the polar coordinates of codependency.

Learned helplessness finds children blaming parents, parents blaming children, teachers blaming both with everyone attempting to dump the problem on to someone else. It is the same blame game at work. In this landscape, solutions have many critics with few authors with everyone blind to the obvious problem. This might explain why so many books are written on the subject of society's ills without a consensus definition of the problem situation.

We are crippled with our dependence on analysis when we need to design our way forward out of this mess. Designing suggests action, not reaction to calamity. The pejorative cliché "if it isn't broke don't fix it" has given birth to the United States of Anxiety.

There isn't an author who pens a book, who is not guilty of many of the behaviors selectively mentioned. That should give the reader little comfort, as the book is not about the author. It is for the reader and only for the reader. The reader brings his own mindset and experience to the subjects discussed, and hopefully this leads to a deeper appreciation of things as they are. Only the reader can define his problem situation clearly because he has the data. Carefully defined, the problem solution is within his grasp. It will not be found in generalized descriptions, or in watered down logic. The reader must come out of his cups and rally himself into action. This is not easy.

When suspended in learned helplessness, we are parent-dependent, teacher-centered, and later management dependent and counter dependent on the workplace for solutions to our difficulties, looking for answers from second hand sources outside our experience. There are supportive and abusive parents, supportive and abusive peers, supportive and abusive teachers, and supportive and abusive bosses. I say, "So what?" Forget about the blame game! It will only dissipate your energy.

Somehow in this brief experience called "a life," we must get past impediments constructed along the way, and find our way to self-dependence. This includes enduring pressures from family and friends, teachers and bosses, who are certain they know what is best for us. They may use guilt or intimidation, or hit us with, "how could you think of doing that when all we (I) have done so much for you?" Such an accusation is actually a compliment as it indicates you are on your way to being your own person.

THE KAFKA LAMENT

The first sentence in Franz Kafka's novel "The Trial" (1937) has reverberated with societal implications ever since:

"Someone must have been telling lies about Joseph K., for without having done anything wrong he was arrested one fine morning."

"The Trial" is a symbolic psychological study of a system of judicious righteousness against the "learned helplessness" of Joseph K who finds himself complicit in its design. The book's message is that the plight of a man, any man, has "the system" to blame for his homelessness, his loss of direction, or a reversal of his circumstances. Kafka's "Joseph K" is always denied his rights without ever realizing "he is the system," and if the system is wrong than his wrong headedness must be factored into its construction. It is well to keep this in mind:

When other people make us feel miserable about ourselves, no matter who they are, they do not have our best interest at heart. Nor can we pine our lives away about what our parents did or didn't do for us, using this as justification for our miserable lot in life. Grow up!

Accept the fact that once we are on our own, we are alone, and being "al-one" is the beauty of being al-together, whole, and ready to face the world and contribute to it.

Likewise, I have heard so many people tell me they never had good teachers. This is horse hockey! It is meant to convince ourselves that it is someone else's fault that we have failed to be educated, that we never developed a passion for learning. Grow up!

There is also no point in blaming the Church, the State, the rich and powerful, the well connected, the depraved and indifferent, the moral degenerate, nor those more fortunate and successful than we are. Grow up!

Life doesn't work that way. There is a saying the teacher will arrive when the student is ready. This places the burden on the student. There is not a more important, or more difficult or more thankless job than that of a teacher.

Teaching is very hard work. It requires a lot of time and attention that must be committed outside the classroom. Because it is the most important profession in all of society it should be the best appreciated and compensated profession, when, in fact, teachers enjoy little appreciation or remuneration consistent with their vocation. Why is it that education is made so important in lip service but teachers are not esteemed equal to other professions?

The answer is obvious. Society places a higher premium on material wealth than intellectual acumen, on the product (wealth) rather than the process (learning). It is that simple. Alex Rodriguez of the New York Yankees baseball team makes more in one year than 400 teachers at $50,000 per annum make teaching school with master's or doctorate degrees in the Florida's public school and university system. Something is wrong with this picture.

When manufacturing went elsewhere in the world to produce hard goods, worker dependency in all its sorrow was revealed. Millions on the assembly line and in well-paying manufacturing jobs found these jobs gone forever. Was this cruel and inhuman treatment? No, this was reality in a global economy. It was a process that has been underway for the past sixty years. It did not just happen. Any worker that did not see it coming has been asleep at the wheel. Grow up!

I saw it first hand in Detroit, Michigan when I was a youth during my summer vacations there. Factory workers were economically competitive with professional men and women with college degrees and graduate educations. Indeed, these factory workers had better incomes and better homes than my uncle, a man with two Ph.D.'s and the chairman of his department at the University of Detroit. I saw the sons and daughters of assembly line workers going into the factories right out of high school without a thought to improving their intellectual skills or preparing for the future. *"Paradise Lost"* would not be a Milton poem, for they could not imagine anything untoward happening to them in their American industrial lives.

No one wanted to talk about it. Everyone believed, "as Detroit goes so goes America!"

So, Detroit continued to make automobiles that were designed primarily for American roads feeding the American love fest for big gas guzzling machines on what was then cheap gasoline. Detroit believed, as did Americans, "if it ain't broke, don't fix it!" Detroit, the hub of American manufacturing, wore blinders as if part of its anatomy.

No attempt was made to educate the buying public to think differently. It was the codependent parent giving the American baby what it wanted. So Detroit, the car, the industry, the assembly worker, and the car buyer have all been complicit in the downturn.

While learned helplessness plagued Detroit, other American industries dominant in the aftermath of World War II were feeling the pinch. Steel mills, shoe factories, linen producers, appliance makers, and airlines have been forced into bankruptcy proceedings or out of business. Industrial workers once received generous employee benefits that were not a function of productivity but guarantees for surrendering control of work.

In the 1960s, the steel industry, for example, had a policy of giving its veteran industrial workers 13-week furloughs with pay every five years. Mind you this furlough was in addition to their regular accrued vacation.

What do you think the majority of these workers did with the extra time? Go back to school? Take a sightseeing vacation? Catch up on a hobby? The majority got second jobs, adjusting their lifestyles to the added income. When it was time to return to work, many attempted to balance the regular and furlough job, and became angry when the company insisted they give up the second job. Grow up!

This is academic now that most of these jobs are gone and the furlough program long ago scuttled. John Strohmeyer writes in *"Crisis in Bethlehem"* (1986):

> *"The furlough experiment at Bethlehem Steel and Aluminum Company of America explains how such steel industry excesses actually crippled the goose that laid the golden egg."*

Such policies were created during the 1960's euphoric era of plenty. That was before anyone noticed the economic invasion of Japan. Twenty-eight years later, an editorial

cartoon captured the significance of this with the lead story
of two newspapers in bold headlines:

JAPAN BOMBS PEARL HARBOR (December 7, 1941)

JAPAN BUYS PEARL HARBOR (December 7, 1989)

By the time this economic and industrial reality hit the American conscience, workers were already conditioned to counter dependence on the company for their total security and well-being. The more workers made the more they spent, keeping the economy healthy, but not saving for a rainy day. In fact, personal saving for most Americans became a negative proposition.

Meanwhile, companies increasingly operated on the margin even borrowing from pension funds to finance optimistic expansion, as if the dog days of summer would never end. Now we see the fall out of this excess in bankruptcies and empty pension fund coffers with workers left high and dry. Whose fault was this?

It is easy to blame the companies who couldn't say "no" to workers or stockholders. They tried to have it both ways and ended up having it no way. Many played quick and dirty with pension funds making them complicit in these developments. Others cooked the books. Still others became involved in creative financing believing they could never be caught. And, sad to say, not all of them ever were.

Corporate guru Peter Drucker once said that management demonstrated exemplary restrain through World War II, and into the 1960s and then went haywire. It is hard to imagine now, but CEOs once made only ten to twenty times what the average worker earned, now executive compensation, by comparison, has gone into the stratosphere.

More basic to this extravagance is that management and unions were in collusion. They allowed wage and benefit demands to spiral out of control to the point that many companies are no longer competitive if in business at all. The fault line can be found in entitlement programs.

Once benefit programs became "rights" rather than privileges; once a quarter or more of what a worker earned had next to nothing to do with productivity, the spinning top left the deck.

I can recall practically a rebellion when Honeywell went from paying 90 percent of all hospital costs without co-pay, and transitioned to modest co-pay, while still paying 80 percent of such medical expenses. Workers did not see this as income, but only "rights" upon which they were not willing to compromise.

Many factors contributed to the demise of the American automotive industry but none more directly than the entitlement programs. Every General Motors vehicle off the assembly line has $1,500 price tag added to pay for entitlement programs for current and retired workers. It would seem as if no one expected the rest of the world to catch up. This has proven worse than naive; it has proven nearly the death knell to an industry.

In that sense, it points to a fatal flaw in the American character when it comes to problem solving. American workers treated management as surrogate parents, suspending themselves in permanent adolescence in learned helplessness, totally reactive to demands, being good hires, staying out of trouble by being polite, obedient, submissive, and conforming.

Management not only encouraged this behavior, but also systematically programmed it into workers. A powerful assist came from primary and secondary education, as Alvin Toffler points out in *"Future Shock"* (1970). As the United States revved up to be the dominant industrial power of the world in the early twentieth century, compulsory education was essential for students as workers entering the workforce. The academic curriculum included reading, writing and arithmetic, but also the social curriculum of being polite, punctual, obedient, submissive, conforming and obliging to authority Now, one hundred years later, when workers need to take the initiative, demonstrate creative verve, be confrontational, manage conflict, and be self-motivated problem solvers, these distinctive characteristics have been weaned out of their sociobiology gene pool.

Instead, what we see are American workers moaning the "Kafka

Lament" of having done nothing wrong. You hear them on television moaning about their plight with no sense of being complicit in the affair. Management, they claim, made promises, promises they didn't keep. Workers never developed the caution, "If it sounds too good to be true, it probably is." This differs little with parents who pay the car insurance and half the rent for their grown up children.

If you don't have to grow up, you won't, and American workers have never been asked to grow up in my lifetime. Now, they have no choice, but to grow up and it won't be easy. They have what it takes. Now, they have to discover it.

Journalist Thomas L. Friedman is certainly a creative thinker as well as an apologist for the global economic transformation. I have heard from out-of-work workers who have read *"The World Is Flat"* (2005) as if it were the Bible. The world, however, is far from flat, and as enamored of technology as Friedman is, much of the world lives beyond and below the electronic boom. My greatest problem with the book is not its premise, which I flatly reject, pun intended, but the passion with which those so disadvantaged with the swift currents of change use it as an apology for their plight. This disruption will be assimilated into our social, political and religious, and militarily fabric as was Gutenberg's movable type half a millennium ago. Then, more than 90 percent of Europeans were illiterate and had little choice but to "go with the flow." That is not the case today. We can embrace the currents of change and soar above the chaos they create if we have but the will.

It is easier for workers and managers to find fault with the global economy then to find any fault within themselves. Technology throughout history has eventually covered the four quadrants of the globe. It is just doing it a little faster now. The Kafka Lament won't fly.

FALLACY OF THE COMPANY "AS A FAMILY"

Companies encouraged the prevailing attitude of dependency by creating the impression that the company "is a family." No company or workplace "is a family." No organization in any type of enterprise "is a family." The idea that an outside authority is family to the man is an illusion. The symbolism of "family" is powerful. It was formed in childhood and has been altered little to become something of a truism. Unfortunately, the truism has no legs.

You don't throw the family out on the street, don't make family members redundant, don't move everything to another state or country, and claim you had no choice. With family, there is no such thing as "outside authority." Family is blood and destiny with no special lifeboats for select members when the ship is going down. Family controls its destiny if it has the courage to do so. Companies often lack such gumption.

We are born alone, we live largely alone, and we die alone. We all have peers, but the child is parent to the man. Each man is sovereign in his own way and life and right. The illusion of "family" or outside authority that wraps its magnanimous arms around us and looks after us is the romanticism of the utopian dream. It is the safety net that we crave seeded with the hope of escaping personal responsibility and saved from ourselves. English poet John Doone (1571 - 1631) *"Triple Fool"* touches this woe:

> *"I am two fools, I know for loving, and for saying so in whining poetry:*
> *But where's that Wiseman, that would not be I, if she would not deny!*
> *Then as the earth's inward narrow crooked lanes do purge sea water's fretful salt*
> *   away, I thought, if I could draw my pains through rhyme's vexation, I should*
> *   them allay,*
> *Grief brought to numbers cannot be so fierce.*
> *But when I have done so, some man, his art and voice to show,*
> *Doth set and sing my pain, and, by delighting many, frees again, grief,*
> *   which verse did restrain.*
> *To love and grief tribute of verse belongs, but not of such as pleases when*
> *   `tis read,*
> *Both are increased by such songs: for both their triumphs so are*
> *   published,*

And I, which was two fools, do so grow three; who are a little wise, the best fools be."

I've often read this when I've become down on myself. People that utter this "family" sentiment are apt to believe it because they see themselves as rescuers or strong parents. They consider their lot to protect their weak and vulnerable children. As employers, they attempt to free employees from the ravages of life, ravages that made them strong and straight and wise and courageous. They were made that way because they were allowed to fail to fall and to pick themselves up again and again. Why deny that of one's children, of one's employees? It is the "god complex" in the CEO as parent.

It is why parents still control their fifty-year-old children, and why CEOs make 500 to 1,000 times as much as the average worker. We are willing to pay that heavy price to an "outside authority" to maintain the approval of a parent or stay in the good graces of the boss. When we do, we abdicate our "inner authority" with consequences.

We hear and believe the CEO when he says, "It is only a rumor that there will be massive layoffs. We are optimistic about our future." Countless examples of these dissembling lines surfaced in the 2007-2008 global economy meltdown. A generation ago, Enron's founder and CEO said those precise words repeatedly before he and the Enron CEO team vanished into scandalous infamy in 2001. In fact, President Barak Obama lied dozens of times from 2008 through 2013, when Obamacare was being implemented stating, *"With Obamacare, you can keep your health care plan if you want, period!"* Dissembling has become second nature to those in leadership positions, while paradoxically advocating transparency.

Notice the pageantry, the pomp and circumstance when the CEO of a company visits one of his far-flung satellite operations. You can see the trusting eyes of the workers as the CEO utters his reassurances. He is their father figure, affable, approachable, but always godly. Workers place him on a pedestal so his head is always higher than theirs; his reach always farther, his horizons always wider, and his words balm for their worried souls. They believe because they want to believe, like children.

The CEO entertains select questions collected beforehand. The questions have the implicit character of infantile demands: "Is this plant going to stay open?" "Will we have the option to continue working if we don't want the buyout?"

Workers want the reassurance once provided by their parents. The CEO, coached by his public relations people, answers as if a politician on the stump:

> *"I looked in our three acre parking lot this morning and I saw it full of vehicles, not an empty space. Does that answer your question?"*

Of course it didn't, but only laugher, clapping, and even a few hoorahs follow this non-answer.

The child-in-the-worker says, *"He means we're in business for the long haul."* Wishful thinking, fueled by the CEO's comment, can become a deadly disease. Then, to the second question about a "buyout," the CEO grows merry; his countenance takes on the demeanor of a cherubic archangel. *"I've been looking at those buyout packages, and think I'd be tempted to take one and go fishing myself."*

Laughter again rises from the floor to another non-answer to the question. It lifts the CEO off his throne and carries him through a sea of complacent idolaters. No one dare break the spell.

Companies have paid dearly for this, as we now know. The only guarantee a worker should truly expect is a full day's pay for a full day's work. There are no guarantees in life, and why should work be any different? It puts the worker on his mettle when he knows he always has to perform. When I was a college student, and something of a grind, I was often asked, "Why do you study so hard? You've already clinched an 'N. You could flunk the final and still ace the course."

First of all, it was my nickel that put me in school, all my own nickels. Secondly, I was determined to learn as much as I possibly could. And thirdly, and this was important, I believed in my own heart that I could flunk out at any time. Nothing was ever taken for granted because I knew I could never charm a professor to get a good grade. I was stuck with me, and that me was not always too easy to take.

It will take some time, and I'm sure, reprogramming, if workers are to assume responsibility for their own security and future. It is clear they must find a way to add value status to their job. This will promote individual security, and by extension, company stability. Somehow this got lost in post-World War II euphoria, and now everyone is suffering for this failing.

It has been my observation that for every hard working person, there are four that are dogging it.

What is sad about this is that everyone knows who these people are, but no one does anything about it. Mired in learned helplessness, hard workers don't want to be labeled snitches, while loafers know how to play the system to their advantage. Since loafers are paid the same, they busy themselves looking for ways to redirect attention by constant complaining or flattering their bosses. Like the disruptive child that used tears to get its way, these workers know the squeaky wheel gets oiled. So, while hard workers are focusing on work they are nitpicking or focusing on making an impression. Loafers have killed the golden goose, and now, with matters as they are, with a global economy in full swing, the blame game has no fire or audience.

WILLIAM GEORGE MOSLEY'S INCREDIBLE PASSION FOR THE POSSIBLE

Michelle Bearden, a journalist with "The Tampa Tribune," wrote a remarkable article (July 9, 2006) on an African American man that, while inspiring, is indicative of the resilience of the human spirit under the most trying of circumstances.

Mr. Mosley's journey epitomizes the beauty and breadth of Confident Thinking problem solving, and for that reason, it is included here.

Mr. William George Mosley is 87. When he stubbed his toe and infection set in two years ago, doctors had to remove his left leg. For a time he got down and let his health go, but now he works out religiously at the Interbay-Glover YMCA in Tampa, and attends church in his best dress clothes every Sunday.

The simple rules provided by his grandmother have guided this man throughout his life. She told him to keep his head up and face his problems. "I just may be the luckiest man around," he declares. "And I ain't got but one leg, no teeth, and no money, but I know God is blessin' me, as sure as I know anything."

He believes to understand where a man is; you have to understand where he came from. Mr. Mosley came from Macon, Georgia, where he was born September 21, 1918. His daddy, a Pullman porter, died of a heart attack that very day. Three months later, his mama passed away. His maternal grandmother in Tampa took him in and poured on the love.

She taught him pretty much all he would ever really need to know: "don't smoke cigarettes, don't cheat, don't steal, don't lie, don't drink no liquor, and don't do no drugs, don't hang out with no crowd, don't do nothin that will land you in jail, and surely don't do nothin' that will land you in an early grave."

When he was four going on five, his grandma passed away. An aunt took him in, but he doesn't remember much love in that house. "She beat on me bad, like a dog," he says. "So, I grabbed me a knapsack, and I ran away." He was five going on six.

He spent days foraging for food in Ybor City (Cuban suburb of Tampa), and running errands for Cuban shopkeepers to earn a few coins, always mindful of his grandmother's rules. When darkness came, he bundled up in a potato sack and slept under front porches and produce trucks and in outhouses. When the stink got to be too much, he'd open the door a crack and stick his nose out to breathe in the fresh air.

He tried once to go to school. He got in line with the other children in the schoolyard, but a teacher noticed how filthy he was and delivered him to the principal's office. "They told me to go home to my mother and father and take a bath," he says. "I walked right out of there and never looked back."

Instead, he taught himself to read and write. He would study a word in a newspaper or comic book, and when he saw a friendly face, he'd ask what it meant. His Cuban friends taught him Spanish, too. He learned to count money and take care of his own finances. Never bothered with a bank account; a money belt did just fine.

Grandmother had always told him to watch his back; don't rely on no one but your own good sense. "Nothin' more than put-tin' your mind to it," he says.

From time to time, a kind family took him in and treated him like one of their own. "There's good folks out there, wherever you go," he says.

As a young man, he ventured down to Opa-locka (Florida) where he worked for $15 a week for Mr. Cook, a white man from Tennessee who owned a car lot. He washed cars for a while, before admitting to his boss he would rather be selling them.

One day, he got that chance. "A black man was in the lot from 9 in the morning `til quarter to 2," he recalls. "And Mr. Cook, he told me to see what was up. The man bought two Coup de Villes, one for himself, and one for his wife. Then he told me he'd pay me $150 to drive one of the cars to Fort Lauderdale (Florida)."

When Mr. Mosley returned, his employer gave him $400 cash commission for each car. He had never seen so much money in his life. "Bill, you got yourself a job selling cars. And I'm making you my assistant manager," Mr. Cook proclaimed. Two of the other three salesmen promptly quit. They would have no part of working for a black man. The next day, the remaining salesman fetched Mr. Mosley a cup of coffee.

Serendipity continued to follow him. One time he was on his way to Tuskegee, Alabama to pick up some cars, when he got caught up in Martin Luther King's Selma-to-Montgomery march for civil rights. He remembers it as a beautiful thing with hundreds of people, black folks and white, marching side by side. He also remembers the police using fire hoses and fierce dogs against the marchers. He could hear his grandmother's warning about staying out of crowds and away from trouble. Still, he felt it was important to be there, make his stand for equality. "But it was real scary," he says.

He didn't want trouble on his travels, so he took to dressing like a chauffeur, "white shirt, black pants, black cap," when he drove one of his beloved Cadillacs. He didn't want anyone thinking he was uppity. When he gassed up, he would always tell the gas station attendant that he was driving for Dr. Mosley. Only when self-service stations opened along the interstate did he let his guard down. "Best thing that happened for us," he says, "didn't have to rely on the eyes in the back of our heads."

Eventually, with the entrepreneur spirit, he had a fleet of limousines, driving for such celebrities as crooner Nat King Cole and Muhammad Ali. "You call him Cassius Clay and he'd knock you out," he says.

And so now, Mr. Mosley in his eighty-eighth year is still smiling, still living by the code of his grandmother, and still always finding something happening to brighten his day.

Is Mr. William George Mosley unique? I don't think so. He was blessed very early in his life with programming from his beloved grandmother. It sustained his spirit under the most trying circumstances. He has been a confident thinking problem solver engaged in a passion for the possible. Resilience has blessed his life, and all those he has touched. His moral compass was set firmly in place in his heart by a grandmother he lived with for only three years. Imagine that! What lessons his life teaches us. Michele Bearden has written a moving story.

James R. Fisher, Jr., PhD.

CONFIDENT THINKING
CREATIVE STAGE NINE

PLAN YOUR WORK, WORK YOUR PLAN!
WHERE DO YOU WANT TO GO IN LIFE?
THE PURPOSE OF YOUR LIFE IS
WHAT YOU DO!
LIVE YOUR OWN AGENDA!

"Thoughts lead on to purposes; purposes go forth in action; actions form habits; habits decide character; and character fixes our destiny."
—**Tryon Edwards** (1809-1884), American Theologian

YOUR LIFE AS A NOVEL

I F YOU ARE not organized, you are going to get somewhere but not necessarily where you expect to go. Ask yourself, "Am I in the driver's or passenger's seat?" You don't have to be a captain of industry, only the captain of your own boat to get to where you want to go.

Be patient! Your patience will be returned tenfold. Don't be taken in by the tough exteriors of others. We all walk this earth with great vulnerability It is therefore an asset to be acquainted with your own vulnerability, not to be embarrassed by it, or apologetic for it, but only to understand and be able to use it as unique to you and your character. To be vulnerable is to be alive and receptive to the possibilities of experience.

When we think of planning a life, and working a plan, we often think of something grand or written in concrete—I'm going to get an education, have this kind of career, retire with this type of portfolio, and live out my dream. Surely, this is a plan, and a well-defined one, but it leaves out the wonders of chance. Notice the plan here is always focused on the future, not what you are doing and plan on doing, right now!

The future can only exist in the mind. Moreover, it is likely to be a chronological plan rather than psychological plan. A plan that works is open ended. With a plan as with life, we must first crawl then walk then run and then climb. During it all, we must also stop, rest, reassess and start again, and always, fall and rise, again and again. We are likely to be too busy to notice much less smell the roses along the way until often it is too late. In such a case, we are slave to the plan and the plan owns us instead of our owning the plan. The way to avoid this is to seize the day—everyday—

like George Mosley.

Worry less about progress and more about *carpe diem*, i.e., making the most of every day, enjoying the present, trusting as little as possible to what the morrow may bring. Implicit in this is love: love of self, life, family, friends, country, school, church and community. Love also of sport, hobby, and work, of everything you are doing right now. Love is the calculus to what you are and can be.

One of the wonders of life is that which gives us order and balance also gives us pleasure and satisfaction, and it is usually what we are doing, or we would be doing something else.

This open ended plan can be derailed when someone decides to structure a foolproof plan. If you read biographies of "great men," you will see that they march to their own drummer with the plan as much unconscious as conscious, more psychological than chronological.

Poet Walt Whitman (1819-1891) took the risk of self-publishing his famous poem *"Leaves of Grass"*(1993) in 1855. It didn't sell well. It did succeed in getting him fired from his job with the Department of Interior for its offensive content.

Whitman kept adding poems and republishing throughout his life, the editions growing from an initial twelve poems and 95 pages to a hefty tome of 400 poems and nearly 500 pages shortly before he died.

"Leaves of Grass" is important for establishing an American prosody style departing from the symbolism, allegory, meditation and religious spiritualism of European poetry.

Benjamin Franklin, one of America's first notable autodidacts, managed to define the American character while departing from its standards. His formal schooling ended when he was ten, yet he became a leading author and printer, satirist, political theorist, politician, scientist, inventor, civic activist, statesman, soldier and diplomat.

As a scientist, he was a major figure in the history of physics for his discoveries and theories regarding electricity. He invented the lightning rod, bifocals, and the Franklin furnace. He formed the first public lending library in America, the first fire department in Pennsylvania. As a political writer and activist, he supported the idea of an American nation. As a diplomat during the *American Revolution*, he secured the support of France in that war to make independence of the United States possible.

Impressive as these achievements, more impressive is the way he built his life, knowing intuitively when to cut and run, change courses, and go forward. As a ten-year-old, he worked for a time with his father a candle maker, quit that job at the age of 12 and became a printer apprentice to his brother. When he was fifteen, he and his brother started a newspaper, The New-England Courant, the first independent newspaper of the colonies. When his brother refused to let him write a letter to the newspaper for publication, he adopted the pseudonym of "Mrs. Silence Do Good," and wrote letters-to-the-editor, which became conversation pieces in the community. His brother was unhappy when he found this out. So, Franklin left his apprenticeship without permission, and in so doing became a freelancer.

At age 17, Franklin ran away from Boston to Philadelphia to seek a new start, and as the saying goes, the rest is history.

A voracious reader since a little boy, he got ideas from what he read, found he had organizing skills, a marked facility for humor and composition as well as a natural acumen for business. He would set up his own printing shop, publish his own newspaper, organize his own bank, and set up a philosophical society. Then in the same esprit fort of Ray Kroc of McDonald's franchise fame, he established printing shops throughout Pennsylvania creating franchise dealerships. This along with the success of his writing allowed him to become independently wealthy before the age of forty. No longer having to work, he devoted the rest of his long life to public service, science and the arts.

It is easy to forget that Americans such as Andrew Jackson, Abraham Lincoln, Thomas Edison, Henry Ford, and yes, Ray Kroc, et al, displayed similar esprit fort to that of Benjamin Franklin. All these men were autodidacts, self-educated trailblazers, strong-minded persons and freethinkers. They invented their plans in the fluidity of the moment or as opportunity presented itself, and little time before.

Planning is not about the ultimate goal, but rather preparation for and being ready as opportunities unfold along the way.

A well-planned life is first of all an exploration of the many sides of our unique character, disposition and talent. The two defining parts are our essence and *personality,* which have been mentioned before but will be discussed in more detail now. Personality and essence must be in some balance to prosper in life. If one is developed at the expense of or at the exception of the other, then we experience difficulty.

THE ACQUIRED SELF OR YOUR PERSONALITY

Personality is the acquired self. It is the many masks we wear in public given the situation and the circumstances. There is a time when personality displays its assertive side, other times its conciliatory side, and still other times its light-hearted humorous side. It is when one of these sides on display is inappropriate that a person can be perceived as a tic out of sync, or off center to what is expected.

With personality, there are numerous unwritten but well-defined behavioral expectations that make others comfortable or uncomfortable. A person can become so obsessed with rules, wanting so desperately to behave as expected that he is so uptight as to behave the exact opposite.

One time in undergraduate school, the most brilliant member of my class, who had this inordinate need to please and fit in, invited me to have a coffee with him. Once we were seated, he grabbed my shoulders and looked me in the eye, and said, "Teach me how to be sincere!" He thought sincerity was another personality algorithm, when sincerity rises out of one's essence.

THE NATIVE SELF OR YOUR ESSENCE

Essence is that raw indefinable yet not realized sleeping talent in a person crying out to be expressed. Virtually everyone has a deep reservoir of talent. The problem is that the talent a person has is never the talent another person has. It is therefore futile to compare and compete to be "just like somebody else." The results are bound to disappoint. So often the native self lies dormant and untouched because we're trying to be like everyone else.

It takes awareness, judgment, diagnostic skills, and risks as well as self-acceptance to wrest this native talent from its dark chamber and put it to some kind of use. This, of course, always begins with a test. The pleasant thing about talent is that we often discover we have it quite by accident, or in our play. We find out what we do well by exploring life like every other animal.

- We may be doodling the time away, and discover we have the ability to draw.

- We may like organizing the kids in the neighborhood to create pretend dramas, and discover we have the nascent skills of the dramatist.

- We may be humming away something we hear on the radio or television and find we have a voice that can carry a tune.

- We may be tinkering with an old radio or television set on the blink and find we can think in three dimensions with mechanical precision.

- We may read a few lines in a book, or hear a teacher speak and find later we can repeat nearly every word as if we had a recorder in our head.

- We find that people listen to us and always want to be around us as if we know something they don't or they want to go where we are going.

- We may find mathematics not only a stimulating language that speaks to us but that chemistry, physics and biology are a natural application to our wondering.

- We may see a motion picture in our heads that is like our own private screening studio, rolling out stories as if they were already in print.

- We may find ideas, diverse, controversial, absurd or contradictory appealing to us because we feel confident we can weave them into a conceptual narrative that speaks beyond their isolated significance.

Each of these talents mentioned here has been expressed in biographies of individuals who came quite by accident to find that they were special. But the point is that although everyone is special only a few run so far and so hard and so long with their specialness.

LET ME INTRODUCE YOU TO YOURSELF

Then there are others that have absolutely no idea they have a special talent. They need someone else to point that out.

One time I was in Denver giving a seminar for the American Management Association, and my cousin, an electrical engineer attached to the Atomic Energy Commission, invited me to a party of his friends. They were all talking about an individual not there who apparently had incredible skills in applying quantum mechanics to engineering problems.

He did astounding work in the laboratory, yet they thought he undervalued and underutilized his talent.

"There is no question in my mind," said one, "if he focused on this discipline he'd win the Nobel Prize." All heads nodded in agreement.

I had remained silent, so they were surprised when I said, "It will never happen."

They turned and looked at me suspiciously, me the intruder disturbing their consensus, the outsider with no relevance to the discussion. Then I smiled, "That is, until someone introduces him to himself."

They looked to my cousin, as if to say, this guy is certainly not one of us! Undismayed, I continued, "Most of us need someone to point out our essence, otherwise we think we're all the same when it comes to talent. Well, that isn't the case, as you point out in this instance." They seem to take this with some degree of cynicism.

"I wonder," I said finally, "has anyone here ever talked to him the way you are talking about him?" The nods made it apparent no one had. "Well, there's the problem. Insight isn't gained by osmosis."

Years later I asked my cousin if anyone had ever taken up my challenge. "I did," he said, "and he was impressed."

"Did he do anything about it?"

"Well, he didn't win the Nobel Prize, but he became head of our department, and then went into intelligence work for the government."

THE WISDOM OF AN OPEN ENDED PLAN

A few years ago, there was a twenty-two-year-old baseball player by the name of Scott Kazmir. He then played for the Tampa Bay Rays in the American League.

When he was a boy of nine-years-old trying out for the Little League team, the coach was hitting ground balls to each player at shortstop. When the ball was hit to Scott, it went through his legs and rolled all the way to the center field fence. He ran out and picked it up and threw a strike to first base. The throw traveled more than 200 feet away on a straight line.

This was no small achievement for a boy so young. His coach told him that few boys have such a good arm. "I'm going to make you a pitcher," he declared, and he did.

Up to that point, Scott had no idea that his arm was special. In 2006, he was a member of the American League all-star team, having won ten games in the first half of the season. Only ten other pitchers so young in the more than one hundred year history of major league baseball had won so many games in so short a time.

So, this scrawny little kid, Scott Kazmir, whose talent was first noted as a boy, was molded into a pitcher and made a major league baseball player. The second half of the 2006 season did not go so well. Most of his time was spent on the injured reserve list winning only one more game. Surgery on his arm in the offseason makes his baseball future an open book. It has not been an easy ride for this young man. In 2012, he dropped out of Major League Baseball, working on his mechanics playing in the minor leagues and in winter baseball. In 2013, the Cleveland Indians acquired him where he went 10-9. He has a two-year contract with the Oakland Athletics at $22 million for the 2014 and 2015 seasons. Kazmir turned 30 in January 2014, still focused on the possible.

What Scott Kazmir has still remains a rarity. Few aspiring athletes ever make the major leagues at all much less come on hard times and fall out of baseball but fight their way back into the major leagues with a substantial contract.

When I was a boy, I played baseball on the courthouse lawn. This was located between the jail and courthouse, which sheriff Ky Petersen had converted into a playground. There I saw Dick Tharp demonstrate an arm not unlike Scott Kazmir's. Only it was Dick's misfortune that his talent was noted among his peers, alone, as no adults were involved to assess such skill during World War II, when there was no Little League, and no organized sport for boys of ages nine to twelve to profile such talent.

Dick Tharp in fact at age ten had an arm that could throw a baseball 300 feet on a line, which many of us watched repeatedly in awe. One time he even threw the baseball from home plate in Riverview Stadium, when he was eleven, hitting the scoreboard on the fly 390 feet away. But there was no major league scout assessing such talent in Clinton, Iowa, only the Courthouse Tigers, a neighborhood team, playing against other neighborhood teams in the city recreational league.

Dick turned out to be a good pitcher but without guidance, mentoring, or anyone promoting his talent. It was never developed to the point that it could become the basis of a career. Instead, he became a cross-country truck driver, which became his life's work.

A moment of déjà vu was experienced when I was invited to his home outside Orlando (Florida) to celebrate his fiftieth wedding anniversary.

I hadn't seen Dick since we were kids. It was a country home with a large open field behind the house with a pasture for grazing horses. After dinner, I mentioned to his wife, whom I had never met before, what a great arm her husband had as a boy, only to have his thirty-three-year-old son interrupt, "I've got a better arm than dad had, don't I, dad?"

Dick smiled, and said nothing. His son, a devil-may-care kind of guy, a smoker and drinker, who admitted to not liking the idea of being nailed down to anything permanent, looking to be out of shape, prompting me to say. "I don't think so."

"Want me to prove it?" he asked. Dick's son picked up a new baseball with his left hand; Dick having been right handed, took the cigarette out of his mouth, rolled up his left sleeve, and said, "What do you want me to hit?"

The red wooden fence at the edge of the pasture was at least 300 feet away. I said in an incredulous tone, "Hit the fence."

Undaunted, ignoring my sarcasm, he said, "Where do you want me to hit it?"

I couldn't help myself; I roared with laughter, "Where do I want you to hit it? Anywhere, okay?" I thought at that point he was putting me on.

Sensing this, he said, "I'm serious. Where do you want me to hit the fence?"

Well, there was a red post that joined the two sections of the fence together with about a foot in diameter. "Hit that post!" I laughed again. It was obvious that he now felt the challenge.

"Where do you want me to hit it, high, low, or in the center?"

"Come on now, this has been enough fun," I said, "You don't have to hit it at all. I apologize for putting you on like this."

I was ready to go back into the house when he said; "I'm going to hit it about in the middle if that is okay with you." And he did. On the fly. It was simply beautiful to watch. That white baseball flying through the air as if it had eyes, as well as wings, a jet propulsion motor and an electronic tracking guiding system.

It was as if I was back at the courthouse those many years before, and Dick Tharp, with that beautiful arm, was displaying his talent. I got tears in my eyes. I don't know why. I don't know if it was nostalgia, or disappointment seeing one great talent wasted, and another wasting before my eyes. Father and son were gifted by genetics but not visited by Providence.

Scott Kazmir received a $2 million signing bonus with his professional baseball contract. Dick's son has never pitched professionally. He confesses he wasn't interested, but I suspect he didn't want to submit to the discipline. His arm was simply something to show off, and to stay loose from any formal commitments.

Athleticism is one talent. There are many others. Musical talent. Talent to write. To paint. To draw. To acquire foreign languages. To excel in mathematics and science. To think conceptually. All of these talents can be realized only if recognized and then developed.

Talent demands discipline, organization, and resolute drive to bring out its latency. It takes stamina and patience to perfect it as something special and useful to others. It means taking the inevitable bumps in the road when the pavement ahead is not always smooth and is dotted with potholes. Continuing the metaphor, it means some bridges will be down, and so other ways to cross and continue the journey must be found. Malcolm Gladwell in *"Outliers"* (2008) writes of the "10,000-hour-rule," claiming the key to success in any field is a matter of practicing a specific task for a total of 10,000 hours.

Some stop once they run into an obstacle and stay there for life. Others allow a single misfortune to derail their effort because their plan is one-dimensional. Planning like life is multidimensional and exciting because it is so.

MENTORING YOUR WAY TO FULFILLMENT

Some of us have minders who put us back on track when we appear lost. These mentors recognize special talents and want only what is best for us. They are not in competition with us. I once had a boss, Dr. Francis Xavier Pesuth at Honeywell Avionics, a wonderful mentor and the first man that ever got me to behave, who claimed he always hired people smarter than he saw himself. It was of course not true, but it demonstrated he was a catalyst rather than retarding agent when it came to talent development.

Dr. Pesuth was one of many mentors it has been my good fortune to have had. He assessed accurately what I could and would do. That was his coaching aspect. He assessed how far I could go, and created a climate for that possibility. It meant taking risks and allowing me to fail, and therefore succeed. That was his management aspect. He created benchmarks to assess my competency. That was his leadership aspect. He made others aware in the corporation of my readiness for challenging assignments beyond his authority. That was his corporate aspect. He developed a career track with me and we monitored it together. That was his educator aspect.

That doesn't mean I always heeded his advice. In fact, I've been called a difficult person to manage. Someone once asked me why Dr. Pesuth was the exception. I answered simply, "I love the guy." I discovered that love is a great motivator with me, and the love was derived from his being consistently firm, fair, honest, and in your face if he had a problem with you. He was passionately loyal to the company and displayed this same passion in activities outside of work. For example, he was chairman of the Pinellas County School Board, supervising an ambitious school construction and school renovation program. He also taught at the University of South Florida and St. Petersburg College as an adjunct professor, and was an advisor to the Bishop for the Archdiocese of St. Petersburg.

When I was an undergraduate student at the University of Iowa, taking a required course in "Modern Literature, Greeks, and the Bible," my professor suggested it be an oral rather than a written examination. I had lost classroom time being in the infirmary with an infection. It was at the end of the term and I sensed the professor didn't want to grade another paper. My essays tended to be voluminous. Previously, I had written a paper on "The Influence of Religion in My Life," which was long and complex and I think this was factored in to the request.

In any case, the examination was on James Joyce's *"Portrait of the Artist as a Young Man"* (1916). It started with him asking a few routine questions, which I answered, then I stopped abruptly and said,

"Would it be possible to explain what the book meant to me in light of my own experience?"

Smoking a cigarette, behind a veil of spiraling mist, I couldn't quite make out his face. I thought I heard a sigh, and then, "Go on." So, I did.

For the next forty-five minutes I weaved the story of Joyce's artist, Stephen Dedalus, obviously the author himself, and his war with Irish Catholicism, priests, his family, his youth, and the fury of his tormented soul, which resonated completely with me.

I had not only read the book, but also returned to it repeatedly as if a bible, sensing that something of an epiphany was being experienced. I had never read anything like it.

Here I was, a lad, who had come from a small Iowa town with no books on literature in my home, who had never heard of James Joyce (although later I learned my mother read him), but could see in the book a sympathetic soul parallel to my own.

It astounded me that an author's words could speak so profoundly to what troubled me. That someone could describe what I thought had no language but gnawed at my conscience every day.

I was ashamed of my impurity of thoughts; amazed that someone could be so honest and forthwith about such things, and yes, so gifted, to speak to my most private self. My face burned with passion as I concluded my remarks and looked to the professor.

For the longest moment, the room was silent. Then the professor asked, "How do you explain your sense of Joyce?" Before I could answer, he added, "This is quite remarkable, you know." The room had the pungent smell of cigarette smoke as he lit another cigarette on the burning tip of his stub.

Somewhat in a trance, I answered, "I am Joyce."

"You are Joyce?" he chuckled. "That's good." When I didn't elaborate, he picked up his papers. "By the way, what is your major?" I said that I was a chemistry major. He replied, "What are you doing in science?" I said self-consciously if not a bit arrogantly, "I'm good at it." He said flatly, "You should be in the humanities, not science."

The professor said he would like to recommend me for the Honor's Program, a University of Iowa humanities curriculum with an international reputation, where I would pursue literature and possibly go on to become a writer.

When I broached the subject with my railroad brakeman da, he was incensed, claiming such people rode his trains: "Reading books, long hair, dirty, unkempt, and hanging on each other." Then he exploded my idealistic trance with this question, "Jimmy, you're not a goddamn fag are you?" It didn't matter that I wasn't. It was clear he would be ashamed of me if I left science for the arts. I didn't. I became a chemist.

The professor's recognition of this essence found me becoming a reader to which I have been loyal all my life.

Writers who have influenced Western thought have been my constant companions. It has also made me a student of culture and its impact on behavior. You could say it was a combination of my reading and my international career that found me abruptly retiring, the first time, in my thirties to assess where I was and where I was going.

I wrote some including one book, but after a two-year sabbatical returned to the university to earn my doctorate in industrial and organizational psychology. Armed with this training, I returned to industry, and then retiring a second time in my fifties to once more pursue the field my good professor suggested so many years before. I share this with you because it is never too late to reacquaint yourself with your essence, and to allow it to blossom.

As long as the mind is alive and the body healthy, and soul not ignored, it is possible to do what you have always postponed doing. The time is right, right now!

COUNTERINTUITIVE WISDOM, THE MIND'S PLAN SET FREE

There are many factors that go into a life's plan. Often they are composed of ideas we believe we should do with little variance. It is counterintuitive to think that the best plan is a plan that has no rigid construction, a plan that breathes and allows essence to rise when it is ready, and not before.

Sometimes, that is never, as pointed out earlier, if no one is there to remind us of our essence. I think that is rare. More common, I believe, people remark what we do well, but we aren't listening. We have our mind made up and that is all there is to it. We see the road we have in mind as the safe road, the road most traveled, the road for us.

In my day, the safest road was to become a doctor of medicine. That was a guaranteed income, with the prestige of the community as a healer, and with the recognition as a person of substance, intellect, compassion, and caring.

MDs, over the last half-century, have come in for a lot of heat and with many leaving the profession because of the exorbitant malpractice insurance costs, the administrative demands, and other complexities of running a small business irrespective of the practice of medicine. It was once a male-dominated profession, but now more women than men are in the medical schools across the land.

Men like certainty and the prospects of soaring like angels. Western man, in particular, has been guided by left-brain thinking: logical, analytical, rational, sequential, digital, predictable, a veritable walking computer. And like a computer, a lot that is going on can be missed, driving the good doctor into malpractice suits, bad investments, and missed opportunities because of poor management skills. Women, on the other hand, while being left-brain efficient, are equally comfortable being right brain thinkers: holistic, intuitive, conceptual, non-sequential, spatial, and analogical. Western woman, like women in general, is comfortable with her feet planted firmly on the ground, pragmatic dealing with the possible, while realizing the advantage of good interpersonal skills.

The medical analogy is given because both hemispheres of the brain can and should be used by everyone in concert instead of being at war with each other.

We are moving from *"Machine Age"* thinking where there is a place for everything and everything in its place to everything in a state of flux. Where you are today doing what you are doing may have little to do with what you are doing tomorrow, but in another sense be the reason you are doing it. Permit me to explain.

Psychologist B. F. Skinner was at first passionately into music; Albert Schweitzer was at first a world renowned classical organist, then a theologian, then a medical missionary, and finally a philosopher. There is a musicality to Skinner's behavioral theories, as there is to Schweitzer's philosophy.

It is my belief that nothing we learn at any level is lost or discarded but is more likely integrated into new patterns of thinking as we venture forward away from our initial training and experience.

Chemists and engineers who eventually become psychologists manage to build their earlier disciplines into related theories, such as David McClelland's theory of *"expectancy valence motivation."* Valence is the charge on an atomic electron, which dictates its activity. Expectancy valence is the theory that little successes build to greater successes, which in turn encourages the individual to seek new challenges and higher expectations. In chemistry, the higher the valence the greater the electronic activity.

Malcolm Gladwell, a trained journalist, has discovered a new career by thinking outside the box, explaining the unexpected implications of social science research, implications social scientists have missed. Consider these consciousness expanding books of his in an unconscious age:

"The Tipping Point: How Little Things Can Make A Big Difference" (2000); *"Blink: The Power of Thinking Without Thinking"* (2005); *"Outliers: The Story of Success"* (2008); *"What the Dog Saw: And Other Adventures"* (2009); *"David and Goliath: Underdogs, Misfits, and the Art of Battling Giants"* (2013).

Gladwell is Colin Wilson's consummate outsider, who has become an insider. College was not an intellectually fruitful time for him, but paradoxically, he saw academics walking on diamonds but not having the good sense to bend down and pick them up. He has done this for them, and for the effort has proven the ultimate confident thinker.

If you have occasion to read sociologists, it should not surprise you that many first pursued a career as "number crunchers," or accountants with a flair for statistical correlations and validations. It would appear that they have trouble getting inside the numbers, as Gladwell has.

Counterintuitive thinking suggests there is an unrevealed plan inside everyone's mind that is waiting to be unfolded. It is a plan of many roads and many junctions, and even with a timetable as to when best to take one or another road, while making it clear that you can always double back if you should choose.

This life map has four-way stops and two-way roads going in all directions with suggested signs but only suggested signs for the traveler. The signs indicate the possibilities ahead, which might be read intuitively or counterintuitively. Taking a given road may not be consistent with logic, good sense, or pragmatic consideration, but it may be the best road for you.

Such was the case when I retired the first time, after completing an assignment in South Africa. Life made no sense to me. I was making a good living but I was not happy with where I was, what I saw, and what I had experienced as it clashed with my beliefs and values. It was the era of apartheid in South Africa.

My options were: (1) ignore my unease and simply go on with my career; (2) rationalize that I had too much to lose to do otherwise; or (3) take a "time out" by resigning. I chose the third option. Logic told me that I was too young to retire, making too much money, and should appreciate my success, and deal with it as an adult. Logic also reminded me that I had a wife and four small children to support.

My extended family was openly hostile to the idea of my dropping out, yet that is what I did. I took a two-year "time out," and then backtracked on a road I had already taken, going back to school full-time, year around, for six years, treating the pursuit of a doctorate in psychology as my therapy while consulting on the side.

It has all worked out well, but the road was bumpy with many potholes, washed out bridges, and sometimes roads closed to traffic. In the world of counterintuitive wisdom the mind is free and may sometimes find itself in surprising territory. After a second executive career as a corporate executive, in which I saw Europe up close and personal in its struggle to become the *European Economic Community* (EEC), I retired a second time (1990) to write about the conflict:

Between managers and the emerging professional class;

Between old European national work federations with the new European Economic Community.

Work Without Managers (1991) gained international exposure as it announced the death of "corpocracy" (i.e., top-down executive authority), and the emergence of the knowledge worker with power, on the one hand, and the decline and fragmentation of feudalistic Europe and the emergence of the European Economic Community as a viable alternative on the other.

The impetus for writing *'In the Shadow of the Courthouse: Memoir of the 1940s Written as a Novel"* (2003) was the death of a boyhood friend, Bobby Witt. It reminded me of my own mortality. During the middle of the 20th century, in the middle of the United States, in a neighborhood in the middle of Clinton, Iowa, during World War Two, we as adolescent boys played baseball over at the courthouse grounds.

Were it not for taking that road less traveled that book would not have been written. The book is frozen music of a time, place and space. It cannot be changed even though there is no longer a courthouse lawn, no longer a St. Patrick's School, Rectory and Church. A large public safety building has replaced the baseball diamond of the summer, which became an ice skating rink in the winter, thanks to sheriff Ky Peterson. He had the grounds between the jail and the courthouse flooded in the winter for our entertainment. St. Patrick's church and school, the other center of our young lives, has since been razed, leaving these halcyon days alive only in our memories.

The book is a snapshot of a period (1941-1947) when we came of age in the shadow of that courthouse while the United States struggled to come of age in the shadow of the atomic bomb.

SERENDIPITY AND WHY THE BEST LAID PLANS GO AWRY

Planning in terms of Confident Thinking is a learning process in constant motion, a journey not an end, a surprise filled series of happenings along the way with correcting vision fueled by the effective utilization of one's inherent ability in the service of others.

Alas, our vital essence is not usually revealed to us whole. Obstacles are placed in our way that challenge our passions, test our resolve, and hide our authentic self from us.

So, in planning your work and working your plan, remember you are in the learning business from the beginning to the very end.

CASE OF SEAMUS FARRELL

Seamus (pronounced *sham mus*) was a good high school student taking a college preparatory course of four years of English, two years of Latin, four years of mathematics, physics, chemistry, social science studies, psychology and ancient and American history.

He majored in chemistry at a Midwestern university, took a degree in it, and a position in research and development with a food processing company.

The "first obstacle" he encountered was to find he was not a competent bench chemist. He lacked the mechanical aptitude to set up experiments, a crucial skill. Attempting to make the best of a disappointing situation, he applied for and was granted a fellowship to an eastern university to pursue graduate work in theoretical chemistry, thinking he would be happier constructing molecular chemical models than monitoring laboratory experiments.

Already the father of two children under the age of four, he learned his wife was pregnant with a third child when he was to assume his fellowship. Given the size of the grant, the expected course load, there was no way he could satisfy the fellowship and support his family.

Then he saw a job listed in *Chemical & Engineering News* for a chemical sales engineer. So, he applied for the job and was hired, which meant relocating to another state, thinking he could make enough money in the short term selling to supplement his grant, and continue as planned.

Seamus had never sold anything, but had the notion that salesmen made more money than chemists and therefore the detour would keep his plan on track.

The youngest member of a district sales staff of eight seasoned sales engineers, the first two weeks on the job he rode with the area manager. At the end of this period, he was asked to critique what he had learned. Seamus was by nature opinionated, suffered fools poorly, and had the tact of an alley cat.

He proceeded to point out that the sales calls were little more than social calls, that the area manager dominated the conversation not allowing the customer to express his interests much less his needs, that the focus was always on how wonderful the company's products were, its standing in the industry, but nothing about the cost benefit of the company's products to this customer. If this were not enough, Seamus felt compelled to add, "You never asked for an order."

The following Monday, when Seamus went to the office, only his district and area manager were present, his colleagues were conspicuously absent. It was soon apparent that he was in trouble. He was told that he was obviously not cut out for this kind of work, that technical competence was not enough to succeed in the field, and that he should start looking for another job.

His mind raced. He had disrupted his family, cut off his wife from her parents and friends, and the children from their grandparents. Essentially broke, with no apparent viable support system at hand, his fellowship now in jeopardy, plans his bosses knew nothing about, he reacted by not reacting.

Noting his painful silence, the district manager said that he would give him a workload of marginal accounts to service, which he was free to upgrade for the commission. He could also call on competitor accounts in the area if he liked. "But I want to make one thing clear," his boss said, "This is a 90-day window so you best line up another job ASAP as you will be terminated at the end of this period."

It was also during that session that he learned the company had a three-year sales training program in which the focus was on technical development to work as consultant to major public utilities, paper mills, chemical, automotive and electrical appliance manufacturers, distilleries, and petroleum refineries. The company reasoned out of this technical proficiency demand would come for the company's products and services. "We are not backslapping peddlers," the area manager reminded Seamus. "We are professional engineers."

This ultimatum was both a shock and horrible surprise, as he needed to make commission money now, not three years from now. He never told anyone the job was an interim step to his academic career. Nor did he buy into the company's declaration they only recruited chemists and chemical engineers for selling positions. True, the company had an elaborate screening process, which involved taking an intelligence test, a three-hour inquisition with a psychiatrist, and a full day of interviews with company executives.

"Chemical & Engineering News" had finessed him. Its advertisement had displayed the company's field test kits, which were the reason he had applied for the position. These portable laboratories didn't seem too radical a jump from the R&D lab to field sales.

Now, after this session, he felt between a rock and a hard place. He needed cash and it wasn't in the company's game plan, plus he would soon be out of a job. He had gambled taking a position with a salary less than he had been making in the laboratory. In a way, he thought, only with the company three weeks, not three years, I can earn commissions now! I can upgrade accounts. I can call on competitors. In this nightmarish moment, this nightmarish moment, put a positive spin on things. It was the way he kept his sanity.

His orientation in the company was a month's technical training at the company's headquarters in Chicago. No time was spent on sales training. Complicating matters further, Seamus was introspective, and hardly a hearty fellow well-meant like his area manager, a better listener than a talker, more inclined to observe than impress, more naturally skeptical than likely to join the company's bandwagon.

Seamus was further handicapped in that he did not know his company's products. To his delight, the marginal accounts he was given, all low-tech customers enjoyed the attention he was giving them. They were happy to explain their systems and how the company's products worked or failed to work.

These operations often ran 24/7. He could call on them well into the night. This worked for him because he did not drink or hang out at bars or watch television preferring to spend as little time as possible in his motel room. He also kept copious notes of everything he did complete with comments from customers about the company's products. He was on a steep learning curve, but he was a learner and not a knower.

His district manager was mildly surprised when after the first week he upgraded all the accounts he called on by 25 percent. This was modest in total business because these were small accounts. The second week out he sold an account with three plants in a small industrial town that had been with a major competitor for a quarter century. It also proved to be the largest account sold in the district in the last three years.

More remarkably, he was given a blanket order for products and applications he knew only theoretically. It required his area manager to assist him in surveying these plants, ordering the appropriate proprietary chemicals, feeding and monitoring equipment. While the area manager was making these calculations he kept shaking his head. Finally, he asked Seamus, "How did you do it?"

Seamus said simply, **"I asked for the order."** That stung as it was meant to sting, which only retched up the enmity between them.

It was even more basic than that. He decided that the problems his customers were having with his company's products were the same problems competitors' customers were having with theirs. He used this intelligence as entrée to discussions. Moreover, in upgrading his accounts, customers were showing him how to make his products work better. "You're the first one who has ever asked us," they would say.

Seamus discovered a facility for capturing ideas with schematics of how systems could work with the proper attention to detail. He didn't use company brochures or product bulletins to tell his story but created his own. Customers appeared to like this demonstration of spontaneity.

How he sold that first major account was totally unconventional and counterintuitive. While the superintendent of operations was busy putting out fires, his secretary escorted him to the superintendent's office, which was a bullpen in the middle of a seven-acre plant. Here Seamus could see just how chaotic operations were.

When the superintendent finally appeared, nearly an hour later, he lit a cigarette, leaned on his desk, and said, "Okay, sport, you've got five minutes. What do have for me?"

The previous 45 minutes Seamus observed the frantic behavior of people coming in and leaving the office, the samples of failed equipment on every surface, the constant ringing of the telephone that was never answered, the overflowing ash trays of cigarette butts, the coffee stains of papers on desks and chairs and clipboards, and now the weary look on the face of the superintendent as he challenged him. Seamus found himself saying, "I'm here to save your job!"

The superintendent almost swallowed his cigarette, but then broke into an ear splitting strident laugh that broke the tension and gave him a gleeful appearance. He relaxed and fell into his chair behind his desk. "You're going to save my job!"

"Yes, sir," Seamus replied, and then without preamble he moved around the desk beside the superintendent and began to sketch schematics of systems he was certain were failing. He highlighted these drawings with where he assumed chronic problems were occurring providing a possible explanation of why.

This gained the superintendent's attention. Then he asked for a month's order in which he would install monitoring devices in the processes that would be evaluated on a weekly basis with chemical dosage levels adjusted until all systems were up and running to capacity.

You could say it was serendipity, and there were grounds for such thinking. The superintendent was desperate. More accurately, however, it was *Confident Thinking* boldly on display.

Seamus presented a problem solving strategy on the basis of what he had learned in his own accounts, and what he was seeing here. Clearly, his competitor had neglected this account. The operation was having the same problems of neglect he experienced in his marginal accounts. Seamus never bought into the idea that products differed that much from company to company. Having been a bench chemist, he knew competitors' products differed little chemically with his own. It was application and control that made the difference, not necessarily the superiority of one company's set of chemical compounds to another. He was only with the company a little over a month and already was certain how he would build his success.

There was no way for him to explain his success in salesmanship terms because he didn't know the vocabulary of selling. Other successes followed. Regional managers invited him to explain how he planned and worked his plan in acquiring new business. He had to read selling books, but found they were inadequate, as they all seemed to focus on the customer as adversary, or someone to finesse, and he was not about this at all. He developed a jingle to express his approach:

To sell to Mr. Blue what Mr. Blue buys you must see Mr. Blue through Mr. Blue's eyes.

A TOUCH OF THE RADICAL SOMETIMES IS NECESSARY

So, thus far we have the career of a student who becomes a chemist, finds the laboratory not of his liking, seeks a fellowship to further his training in chemistry, only to be derailed by the pending arrival of a third child, where he attempts to take a detour into selling to keep his graduate plan on course to supplement the fellowship, only to find he is almost fired from day one, but somehow is given a second chance, and succeeds beyond his wildest expectations.

So, he stays in selling. Many are interested in his formula of success. This gives him exposure to the company brass, which he eventually joins, finding him an international troubleshooter for the company, eventually landing in South Africa.

It is 1968, a time of turmoil. The United States seems to be coming apart at the seams. There are riots in Chicago and Miami at the national presidential nominating conventions with riots on college campuses over the war in Viet Nam. Dr. Martin Luther King and Bobby Kennedy are assassinated. Students burn their draft cards, and flee to Canada. African American Olympic Medal Winners raise black glove fists in defiance to a world television audience in the Summer Olympics in Mexico City.

On the morning of October 16, 1968, Tommie Smith of the United States team won the 200-meter race in then-world-record time of 20.7 seconds, winning the Gold Medal, John Carlos, his teammate, came in third winning the Bronze at 20.10 seconds. After the race, the two African Americans went to medals podium with defiance in mind, shoeless, but wearing black socks to represent black poverty.

Smith wore a black scarf around his neck to represent black pride. Carlos had his tracksuit top unzipped to show solidarity with blue-collar workers in the U.S., with a necklace of beads around his neck.

"These (provocations) are for those individuals that were lynched or killed, and no one said a prayer for them that were hung and tarred." Carlos explained, *"It was for those thrown off the side of the boats in the middle passage."*

Both athletes wore Olympic Project for Human Rights (OPHR) badges. Once *"The Star-Spangled Banner"* was played, they raised black-gloved fists with bowed heads in defiance as a Black Power salute, a gesture, which became front-page news around the world.

As they left the podium, the crowd booed them. Gold Medal winner Smith later said, *"If I win, I am American, not a black American. But if I did something bad, then they would say I am a Negro. We are black and we are proud of being black. Black America will understand what we did tonight."*

The aftermath for the two athletes was to be expelled from the games. The U.S. sporting establishment in the following years largely ostracized Smith and Carlos. Smith continued in athletics, going on to play in the NFL with the Cincinnati Bengals before becoming an assistant professor of physical education at Oberlin. In 1995, he went on to help coach the U.S. team at the World Indoor Championships at Barcelona. In 1999, he was awarded a Sportsman of the Millennium award. He is today a public speaker.

Carlos' career followed a similar path to Smith's. He continued in athletics, equaling the 100-yard dash world record the following year. Later, he played in the NFL with the Philadelphia Eagles, before a knee injury ended his career. He fell upon hard times in the 1970s, but was employed by the Organizing Committee for the 1984 Summer Olympics in Los Angeles to promote the games and act as liaison with the city's black community. In 1985, he became a track and field coach at Palm Springs High School, a post he still holds.

In 2005, San Jose State University honored former students Smith and Carlos with a twenty-two foot high statue of their protest. In January 2007, San Jose State opened a new exhibit called Speed City:

From Civil Rights to Black Power, announcing that "from which many student athletes globally recognized as the Civil Rights and Black Power movements, reshaped American society."

The action has had repercussions down to the present day. Two young men became political in their innocence, and with that radicalism, had a hand in changing their times. Forty-five years later, we have a black president in Barak Obama.

When nothing makes sense, there are two options: deny it and go forward as usual, or deal with it and act accordingly to the dictates of your will. In either case, it implies a bit of radicalism. Radicalism can be self-creative or self-destructive.

The internal conflict can build to the point that a person, who has never been a drinker, turns to drink or drugs, who has never been a smoker, takes up smoking, who has never been promiscuous, becomes preoccupied with pornography, who has never been unfaithful, becomes adulterous. Such radicalism destroys. Equally destructive is to give up and give out and become embittered with life and everyone in it as if this chaotic state will never pass.

Radicalism can also involve simply taking a break from the grind, going on holiday, visiting the old neighborhood, and reliving an earlier time of calm, connecting with old friends. This sometimes works because life can take you out of the neighborhood, but never the neighborhood out of you, as it is part of your geography and baggage.

Or you could take a total break as I did. In the back of my mind, once I was no longer working for a company, was the idea that I would become a writer, having no sense of what a ludicrous idea that was. I had published a book and a few articles, but it was clear that a freelance writing career was not sufficient to support my family.

My radicalism was then compounded when instead of seeking a full-time job; I went back to school full-time for the next six-years. I thought I would find answers at the university. I did not. I was looking for an escape from myself but kept running into that self, and the university was no exception. Society had programmed me to occupy a well-defined slot. I didn't fit in that slot and was running faster and faster from myself only to find I could not out run that self. I came to realize I had to go against the grain of my cultural programming and embrace my fear of self-knowing.

It is counterintuitive to please oneself before pleasing and serving others. We are conditioned to be self-effacing, humble, to sacrifice and be selfless when that goes counter to our self-directed nature. For this self-rejection, we have a society of counter dependence, which has produced a large body of codependent people waiting for others to do for them what they might best do for themselves.

The unintended consequences of this inner emptiness have been to spawn an acquisitive society, often a devious and avaricious society on the brink of being a corrupt society, where few are content with who they are. Inner emptiness needs outer validation. The option of making choices was always there, but the will to make choices pleasing to oneself has not been enough to resist societal programming, and so sickness on the brink of madness has possessed people of this land.

We see this in escalating neighborhood violent crime; in a higher degree of lifestyle diseases; in more mental illness; in more corrupt politicians and corporate executives; in more people on the dole; in more illiteracy; and in more embarrassing crimes of the clergy than nearly anywhere else. We also cannot explain why so many become victims of cancer or other rare and debilitating diseases.

The year 1968 was chosen because that was the year that shaped a generation. Journalist Lance Morrow in Time magazine compares 1968 to a knife that severed the past from the future (January 11, 1988). Bob Kirkpatrick claims in *"1969: The Year Everything Changed"* (2009) that it was the birth of modern America. For those not yet born in 1969, it was the year of revolution, apocalypse and the end of *The American Century* more than thirty years early. It was the commencement of what I call the "unconscious age," for all the madness that has transpired since, as American society seems incapable of breaking the circle that finds it chronically and constantly circling back on itself to that period.

James R. Fisher, Jr., PhD.

CONFLUENCE OF ESSENCE AND PERSONALITY

Everything starts with the individual. The science of people in general and the individual in particular has not made equivalent progress to that made in the material world. Dealing confidently with complexity in this new century has left much to be desired.

Man remains essentially lost in description, an object analyzed, categorized, labeled, and identified, a subject opened to conjecture, bias and fantasy, but hardly understood. The idea of man varies according to metaphysical beliefs. A physical scientist and theologian accept the same definition of a crystal of sodium chloride. They do not agree on the same definition of man. The sociologist, psychologist, anthropologist, ethnologist and etiologist have their definitions as well.

We are late to make man a subject of pressing concern. Astronomy was already far advanced at a time when man's physiology was relatively primitive. Copernicus, Galileo and Kepler reduced the earth from the center of the universe to a humble satellite of the sun, while their contemporaries had little idea of the elementary structure or function of the brain. Even earlier, the study of spiritual life and philosophy attracted greater men than the study of science and medicine.

Our mind is designed to contemplate simple facts and solve simple problems.

There is a reluctance to unravel the contradictions and aberrant behaviors of man. French philosopher and Nobel Laureate Henri Bergson (1859-1941) stated flatly, *"The intellect is characterized by a natural inability to comprehend life."* He claimed we love to discover in the cosmos the geometrical forms that exist in the depths of our consciousness. "You can see it," he said, "in the exactness of our monuments, the precision of our machines, and the purity of our algorithms, all a fundamental character of our minds. Yet, geometry doesn't exist in nature. It originates in us."

We abstract from complexity simple systems that bear certain relationships to one another and reduce them to pure mathematics.

Alexis Carrel, Nobel Laureate for Medicine (1912) writes in

"Man, The Unknown" (1935), *"The knowledge of ourselves will never attain the elegant simplicity, the abstractness, and the beauty of physics."*

Three-quarters of a century later, little has changed. Carrel's point was that while our universe is exclusively mechanical; man is not. He claimed that with each technological advance civilization was threatened with more mental deterioration than any infectious disease.

Carrel goes on to say, "Modern civilization seems to be incapable of producing people endowed with imagination, intelligence, and courage." Is this simply Nietzschean or are there grounds for concern? Perhaps a better question might be: has man's development kept pace with his technological advancement? Science and technology have sprung from man's brains, but what is the status of man's moral equivalent?

Imagine if Galileo, Newton and Einstein had applied their intellectual gifts to the study of man, would our world be the same? Men of science do not know where they are going. They are guided by chance, curiosity, craving to explore the unknown, but always outside themselves, as men.

Each is in his own world governed by his own laws.

From time to time, obscurity is penetrated with some meaningful discovery without prevision to its consequences. Einstein admitted as much. "I made one great mistake in my life when I signed the letter to President Roosevelt recommending that atom bombs be made; but there was some justification—the danger that the Germans would make them."

We are now in a postindustrial society moving further from the idea of man while our factory programming and mentality continue to dog us, structured to operate as if our institutions were living factories with a physiology and mental landscape impossible to alter for fear the corpus might die.

Modern industry has been based on the idea of progress, progress in school, in health, wealth and happiness, in our careers, in production at the lowest cost so that the individual and the company can earn as much as possible. The individual who runs the machines with little consideration as to the long-term effects to his existence has embraced this concept.

Education today is essentially job training to package man as a conduit component to Electronic Age fruition. Man was passive before and after the Industrial Revolution. Now, he has taken a great leap backward to complete passive receptivity. We see this in his electronic games of virtual reality, spectator sports, celebrity watching, Internet surfing and vicarious recreation that makes atavistic television couch potatoes appear as activists.

The microchip continues to be reduced until it will be little more than the size of a grain of sand. Videophones, video watches, and lapel pin sensing devices will soon be as common as McDonald burgers leading to an obesity of the mind to match that of obesity of the body.

Inert science of matter has come to be matched by our own physical inertness. The power to clone animals has resulted in our cloning without having to undergo the procedure.

Protagoras was confident that "Man is the measure of all things," when it seems he is a stranger in the world he has created. Man is capable of organizing this world for himself but not himself for this world. Why? It seems he does not possess the practical knowledge of his own nature.

Technology soars on the great advancements in the sciences of nature while nature through tsunamis, earthquakes, typhoons, hurricanes, mud slides, avalanches and floods become increasingly hostile to man.

"Man has lost the capacity to foresee and forestall," observes Einstein, *"He will end by destroying the earth."* The science of matter has taken precedence to the science of man. Science has opted for the less challenging conundrum.

That said we shouldn't wait for science to create a definitive mind map to guide us. We should instead develop confluence between our essence and personality on our own. There are certain facts we know:

- Everything in Nature is connected to everything else.
- Everything in Nature has to go somewhere.

- Nature knows best.
- We cannot change Nature.
- There are no free lunches in Nature.

This is as true of matter and it is of man. *Confident Thinking* is not rocket science. It is a practical guide to better understand and leverage us to more satisfying and effective behavior. While neurophysiologists dig into the neurons of our brains, theologians into our souls, psychologists into our consciousness, and sociologists and anthropologists into our work and play, we have the important business at hand of living and saving our planet from ourselves.

Society gets better one person at a time. To be useful to others we must first be useful to ourselves. To be comfortable with others we must first be comfortable with ourselves. This means we must know, understand and accept ourselves, as we are in order to accept others as we find them.

We are all more alike than different. We are all a product of our experience. We are inclined to see others as reflections of what we see and understand in ourselves.

A society is an organism as real as the individual. If a society can only see other societies in its own image, then it is a blind society. Whatever its plans it will quicken its doom and ultimate demise. We as individuals must recognize this flaw. We must plan our work and work our plan to connect rather than to divide us.

Nothing is ever wasted. Curiosity is a blind impulse that obeys no rule. We may go down many false roads before we find the right one. Our minds are as naturally given to exploration as lower animals. We are intrigued with machines but forget we mirror the same complexity in our human anatomy and physiology. Our curiosity extends quite naturally to outer space but not so naturally to inner space. We are drawn to the terrain of the unknown. But it seems to stop when the curiosity turns to human behavior. We remain a puzzle to ourselves. Cartoonist Walt Kelley's Pogo states the obvious, *"I have seen the enemy, and he is us."*

We echo a variation of this, "We are our own worst enemy!" No matter how many false turns we make we are picking up valuable material along the way.

No one escapes the morality of his time. It surrounds us and bombards our senses with its stimuli while we think we are exercising free will. Therefore, we should give pause before we make choices recognizing that the influence is always present. There is a natural confluence between our essence and personality, which is our failsafe protection to sanity and survival.

THE PRUDENCE OF DESTINY

Confident Thinking is not about impressing, but expressing our usefulness to others in action. If our plan doesn't have the confluence you desire, then rework the plan. A plan should be a happy collaboration between our personality and essence to a satisfying purpose. I saw this happen when a nephew planned a celebrity golf tournament for his favorite charity. He was also looking for customers in his computer consulting business. He was pleasing himself and pleasing others as well.

Some people are always looking for the lucky break. They are waiting for something "real" to happen, something that will move them off the dime. They are looking for answers in all the wrong places. When they are not discovered, they collapse in self-pity and fold up into bitter retreat. They have had plans but the plans have gone awry, and it is not their fault.

My nephew was rebuff by John Elway who had been named the MVP of the previous Super Bowl. He took it in stride, commenting, "I must have caught him at a bad time." The important point is he wasn't dissuaded from his plan.

Ask some people what would they like to do, and they are quick to reply, "Certainly not what I'm doing now." Press them further, and they are apt to say, "Making enough money to take a vacation now and then."

"Do you have a plan?" I ask. This always confuses. So, I add, "What would be your ideal situation?"

"Being my own boss."

"Doing what?"

"I don't know, something important, something where you get some respect."

None of this is real because there has been no serious thought given to a plan. The confident thinker has thought about it, and recognizes that success and happiness is a journey, a segue from little success to larger ones, always recognizing setbacks are part of the drill as well as periodic detours in quest of an objective that may be fuzzy at first, but takes on greater clarity as time, energy, patience, and will are dedicated to it. The confident thinker knows that he can start at any time in his life to reboot his existence to another plane and other circumstances.

IT IS NEVER TOO LATE TO START

So, what is the age when you can start becoming a Confident Thinking planner? There is no such age. Anna Mary Robertson, better known as "Grandma Moses," began to paint childhood country scenes at about the age of seventy-five, when arthritis made it too difficult for her to sew. Two of her famous paintings are "Catching the Thanksgiving Turkey," and "Over the River to Grandma's Home." She had her first show in New York City at the age of 80 in 1940, and lived to 101, dying in 1961.

There is no certain age that you can move in the direction of your talent. Likewise, there is no activity useful to others and self-generating that is not of great consequences. I have known people who have turned hobbies into livelihoods.

Eric Hoffer became blind as a youngster of seven with his sight not returning until he was fifteen. When his eyesight returned, he was seized with an enormous hunger for the printed word. He went to the library and checked out the largest book of essays with the smallest print, and relished the stylish sentences of Montaigne.

During the subsequent years as a migrant worker, gold miner, and longshoreman, he began to capture his insights into thought provoking epigrams and poignant sentences. In 1950, he sent a handwritten manuscript to what he thought was the best publisher, Harper & Row, which published *"The True Believer"* in 1951. He was 49-years-old. His work was modestly successful. It wasn't until he appeared with Eric Sevareid in an hour-long conversation on CBS TV in 1967 at the age of 65 that he actually became famous. Hoffer came on the American scene in the confusing and chaotic 1960s. He pulled aside the veils of supposed intellectual and societal sophistication and, in new ways, showed Americans her old truths, and why they were still valid.

There is no limit to what talent lies right under a person's nose. It could be a painting or the written word, or it could be a talent for systematic thought, creating mechanical objects, homemaking, or a zillion other possibilities. It is ordinary people as visionaries who create things that have changed the way we think. Even the revised popularity of our comic heroes is part of this precedence. A Jewish impressionist, Joe Schuster, could not find his niche as an artist because there already was a Marc Chagall. He collaborated with writer Jerry Siegel to create "Superman."

In February 2010, an original 10-cent Action Comics No. 1 edition (1938) of Superman sold at auction for $1 million, in March, a copy in better shape sold for $1.5 million.

The creator of *"The Twilight Zone"* of television, Rod Serling, couldn't find a sponsor for his work, or a network amendable to his stories because they were too controversially political. He got around that by creating the same ideas in trenchant sci-fi fantasy parables. He was free in this medium to explore human hopes, despairs, prides and prejudices in metaphoric ways conventional television considered too sensitive.

So it is and so it will always be, people will find their niche by exploring their latent talents. When they encounter resistance, they will create a way to circumvent it and stay on message. That is why planning is one of the ten stages to Confident Thinking. Planners think of ways to circumvent obstacles and have fun in the process.

CONFIDENT THINKING
CREATIVE STAGE TEN

PALLIATIVES IN AN
ANXIOUS AGE

"Today Americans are overcome not by the sense of endless possibility but by the banality of the social order they have erected against it. Having internalized the social restraints by means of which they formerly sought to keep possibility within civilized limits, they feel themselves overwhelmed by an annihilating boredom, like animals whose instincts have withered in captivity. A reversion to savagery threatens them so little that they long precisely for a more vigorous instinctual existence. People nowadays complain of an inability to feel. They cultivate more vivid experiences, seek to beat sluggish flesh to life, and attempt to revive jaded appetites. They condemn the superego and exalt the lost life of the sense... Outwardly bland, submissive, and sociable, they seethe with an inner anger for which a dense, overpopulated, bureaucratic society can devise few legitimate outlets."

—**Christopher Lasch**, The Culture of Narcissism (1979)

We can easily forgive a child who is afraid of the dark; the real tragedy of life is when men are afraid of the light.

—**Plato**

PATHOS OF SELF ABSORPTION

E VERY AGE HAS its peculiar forms of pathology. It expresses in exaggerated form its underlying character flaws. Ours seems to be schizophrenia. In Freud's time, it was hysteria with the emergent of women in their own right out of the chastity belt of the Victorian Age.

Webster defines hysteria as: "A psychiatric condition variously characterized by emotional excitability, excessive anxiety, sensory and motor disturbances, or the unconscious simulation of organic disorders."

Freud would concentrate on what we call today "psychosomatic" illnesses, that is, seemingly organic but in fact having a purely psychological origin. He took issue with the emphasis on nature as the precondition for hysteria and tried to shift the focus to questions of nurture.

Hysteria is exclusively a female disorder with the disease derived from the word "hysteria" or womb. Freud first put forth his "seduction theory" claiming real acts of seduction during childhood led to sexual trauma.

He later abandoned this theory to believe traumatic sexual events did not have to have been real to have lasting pathological effect. Sexual trauma can be merely imagined. It can be the product of fantasy. He opened a real can of worms with this and seeded some say the sexual revolution, which is ongoing to this day. We are consequently absorbed in our sexuality, which has become tantamount to an addiction.

Personality disorders follow wars. Combat veterans were said to be "shell shocked" after WWI, suffering from "gross stress reaction" after WWII, and "post-traumatic stress disorder" (PTSD) since Vietnam.

On the other hand, once combat veterans are back home, schizophrenia has become the disease most threatening to a normal life. It is a mental disorder characterized by abnormalities in perception of reality, commonly shown as auditory hallucinations, paranoid or bizarre delusions, disorganized speech and thinking. This can lead to significant social and occupational dysfunction. There is an army ready to treat people with these real or imagined symptoms.

Bernie Zilbergeld calls this army, *"The Shrinking of America"* (1983). He sees combat veterans as well as ordinary citizens turning to the soft sciences as a coping mechanism with a smorgasbord of prescription therapies to deal with their uncertainties and nightmares of terror. Psychiatrists, psychotherapists, clinical psychologists, and social workers are directly involved with pre-schizophrenic, borderline personality disorders more than with full-blown schizophrenia.

There is controversy as to whether schizophrenia is exclusively an organic disorder or the result of life experience as well. People with a pre-schizophrenic condition function adequately in society augmented by medication. Indeed, several years ago a New York City Street Survey was taken of ordinary New Yorkers asking them if they had two or more of these symptoms:

Delusions
Hallucinations
Disorganized speech
Negative symptoms
Paranoia

Some 80 percent claimed to be suffering mild to serious forms of these symptoms. Since only one percent of the population is said to be suffering from this disease, what does this tell us?

Complicating matters further, for a disease that has no apparent cure, professionals cannot seem to agree on either the nature of the disease, its diagnosis, definitive symptoms, or the proper treatment.

Schizophrenia is the fourth leading cause of men and women to be sick to death with life, the second leading cause of international terrorism, and the leading cause of war.

Incidentally, the sensory and physical abnormalities listed above are characteristically inherent in attorneys, politicians, mental health professionals, children under five and adults over seventy. Is it inappropriate to diagnose these people as suffering from schizophrenia? Could it not be their natural state? Self-absorption has a peculiar construction in our culture. Take the:

- Stimulation of infantile constant cravings through

subliminal television and Internet bombardment by advertisers;

- Commandeering of parental authority by the media and school change masters to meets its agenda;

- Rationalizations of presupposed inner life demands by those that know accompanied by false promises of personal fulfillment;

- Creation of a new type of social individual to meet the market's anxiety by translating unquestionable wants into necessary needs.

It is obvious in children, but it is equally obvious in workers, who refuse to grow up and take charge of their lives. Such neuroses were previously nipped in the bud by parental authority, and societal reinforcement, but not anymore. In the modern climate, such impulses are stimulated and then perverted into insatiable needs with no chance of satisfaction or coherent forms of control.

We have had waves of the self-indulgent from the "baby boomers," to the "Sexual Revolution," from the "me" generation, to the hippies and yuppies, where anything goes, and yet it has not reduced anxiety but only increased its variations and forms.

THE SECOND SIN

During the last half of the twentieth century, the movement away from us, as cohesive and civil societal individuals, was so swift that flight became the norm. We gave it a name. We called it the "alpha personality," the go-getter, the doer, the workaholic, the change maker, and the leader. Of course, it wasn't anything like it pretended to be. It was the epitome of self-estrangement on the quick and dirty.

We have had the myth of mental illness in a collection of "diseases," so labeled by vote of the American Psychiatric Association of the American Medical Association. At one point, the APA voted homosexuality as a disease, on another occasion as a lifestyle.

Scientific research is not supposed to be designated by a vote of peers, but based on objective science and research. Then there was the wild dash to deify Sigmund Freud and his psychotherapy of the talking cure.

Psychiatrist Thomas Szasz, who would have none of this, and who was essentially ostracized by his colleagues wrote in *"The Myth of Mental Illness"* (1961) that brain damage or brain disease cannot be cured by conversation.

"What so many doctors call mental illness," he states, *"are human conflict expressed in ways society can't live with."*

Szasz believes that the science of man belongs on the side of the people it studies, rather than aligning itself with a society that wants to control differences. He has this to say in *"The Manufacture of Madness"* (1970):

> *"What we call modern, dynamic psychiatry is neither a glamorous advance over the superstitions and practices of the witch-hunts, nor a retrogression from the humanism of the Renaissance and the scientific spirit of the Enlightenment. In actuality, Institutional Psychiatry is a continuation of the Inquisition. All that has really changed is the vocabulary and the social style."*

In his book, *"The Second Sin"* (1974) he points out that if, as the Old Testament tells us, the First or Original Sin was the knowledge of good and evil, then the knowledge of clear speech was the *"Second Sin."* At Babel, God punished man for this transgression with the Divine Confusion, and we have been misleading each other ever since. Szasz believes the confusion of language has produced much of the inhumanity, intolerance, and outright stupidity, which today affect everything from our politics to our sex lives.

The *"Second Sin"* is his effort to dispel some of this confusion. It is a collection of penetrating and often humorous thoughts ranging from sex and the family to drugs, schizophrenia, and psychiatry.

Here is a sample:

- If a man says he is talking to God we say he is praying. If he says God is talking to him we say he is schizophrenic.

- Treating addiction to heroin with methadone is like treating addiction to Scotch with bourbon.

- Mental hospitals are POW camps of our undeclared and unarticulated wars.

- Pimp is illegal, but when a so-called sex therapist like Dr. Masters gets you a prostitute and calls her a "surrogate wife," then pimping becomes a form of treatment, which you can take off on your income tax.

- Formerly, Americans charged with murder were considered innocent until proven guilty; now they are considered insane until proven sane.

- Masturbation: the primary sexual activity of mankind. In the nineteenth century, it was a disease; in the twentieth, it is a cure.

Szasz asks in *"Ceremonial Chemistry"* (1975):

Why is it that a man who sells alcohol is a retail merchant, and a man who sells drugs is a pusher? Or why is it that an alcoholic with DT's ends up in a hospital, while a drug user who hallucinates ends up in jail.

Each of his books and his continuing crusade is about ourselves as we are and the way we are, fighting for clarity against the *"Second Sin"* to encourage us to live our own lives by what I call *Confident Thinking*, and not let society take away that right from us. He writes in *"Ceremonial Chemistry"*:

"There is only one political sin: independence; and only one political virtue: obedience. To put it differently, there is only one offense against authority: self-control; and only one obedience to it: submission to control by authority. Why are self-control, autonomy, and such a threat to authority? Because

the person who controls himself, who is his own master, has no need for an authority figure to be his master. This, then, renders authority unemployed. What is he to do if he cannot control others? To be sure, he could mind his own business. But this is a fatuous answer, for those who are satisfied to mind their own business do not aspire to become authorities. In short, authority needs subjects, persons not in command of themselves—just as parents need children and physicians need patients."

It is clear that managers need workers, but it is not clear that workers need managers (see *Work Without Managers*, 1991).

YOUR MAJOR WEAPON IS YOU!

The key to an anxious age is to embrace and wrestle it to your will. The age is not your enemy but your friend and destiny. You live in a time of wonder and magic, splendor and awe, and yes, constant, exploding and imploding change, change that tests the fabric of your will not only to survive, but also to prevail.

It is an anxious time because it is lost in its own creations and moving at mock speed away from itself. The books of Dr. Thomas Szasz are not read today, many are not even in print, but his ideas are as fresh and relevant as ever. Man is in "Nowhere Land" living as "Nowhere Man." Shock and rage have failed to get people's attention. Will this narrative discussion? It remains to be seen.

Small steps can be taken against anxiety:

- Let humor brighten your spirit as tonic to depression.
- Laugh with Folly to neutralize your gloom.
- Become educated and enlightened to expose and dispense with fanaticism.
- Be aware of chronic patterns that cause you to be stuck.
- Allow trust to take the measure of pessimism.
- Give the heart permission to heal the mind and spirit.
- Take hold of confidence because what you think is what

you are and will be.

- Realize what seems accidental and of little moment in the wholeness of life is part of a consistent plot.

- Let the mind weigh the evidence and not the evidence imprison the mind.

- Be a confident thinker and you will be false to no one.

We must avoid the pitfalls of obscurantism to see our problems clearly. We cannot afford to be discouraged or despairing. Sadly, clarity has not always been in our programming. We are forced by necessity to penetrate our cynicism to establish our enthusiasm.

ENTHUSIASM THE PALLIATIVE TO BOREDOM

The word "enthusiasm" comes from the Greek "en + theos," or the god within. So, enthusiasm is our psychic power center connected with the Universal Mind.

Imagine the Universal Mind as a laser connection with the human heart to bring out all the humanity that is in the human spirit.

The virtue of enthusiasm is unlikely to surface in seasons of tranquil circumstance. It flourishes in adversity, awakening in the dark hours of danger to surprise and embolden the individual to a course of action never considered. We see this in natural disasters, train wrecks, plane crashes, floods and other emergencies. The self disappears and the humanity within takes over. Enthusiasm swells to a cause greater than self. Truly, the Greeks had it right as the "god in us" recognizes no odds.

Nothing is more contagious then enthusiasm. It moves mountains and calms rivers. *"Unclimbable mountains vanish before it like smoke before the wind,"* observes Alexis Carrel. Enthusiasm is the genius of sincerity. True endeavor cannot succeed without it, but with enthusiasm, no man need be feared and, therefore, need be despised.

We live in times of mock sincerity. Superstition is seen as the disease of nations, enthusiasm that of individuals. Cynicism seems preferred to enthusiasm as we wax in the false bravado of sarcasm when enthusiasm is the perfect palliative to what apparently ails us, boredom!

HUMOR PALLIATIVE TO DEPRESSION

Humor has always been important to us. Like everything else, it changes to match the times. Out of the nineteenth century we had the folksy humor of Mark Twain and Will Rogers, the early twentieth century silent film humor of Charlie Chaplin, Ben Turpin, Buster Keaton, and W. C. Fields, who bridged into talkies with The Marx Brothers, Mae West, Abbott and Costello, and from vaudeville-to-radio-to-film-to-television of Jack Benny, Milton Berle, Bob Hope, Amos and Andy, Lucille Ball and Red Skelton, and later television's The Smother Brothers, Red Foxx, Carl Reiner, and Flip Wilson into the television sitcoms of Cheers, Seinfeld, Fraser, the King of Queens and still later to Two and Half Men and the Old and New Christine, and into the animation humor of South Park, The Simpsons, and Family Guy, to the sitcom humor of Scrubs, Friends, Everybody Loves Raymond and the Vicar of Dibley. What has made multi-genre programs such as MASH and NCIS work has been humor and an ensemble cast with good chemistry.

Standup comedians such as Lenny Bruce and Mel Brooks set the tone for comedy with bite with black and blue humor, a genre Richard Pryor refined, and then there is Bill Cosby, incidentally holder of a doctorate in education, who has created a series of sit-coms of humor with enlightenment in various genres including animation to bring attention to ideas that interest him.

George Carlin and Dave Chappelle have as well with the use of shocking content to draw attention to the social and socioeconomic divide often to the point of being censored.

We owe a great deal to those who looked into our souls through admittedly stereotypes in such settings as the home, company, office and workplace to put a pin in our discordant ways. Humor, Kahlil

Gibran reminds us, gives us a sense of proportion, which in turn gives us a sense of balance.

Humor is of a genial quality when it dwells on the pathos of character mingled with sensibility With this balance, humor can provide a coping mechanism with infirmities, ill health, and other evils of life that catch us when we are least prepared for them. The humorous laughs with us, not at us. A smile makes life more bearable, but a hearty laugh adds a certain fragrance to the joy.

True humor springs from the heart not the head. It is not contempt for one's situation or one's enemies, but the essence of love. There is certainly no defense against adversity save the humor of putting it into perspective. We cannot all have large bank accounts, live in the best of neighborhoods, or indeed, dress with the most splendid threads, but we can be the best society has to offer with a sense of humor.

We live in a world of perpetual posturing, constant conflict and blatant contradiction. Presence, pretense and pretension have reached legitimacy. Nothing is what it seems, and no one is what he or she pretends to be. That is what humor is telling us, so loosen up! Political cartoonists reduce our leaders to the most absurd caricature exaggerating prominent features. Most telling is that we immediately know who they are. Yet, there is sometimes a special violence to editorial cartoons that would never pass muster in storyboard. A Swedish cartoonist suffered death threats after he published a cartoon of the Prophet Muhammad showing his head on a dog's body.

With change constantly threatening to overwhelm us, we resort to all manner of checks and balances to give the impression we are in control when clearly we are not. This makes us stick figures on stage of a cartoon humorous. The more we deny the absurdity of our ways the more we fall prey to their inventions. The conventional world has been reduced to masks superimposed on reality. The humorous, whatever his or her venue, attempts to penetrate this absurdity and illusion.

In humor, the sublime and ridiculous dance merrily together without stepping on each other's toes, or perspectives. It is in contradiction that efficiency functions. The sublime and the ridiculous are polar coordinates of the reasonable and absurd, the territory of humor where what is and what is supposed to be collide.

No attempt is made to purge the soul of one's biases. They are as much a part of our chemistry as our other aspects. Biases pass through our fragile filtering system and early conditioning. They are then reinforced, turning feelings into facts.

With humor, this travesty is occasionally acknowledged and penetrated to humanize us. A flea landing accidentally on an elephant's trunk or tusk sees the elephant in a different light. The humorous reminds us we are not far removed from that flea.

"IN PRAISE OF FOLLY"- THE PALLIATIVE TO GLOOM

It is healthy to have a sense of humor about ourselves. It is precisely what is needed in troubling times. Folly touches every aspect of our lives. We tend to take ourselves too seriously and matters of urgency not seriously enough.

President Roosevelt said in his inaugural address in 1933 at the height of the Great Depression, "The only thing we have to fear is fear itself." But Plato counters, "Men are afraid of the light."

It is doubtful many Athenians applauded Plato in his day, or FDR in his. Gloom is a subtle deception that simmers rather than burns, frazzles courage rather than destroys hope. It is Folly as palliative that restores dignity and confidence.

Erasmus (1466-1536) wrote "In Praise of Folly" (1511) in a chaotic period in Western civilization. The Roman Catholic Church was corrupt from the papacy to the clergy, while clinging to its vanities. *"Folly"* was published just six years before Martin Luther nailed his 95 theses to the Wittenberg Church door, which ignited the Protestant Reformation.

Today, 500 years later, man's excess and vanity are on a collision course. "Folly" provides the modern reader with inescapable evidence of what happens when conventions and institutions no longer work, are dysfunctional, but still hold on if desperately so.

Neither king nor prince, pope nor priest, aristocrat nor working-man escapes the indignation that Erasmus feels toward the masters of his society. At the beginning of her oration, Folly declares that she is giving a eulogy of herself, and she justifies the impertinence by saying that she knows herself better than anyone else.

The postmodern man has much in common with man in the Age of the Reformation. Sixteenth century man was not interested in leaving Plato's cave of darkness that he knew for the light that might blind him. He preferred to wait until things returned to normal or the way they had always been. This was especially true of the Roman Catholic Church. The clergy, and laity to a considerable degree, continued to ignore the handwriting on the wall, waiting for a miracle. Erasmus knew the folly of this man and circumstance well.

If you can imagine, Catholicism was no longer synonymous with Christianity, nation states were replacing church dominated kingdoms, and capitalism in commerce was replacing church con-trolled feudalism. The lowly merchant class was emerging from the docks to change the complexion and character of society to be performance driven rather than blood and church dependent.

Erasmus's "Folly" was penned in a time of waning morality and scattering loyalties. Folly represented a many-sided symbol that stood for all that was natural in man however misdirected his attempts to get the wrong things right.

Folly revealed the character of man's wisdom and how it could be united with man's action to gain success despite a world domi-nated by folly. Folly was concerned with reason and simple moral advice and how it could be presented. She wondered what secular humanists would make of the supernatural once it was replaced by individual dignity, worth, and self-realization.

Parody, irony, and satire are used to show what man does and what he has harvested for the doing. Folly was obsessed with her passion for Youth, and listed her followers as Drunkenness, Ignorance, Self-love, Flattery, Forgetfulness, Laziness, Pleasure, Madness, Sensuality, Intemperance, and Sound Sleep.

Folly's followers aided her in gaining complete control of all things in society. She was the source of all that was pleasurable in life, and for this she declared, man would never be free from her, as he was ruled by passion and not reason. The two most important aspects of this passion, she argued, were anger and lust, and both shrunk man to his present status.

Folly praised herself under the guise of Prudence because she had allowed man to have first-hand experience with the world. She had freed him from shame and fear, which had clouded his mind and inhibited his actions, thus prevented him from any real experience.

Thanks to Prudence, man, she proclaimed, had gone along with the crowd, which was folly, at the sacrifice of his individuality. Folly had caused all the great achievements of mankind, yet wisdom and learning had not freed man of his anxiety.

Self-love, self-importance, and flattery motivated everything that man had done. Alas, to lead such a life of folly, error, and ignorance were to be only too human. Folly was the expression of man's nature. All other forms of life around man were content with limitations but man was vainly ambitious. Folly concluded the most ignorant men were the happiest and the most deluded men delighted in telling lies.

Erasmus, who was a priest, chided priests, who Folly saw as relying on magic, charms, relics, prayers, saints and particular rites to create the delusion of happiness. Priests were conjurers of deception, Folly chortled, but man had a need for this deception because emotions belonged to Folly and man could not find happiness without them.

The most foolish men, Folly insisted, were those who denied their true nature through religion. Folly proved that religion had more to do with her own nature than with wisdom by showing that children, women, old people and fools took more delight in religion than anyone else. You could tell because they were always nearest the altars.

In the way religion was taught and practiced, man must deny his true nature by disdaining life and preferring death. He must overlook injuries, avoid pleasure, and feast on hunger, vigils, tears, and labors. He must give up and score all physical pleasures, or at the very least take them more lightly than spiritual pleasures.

Folly insisted this was the most foolish way, but also the only sure way to true happiness. Only by forgetting his body and everything physical could man approach this goal. He must give himself up completely to the spiritual aspects of life in order to achieve bliss.

Only a very few men were able to accomplish this task completely while in this world, Folly admitted, for in order to approach such an experience one must be very close to madness. This madness was similar to the heavenly joys that one would experience after death when the spirit had completely left the body.

Erasmus had sympathy for *The Protestant Reformation*, but decided to stay in the Church and lead the *Counter Reformation*. Historians are divided as to whether this was courageous or cowardly.

In this dichotomy, Erasmus is not unlike many of our current opinion makers: a man of reflection rather than action. He wanted to preserve things as they were and to deny intellectually as much as possible things as they were becoming. Unlike Martin Luther, he was unwilling to put his life, reputation and mind on the line. Instead, he retreated into parody. He remained committed to inevitable change but didn't feel obliged to be actively involved.

Luther changed the world. Erasmus put a bite into that world with his sarcasm, but did little more. He composed the work in seven days five hundred years ago (1509), and it is still read. "Folly" was written while recovering from an illness in the home of his English friend, Sir Thomas More, author of "Utopia" (1516). More would be beheaded in 1535 for his refusal to support his friend, King Henry VIII's Church of England in defiance of the Roman Church.

It was not until two years after *"In Praise of Folly"* was written that Erasmus had the book secretly printed in France. The fact that there were at least seven editions within months of this first printing provides a measure of its immediate success and popularity Because of this work Erasmus became one of the most popular men of letters of his time, and consequently, one of the most influential.

We live in an anxious age with many things not only in jeopardy, but also in mass confusion similar to the time of Erasmus:

- Political ideologies
- Economic systems,
- What constitutes a society?
- What defines a nation?
- Military engagement,
- Coping with subversive elements,
- Fragility of the balance of power,
- Rapprochement,
- Individualism,
- Multiculturalism,
- The primacy of religious freedom,
- The prudence of authority.

Erasmus lived not only at the height of the Protestant Reformation, but also during the collapse of feudalism, the birth of capitalism and the rise of great universities in a climate of low literacy. It was a time when science was lifting the fog off mythology. Nations were being formed around discrete languages and common cultures. This disruption was like an earthquake across the Western world. Only a few years earlier, America had been discovered which threw Aristotle's benchmarks into question.

So, in reading In Praise of Folly, it should come as little surprise that its irreverent humor and self-deprecating style should have lightened the heavy hearts of the times. Today, I see no Erasmus-like essayist; no analysis of our follies, foibles and vanities that speaks with such eloquence as his did so long ago. Today, it is partisan politics, partisan academics, partisan theologies, partisan cultures, and even partisan genders, as if the human race were tainted with a divided soul. Dr. Szasz writes in *"Ceremonial Chemistry"*:

> *"It seems clear that only in accepting human beings for what they are can we accept the chemical substances they use for what they are: in short, only insofar as we are able and willing to accept men, women, and children as neither angels nor devils, but as persons with certain inalienable rights and irrepudiable duties, shall we be able and willing to accept heroin, cocaine, and marijuana as neither panaceas nor panapathogens, but as drugs with certain chemical properties and ceremonial possibilities."*

Szasz is not advocating drug addiction, but being realistic in dealing with people as they are. This should extend across the board.

EDUCATION, THE PALLIATIVE TO INTOLERANCE AND FANATICISM

During the 1970s, I consulted police organizations from Hartford, Connecticut to Miami, Florida along the Atlantic coastline. Florida was one of the first states to institute an incentive program for police officers to earn college degrees, paying their tuition and giving a significant boost in salary once degreed. For this policy, the State of Florida issued this assessment:

> College educated officers displayed greater tolerance, understanding, and flexibility in dealing with diversity while exercising better discretion in the discharge of their most difficult job compared to other officers not college trained.

They were more confident thinkers armed with a sense of proportion and passion to serve and protect. It was the decade of the national doctrine of "law & order" with riots on college campuses, draft dodgers escaping to Canada, water cannons used on civil right marchers, middle class children flaunting the law blocking traffic, sit ins in restaurants, with priest and student disrupting the courts and business establishments. Parents no longer had control of their children. Crime was escalating across all socioeconomic classes.

It was also a time of the *Civil Rights Movement*, the *Vietnam War*, and the stunning victory of Richard M. Nixon over George McGovern in the 1968 presidential election. A gulf had grown between the races, the elderly, farmers, the lesser educated underclass, Republicans, white southerners, and fundamentalist Protestants.

"Law & order" became the paramount issue in the 1960s and revved up into an executive order in the 1970s. It agitated and inflamed the American political process driving a partisan wedge between voters. The electorate in the South was being radically restructured along conservative and liberal fault-lines as Southern Democrats abandoned the Democratic Party for the Republican. Pundits claimed McGovern lost the election so decisively because voters believed he might encourage a more permissive society that would fail to provide citizens with safe streets and cities.

My master's thesis in social psychology was based on my empirical work in that disruptive social climate. A white police officer killed an unarmed young black man in a convenient store after a scuffle, which turned into a riot in Herndon in Fairfax County (my thesis: *A Social Psychological Study of the Police Organization: The Anatomy of a Riot*, 1976). Later, I would be involved in diffusing a mutiny of police officers in Raleigh, North Carolina, as well as working other police hot spots writing my doctorate dissertation on that empirical data (*The Police Paradox: Systematic Exploration into the Paradoxical Dilemma between the Police and the Policed*, 1978).

This work afforded me an opportunity to work with hundreds of police officers cruising the streets with them for scores of hours in state after state. The most tolerant and confident officers were invariably college trained. They were disinclined to slip into stereotypes regarding minorities or to profile possible offenders by color, dress or ethnicity. They also were better able to defuse potential violent situations with talk rather than the use of deadly force. This was not easy because the daily test of human combustibles on the job was a test of discretion and resolve as well as skill. Often, I observed officers maintaining their cool in the face of verbal abuse, unruliness and insulting behavior.

Education had not only given them perspective but language and humor to stabilize unstable situations. Education found these police officers equipped to use their discretionary powers wisely.

What these men and women had to deal with daily touched my soul. Imagine discovering the shallow grave of a murdered child, and then be able function much less believe in the job. They did and do. Protect and serve was not only a commitment, but also total involvement. Education appeared to be the linchpin that brought the best out of them.

The paradoxical dilemma of policing I discovered, which may not seem surprising, was that law abiding communities had law abiding police, and corrupt communities had corrupt police. It was never found the other way around. As novelist and former Los Angeles Police Sergeant Joseph Wambaugh puts it succinctly, *"A community gets the police it deserves."*

TRUST, THE PALLIATIVE TO PESSIMISM

Like in the time of Erasmus, the establish order is disintegrating. Moral clarity and moral authority have taken a holiday. Little makes sense anymore. With the world reduced to randomness, paranoia and conspiracy theories abound. Nothing can be taken at face value.

Sixteenth century Erasmus refused to be cynical. He trusted history to prevail albeit he could not see the rise of secular society with budding capitalism. Secularism was a fait accompli, however, when philosopher Friedrich Nietzsche announced, "God is dead."

God wasn't dead. He had taken on the persona of secular science. The difficulties ahead were to balance scientific quest with man's spiritual needs. Confident Thinking is a modest attempt to bridge this divide where cynicism and pessimism reside to arrive at some common ground of mutual trust and respect. Anything is possible with trust, and the person you must trust first is yourself.

The past five hundred years have been traumatic, true, but also exciting and glorious. With the breakup of the European feudal system, people were lifted from bondage. With the rise of Protestantism and capitalism, and the colonization of the New World, Western society was being redefined.

Imagine being alive in that period of transformation. When explorers came back from the New World and told tales of Native Americans living in organized harmony without the Western God, Europeans were shocked, then "went native," imitating the primitives in manner and dress. It must have been absurd and at best comical. It illustrates how fragile our central belief systems are when introduced to contradictions.

The failure of Europe was its ethnocentrism. It couldn't see the legitimacy of another culture in another place to be as relevant to its people and history as was that of Europeans. The problem still plagues the Western mind.

Nature was God to Native Americans. Nature was not something to conquer but to worship for all it provided. Over time, Europeans discovered that the peoples of this new continent were not a monolithic race, but many tribes and nations, diverse and different, and as warring and territorial as Europeans.

Differences, however, led Native Americans and Europeans to be weary of each other, as people of difference are weary of each other today.

The challenge, then, was more apparent. It could be seen and touched and dealt with directly. Today, we live in virtual reality, cyberspace, and don't know if the person next to us on the subway is a suicide bomber or not.

Our enemies no longer wear distinctive uniforms. They may dress and look like ordinary citizens, but have a bomb strapped to their person. Terrorism is not territorial other than the territorial mind, where it can do the most damage.

We don't know who means us harm. We have become a paranoid society willing to give up our freedoms for our suspicions. Yet, perhaps less than one-tenth of one-tenth of one percent is likely so identified. It is a catch-22.

Fortunately, we muddled through the past 500 years. The palliative to pessimism is the trust we will muddle through the next 500 years. War has been the great definer of my life.

Born during *The Great Depression*, an economic war,

An adolescent during *World War II,*

Teenager in the *Korean War,*

A college student during the *Cold War,*

College graduate during the *Selective Service Draft* years,

An enlisted man in the *U.S. Navy* during the *Viet Nam War,*

An American executive in *South Africa* during *Apartheid* where I witnessed a sick culture up close, and our own sick culture from afar during 1968,

Retired after South Africa although only in my mid-thirties,

Raised a family during the *Civil Rights Movement, Sexual Revolution* and *Feminist Movement,* when kids declared war on their parents,

Returned to graduate school during the *War on Crime, War on Drugs, Watergate* and the *Iran Hostage Crisis,*

Reentered industry during the formation of the *EEC,*

Worked as an executive for an American company in Europe in the 1980s,

Retired a second time during the *First Gulf War,*

Assumed senior citizen status during the *Second Gulf War, War in Afghanistan,* and the *War on Terror,*

Was writing a book (*In the Shadow of the Courthouse: Memoir of the 1940s Written as a Novel,* 2003) when terrorist flew two commercial jets into the *Twin Towers in New York City* on September 11, 2001.

The War on Terror mirrors cyberspace in being invisible and without boundaries. It would be easy to lose confidence and retreat into cynicism and pessimism fed by uncertainty and randomness. That would be a mistake. History always triumphs in the end. It just takes time to get it right. Man eventually tires of war, for a while.

PATTERNS, THE PALLIATIVE TO BEING STUCK

There is a transcendental power in patterns. Models slowly emerge unconsciously and then consciously. It has been so throughout history Seneca put it poignantly:

> *"Men trust their eyes rather than their ears; the road by precept is long and tedious; by example, short and affective."*

Where we are now is part of our history No part of history that is all instruction or all entertainment. If the cliché is true that if we don't learn from history we are doomed to repeat, then our history suggests we are slow learners.

A tag line to this is that the more things change the more they remain the same. Opinions alter, manners change, creeds rise and fall, but moral authority is written on the tablets of eternity

Organized religions and temporal civil authorities in contentious conflict are not new: nor is it a new litigious struggle between the West with Islam and with the East over sovereign contingencies.

Let us not forget the *Holy Crusades of European Christians* between the 11th and 14th centuries attempted, unsuccessfully, to recover the Holy Land from Islam.

In the 7th century, the caliph Omar took Jerusalem. Pilgrimages by Christians were not cut off at first, but by early in the 11th century the mad Fatimid caliph Hakim began to persecute Christians, and then profane and despoil the Holy Sepulcher.

Persecution abated after his death in 1012, but relations remained strained and became more so when Jerusalem passed from the tolerant Egyptians to the Seljuk Turks in 1071. In that same year, Turks defeated the Byzantine Emperor Romanus IV at Manzikert.

So there is precedence for our troubles in the Middle East, only now there are no secrets with newspapers, magazines, television, Internet blogs, and conversation on the street recorded by tens of thousands daily on their iPads or iPhones and distributed on Facebook, or by text messages across the globe instantaneously.

French statesman Francois Chateaubriand said, "Grecian history is a poem; Latin history is a picture; modern history is a chronicle." Erasmus might suggest postmodern history is a farce, as there is no give to our give, no ease to our ease, so it behooves us to recognize the charade, and move on.

Since patterns have more followers than reasons, since we trust our eyes more than our ears, we are incalculably influenced by unconscious or subliminal patterns. We take handsome or pretty seriously pretty faces on television, in film, in politics and sport, on the cover of magazines and in the newspapers. We imitate these iconic figures in their dress, speech, manners, behavior, diets, careers, and mating, and conform to their story lines and therefore, paradoxically, copy their stuckness.

New York Times columnist David Brooks does a good job charting our self-mockery ways. He uses the tattoo nation to illustrate how this symbolic nonconformity of the outcast has become a ubiquitous conforming farce. He writes:

> *"Middleclass types have been appropriating the symbols of marginalized outcasts since at least the 1830s. This is no longer a way to express individuality; it's a way to be part of the mob... People adopt socially acceptable transgressions—like tattoos—to show they are edgy, but inside they are still middle class. You run into these candy-cane grunge types: people with piercings and inking all over their bodies who look like Sid*

*Vicious but talk like Barry Manilow. They've got the alienated look—
just not the anger."*

Now, as "tattoo nation," nearly everyone has a tattoo, which means it no longer symbolizes free expression and individuality, but that nonconformity grunge look that is meant to make for feeling special when it conveys just the opposite impression.

THE QUEST TO HEAL OUR BROKEN SPIRIT

We have used consumerism as therapy for our unconscious age, and it has failed.

We have attempted to find happiness in self-indulgent lifestyles and that has made us even more anxious and self-estranged.

We have been on this treadmill, David Brook's informs us, at least since the 1830s when we were transitioning from an agrarian to an industrial society.

We consume a quarter of the world's natural resources while being one-twentieth of the world's population and don't seem to give a fig for the excess.

We are generous to a fault with our money, but we don't save a dime ourselves for a rainy day.

We smile a lot on the outside and cry a lot on the inside.

We play and work hard but have no idea how to relax without making it feel like work unless we take a few pills or drinks that makes us resemble the walking dead for a few hours.

Yet, with all that we have and are, we feel broken inside. This is not my assessment. It is society's assessment. We are a society of the absurd. Two-thirds of Americans are obese, and the most obese are the poorest. More people are dying from obesity-related diseases than from cigarette smoking or alcoholism.

To be more precise, a half-million will die as a result of obesity this year as they did last year. We are a fast-food nation killing ourselves gently with empty calories. Yet, we spend more than $30 billion a year on diet foods and programs. If we are rich, we will possibly endure liposuction surgery to correct a problem requiring only self-management. Erasmus would have quite a time with us.

We are not happy campers. We have lost our moral compass and our way. We are not confident thinkers. We are looking to solve other people's problems having no time to solve our own.

The way to happiness and *Confident Thinking* is not "out there," but "in here," in your center where that internal governor belongs.

Enthusiasm is not rah-rah; it is not, or jumping up and down in a frenzy of joy. It is not frenetic devotion to a fad, or fancy. Enthusiasm is the quiet engine that lights our fire and gets us off to do something, anything, but something.

Enthusiasm is not charisma, although we are impressed with histrionic expressiveness. Enthusiasm is the quiet truth written large on the heart and translated into quiet not always visible action. I was once asked if I was available to give a keynote speech at a large marketing conference. I said yes, and they requested a video. The only video I had was for an appearance on CNBC's *"America's Talking."* I sent the video. I did not get the job. My rejection was polite but with this comment: "We found you not to be charismatic." The note added, "But we did find your observations (on the video) quite sage, but lacking in entertainment value."

No foul, I respected the marketing director for his directness. He made it clear he required a cheerleader, not someone to inspire confidence with content. How did I come to his attention? It was a provocative article written for a journal on leaderless leadership in which I attacked charismatic leadership. He failed to appreciate the irony. He measured appeal from the cold medium of television and not the warm medium of personal engagement. There is a conspicuous difference between an audience in the flesh and the flat screen performance in an empty studio.

PALLIATIVE TO A CHANGING WORLD

Empires have given way to nations, nations have given way to markets, and markets are now giving way to cyberspace where the rules of the road don't match the rules of the airwaves. We are just starting to sense the high crimes and misdemeanors of this new venue with no idea how to monitor much less police it.

These are exciting but dangerous times. We lack the former confidence we had in government, in our common belief system, in the rule of law. People are increasingly gravitating to conclaves whose solidarity depends on common hatreds. Beliefs are no longer enough. As to trust, how can anyone trust anyone else when they don't trust themselves?

For centuries, people have looked to their nation for direction. Now, there are nations within nations of discontented souls that don't abide by the moral authority, or the rule of law, but have their own measure of what is good and evil, right and just irrespective of the greater society. We are in the time of the renegade spirit.

The melting pot, which the United States has always prided itself as being, has never actually existed. We have been a stratified society from the beginning. The only difference is that tolerance for these stratifications is now seemingly at an all-time low.

Economic Man prevails and colors all ideologies. Lost in this mad rush to prosper has been *Spiritual Man*. We define our enemy as someone who thinks differently than we do when that difference is what gives life its majesty.

Transition and transformation has been the story of man: from feudalism to capitalism, from a religious to a secular society, from agriculture to industrialism, from individualism to group norms, from nuclear to post-nuclear age, from nationalism to globalization, and from modernism to postmodernism. Yet, there are places where people still live as they did 2,000 years ago. I find that refreshing.

Each of us is a whole of a piece. Ralph Waldo Emerson saw this in terms of the intimacy of the mind and heart:

> *"Is there any religion but this, to know, that whenever in the wide desert of being, the holy sentiment we cherish has opened into a flower, it blooms for me? If none see it, I see it; I am aware, if alone, of the greatness of the fact."*

Our life and providence are one. We must deal with complexity thinking confidently as we can no longer afford to deny it, as it is the world we have created and now must master. We can. *Confident Thinking* is an introduction of one way we might begin.

A TIME TO PAUSE

Self-examination:
Does your life follow a consistent pattern?

"All that lies between the cradle and the grave is uncertain."

Seneca (4 BC-65 AD), Roman philosopher

NO ONE KNOWS how many more innings he or she will have, but what has been related here is taking place, has taken place, and will continue to take place, in what appears at first blush to be a time of uncertainty.

One word, more than any other connects *Confident Thinking* to our destiny and that word is *consistency*. I am now of an advanced age and can look back over a lifetime to see a consistent order and plan, as though it was composed by a novelist with myself but a character in that story.

Seemingly unimportant events have occurred, of little known consequence at the time, later proving to be central elements of a larger composition, having a coherent plot. Who composed this plot? The philosopher Schopenhauer suggests that just as an aspect of ourselves of which our consciousness is unaware composes our dreams, so, too, our whole life is composed by the *"will within,"* the will that makes all our choices.

It is this will that is key to this missive. We are all authors of our own footprints in the sand, heroes of the novels inscribed in our hearts. Everyone's life, without exception, is sacred, unique, scripted high drama, played out before an audience of one, with one lone actor on stage. The sooner we realize this the more quickly we overcome the bondage of negative thinking, and the loneliness of isolation, to find true friendship with ourselves, and therefore the possibility of meaningful connections with others.

It is a time when we can no longer depend on others to decipher the roadmap of our mind. Our mind has become homeless. That mind, as Milton reminds us, is its own place, and in itself can make a heaven of hell, or a hell of heaven. The choice is ours to make. May you make that prudent connection and soar to grace, greatness and fulfillment.

SELECTIVE BIBLIOGRAPHY

Adler, Alfred, The Individual Psychology, Basic Books, New York, 1956

Andreasen, Nancy, The Broken Brain, Perennial Library, New York, 1984

Appleby, Joyce, The Relentless Revolution: A History of Capitalism, W. W. Norton & Company, 2010

Barrett, William, Irrational Man, Doubleday, Anchor Books, New York, 1962

Bateson, Gregory, Steps to an Ecology of Mind, Ballantine Books, New York, 1972

Beattie, Melody, Codependent No More, A Hazelden Book, New York, 1987

Becker, Ernest, The Denial of Death, The Free Press, New York, 1973

Beckert, Beverly, Changing the Culture, Computer-Aided Engineering, October 1991

Beckett, Samuel, Playwright & Poet, Pegasus, New York, 2009
Beecher, Willard and Marguerite, Beyond Success and Failure, Pocket Books, New York, 1966.

Berger, Peter, The Homeless Mind, Random House, New York, 1973

Berlin, Isaiah, The Crooked Timber of Humanity, Alfred A. Knopf, New York, 1991.

Berne, Eric, Games People Play, Grove Press, New York, 1964, Transactional Analysis In Psychotherapy, Ballantine Books, New York, 1961

Blakeslee, Thomas R., The Right Brain, Playboy Paperbacks, New York, 1983

Blanton, Smiley, Lover or Perish, Simon & Schuster, New York Blumer, Herbert, Symbolic Interaction, University of California Press, Berkeley, 1986

Bono, Edward de, Parallel Thinking, Penguin Books, New York, 1994

Bronowski, J., The Ascent of Man, Little, Brown & Company, Boston, 1973

Burns, Ken, The Civil War (Nine Volumes), PBS Video, New York, 1990

Carey, John, The Intellectuals &The Masses, Academy Chicago Publishers, Chicago, 2002

Carrel, Alexis, Man, The Unknown, Harper and Brothers, New York, 1935

Clegg, Brian, The First Scientist. A Life of Roger Bacon, Constable, London, 2003

Conrad, Joseph, Heart of Darkness, Everyday Paperback Classics, New York, 1995

Csikszentmihalyi, Mihaly, Flow, Harper Perennial, New York, 1990

Dawkins, Richard, The God Delusion, Houghton Mifflin Harcourt, New York, 2006

Drucker, Peter, The New Realities, Harper & Row, New York, 1989

Connor, James A., Kepler's Witch, Harper San Francisco, 2004

Dickens, Charles, A Tale of Two Cities, Volume XII, The Work of Charles Dickens, The Hamilton Book Co., New York, 1908

Doone, John, Selected Poems, Gramercy Books, New York, 1994

Duce, Ivy Oneita, What am I doing here? Perennial Library, New York, 1966

Dusay, John M., Egograms, Harper & Row, New York, 1977

Einstein, Albert, bite-size einstein, St. Martin Press, New York, 1996

Eliot, T S., Christianity & Culture, A Harvest Book, New York, 1976

Emerson, Ralph Waldo, The Writings of, The Modern Library, New York, 1950

Erasmus, Desiderius, In Praise of Folly, Hendricks House Farrar, Straus, New York, 1953

Fernandez-Armesto and Derek Wilson, Reformations: A Radical Interpretation of Christianity and the World (1500-2000), Scribner, New York, 1996

Festinger, Leon, A Theory of Cognitive Dissonance, Northwestern University, Evanston, Illinois, 1954.

Fisher, Jr., James R., Confident Selling, Prentice-Hall, NJ, 1971, Work Without Managers, Delta Group Florida, 1991,Confident Selling for the 90s, Top of the Mountain Publishing, 1992, The Taboo Against Being Your Own Best Friend, The Delta Group Florida, 1996, Six Silent Killers, CRC Press, 1998, In the Shadow of the Courthouse, AuthorHouse, 2003, A Look Back to See Ahead, AuthorHouse, 2007, A Social Psychological Study of the Police Organization: The Anatomy of a Riot, M.A. thesis, University of South Florida, 1976, The Police Paradox: Systematic Exploration into the Paradoxical Dilemma between the Police and the Policed, Ph.D. thesis, Walden University, 1978

Friedman, Thomas L., The World Is Flat, Farrar, Straus and Giroux, New York, 2005

Freud, Sigmund, An Outline of Psychoanalysis, W. W. Norton & Company, New York, 1949: Leonardo da Vinci: A Study in Psychosexuality, Vintage Books, New York, 1947; The Future of Illusion, W. W. Norton & Company, New York, 1961; On Dreams, W. W. Norton & Company, New York, 1952; Civilization and Its Discontents, W. W. Norton & Co., New York, 1961; Beyond the Pleasure Principle, Bantam Psychology, New York, 1972

Gibran, Kahlil, The Prophet, Alfred A. Knopf, New York, 1972

Gladwell, Malcolm, Outliers: The Story of Success, Little Brown and Company, New York, 2008

Goddard, Robert, Borrowed Time, Delta Trade Paperbacks, New York, 2006

Goffman, Erving, The Presentation of Self in Everyday Life, Anchor Original, New York, 1959

Goleman, Daniel, Emotional Intelligence, Bantam Paperbacks, New York, 1997

James R. Fisher, Jr., PhD.

Gordon, William J. J., Synectics, Collier Books, New York, 1961

Gould, Stephen Jay, The Mismeasure of Man, Penguin Books, New York, 1981, Rocks of Ages, Ballantine, New York, 1991

Hall, Edward T, Beyond Culture, Anchor Press, New York, 1976

Hampden-Turner, Charles, Maps of the Mind, Macmillan, New York, 1981

Harris, Judith Rich, The Nurture Assumption, The Free Press, New York, 1998

Harris, Thomas A., I'm OK-- You're OK, Harper & Row, New York, 1969

Hayes, Charles D., The Rapture of Maturity, 2004, Beyond the American Dream, 1998, Proving You're Qualified, 1995, Autodidactic Press, Wasilla, AK.

Healy, Jane M., Endangered Minds, Simon & Schuster Paperbacks, New York, 1990

Henry, Jules, Culture Against Man, Vintage, New York, 1963

Hillman, James, A Terrible Love of War, Penguin Press, New York, 2004

Hoffer, Eric, The True Believer, Perennial Library, New York, 1951

Homans, George C., The Human Group, Harcourt, Brace & World, New York, 1950

Humphreys, Christmas, Buddhism, Pelican Books, 1988

Huxley, Aldous, brave new world, Bantam Classics, New York, 1962, The Doors to Perception, Harper Colophon Books, New York, 1954, Point Counter Point, Penguin, New York, 1955, After Many A Summer Dies The Swan, Avon, New York, 1964

Johnson, Paul, The Renaissance, Phoenix Press, Great Britain, 2000

Joyce, James, A Portrait of the Artist as a Young Man, Viking Press, New York, 1982

Kafka, Franz, The Trial, Penguin, New York, 1986; The Castle, Penguin, New York, 1986

Kempis a Thomas, The Imitation of Christ, Image Books, New York, 1955

King, Basil, The Conquest of Fear, Doubleday & Co., New

York, 1921

Kirkpatrick, Rob, 1969: The Year Everything Changed, Skyhorse Publishing, New York, 2009

Knelman, Fred H., 1984 and all that, Wadsworth Publishing, Belmont, CA, 1971

Krishnamurti, J., You Are The World, Harper & Row, New York, 1972

Laing, R. D., The Voice of Experience, Pantheon, New York, 1962
Larson, Bob, Extreme Evil: Kids Killing Kids, Thomas Nelson, Nashville, 1999

Lasch, Christopher, The Culture of Narcissism, W. W. Norton & Co., New York, 1978

Lewis, C. S., Mere Christianity, Macmillan, New York, 1952

Livingston, William L., Have Fun at Work, 1988, The New Plague, 1985, Friends in High Places, 1990, F. E. S. Limited Publishing, Bayside, NY

Lorenz, Konrad, On Aggression, Harcourt, Brace & World, New York, 1963

Maclachlan, James, Galileo Galilei, Oxford University Press, New York, 1997

Malinowski, Bronislaw, Freedom and Civilization, Indiana University Press, Bloomington, IN, 1944

Maltz, Maxwell, The Magic Power of Self Image Psychology, Prentice-Hall, Englewood Cliffs, N.J., 1964

Man, John, Gutenberg: How One Man Remade the World with Words, John Wiley & Sons, New York, 2002

Marcuse, Herbert, One-Dimensional Man, Ark Paperbacks, London, England, 1986, Eros And Civilization, Vintage Books, New York, 1962

Marius, Richard, Martin Luther, Belknap Press, Cambridge, MA, 1999

Mascaro, Juan, The Bhagavad-Gita, Penguin Books, New York, 1962

Mayer, Jerry, bite-size Einstein, St. Martin's Press, New York, 1996

McClelland, David, The Achieving Society, Van Nostrand Co.,

Princeton, NJ, 1961

Montessori, Maria, The Montessori Method, Paperback Books, New York, 2002

More, Sir Thomas, Utopia, Barnes & Noble, New York, 2005

Morris, Desmond, The Naked Ape, A Dell Book, New York, 1973

Nietzsche, Thus Spoke Zarathustra, Penguin, New York, 1969, Beyond Good and Evil, Random House, New York, 1966

Nirenberg, Jesse S., Getting Through to People, Prentice-Hall, Englewood Cliffs, N.J., 1963

Nisbet, Robert, The Present Age, Harper & Row, New York, 1988 Obama, Barak, Audacity of Hope: Thoughts on Reclaiming the American Dream, Crown Publishers, New York, 2006

Orwell, George, Nineteen Eighty Four, Buccaneer Books, New York, 1982

Ouspensky, P. D., The Psychology of Man's Possible Evolution, Vintage, New York, 1974, In Search of the Miraculous, A Harvest Book, New York, 1949

Parker, Stanley, The Future of Work and Leisure, Praeger Publishers, New York, 1971

Pascarella, Perry, The New Achievers, The Free Press, New York, 1984

Peale, Norman Vincent, You Can if You Think You Can, Spire Books, Old Tappan, NJ, 1974

Peirce, Penny, The Intuitive Way, MJF Books, New York, 1997 Pelletier, Kenneth R., Mind as Healer Mind as Slayer, A Delta Book, New York, 1977

Petroski, Henry, To Engineer Is Human, St. Martin's Press, New York, 1985

Phillips, Adam, On Balance, Farrar, Straus and Giroux, New York, 2010

Plutarch, The Lives of the Nobel Grecians and Romans, The Modern Library, New York, 1950

Prabhavananda, Swami, The Upanishads, Mentor Religious Classic, New York, 1957

Putnam, Robert D., Bowling Alone: Collapse and Revival of the American Community, Simon & Schuster, New York, 1995

Reeves, Richard, President Nixon: Alone in the White House, Simon & Schuster, New York, 2001

Riesman, David, The Lonely Crowd, Anchor Books, New York, 1954 Sartre, Jean Paul, Existentialism and Human Emotions, Philosophical Library, New York, 1957, Sartre & Psychology, edited by Keith Hoeller, Humanities Press, New Jersey, 1994

Schickel, Richard, Intimate Strangers: The Culture of Celebrity, Doubleday & Co., New York, 1985

Schulberg, Budd, What Makes Sammy Run? Robert Bentley, Cambridge, MA 1979

Schur, Edwin M., Labeling Deviant Behavior, Harper & Row, New York, 1991

Schwartz, Gary, Beyond Conformity or Rebellion, The University of Chicago Press, Chicago, 1995

Selye, Hans, Stress Without Distress, Signet Book, New York, 1974

Sennett, Richard, Respect in a World of Inequality, W. W. Norton, New York, 2003

Shachtman, Tom, The Inarticulate Society, The Free Press, 1995 Sheen, Fulton J., Footprints in a Darkened Forest, Meredith Press, New York, 1967

Shermer, The Borderlands of Science, Oxford University Press, London, 2001

Skinner, B. F., About Behaviorism, Alfred A. Knopf, New York, 1974

Slater, Philip, The Pursuit of Loneliness, Beacon Press, 1970 Smith, Robert P., Where Did You Go? "Out" What Did You Do? "Nothing," Lexikos Publishing, San Francisco, 1974

Sorokin, Pitirim A., The Crisis of Our Age, E. P. Dutton & Co., New York, 1941

Springer, Sally P., Georg Deutsch, Left Brain, Right Brain, W. H. Freeman and Co., San Francisco, 1981

Strohmeyer, John, Crisis in Bethlehem, Adler &Adler, Bethesda, MD, 1986

Sutton-Smith, Brian, Toys as Culture, Gardener Press, New York, 1986

James R. Fisher, Jr., PhD.

Szasz, Thomas, The Second Sin, Anchor Books, 1974, The Manufacturing of Madness, A Delta Book, New York, 1970, The Myth of Mental Illness, Perennial Library, New York, 1974, Ceremonial Chemistry, Anchor Press, New York, 1975, Ideology and Insanity, Anchor Press, New York, 1970

Tamny, Martin, Rationality in Thought and Action, Greenwood Press, New York1986

Tawney, R. H., The Acquisitive Society, Harvest Books, New York, 1920

Thompson, William Irwin, Imaginary Landscape, St. Martin's Press, New York, 1989

Thoreau, Henry David, Walden, The Modern Library, New York, 1950

Tillich, Paul, Dynamics of Faith, Harper Torchbooks, New York, 1957

Toffler, Alvin, Future Shock, Bantam Books, New York, 1970

The Torah, The Jewish Publication Society of America, Philadelphia, 1962

Tzu, Lao, Tao Te Ching, Penguin Classics, New York, 1963

Warner, Samuel J., Self-Realization and Self-Defeat, Grove Press, New York, 1966

Watson, James D., The Double Helix, Signet Nonfiction, New York, 1968

Watts, Alan W, The Two Hands of God, Collier Books, New York, 1963, The Wisdom of Insecurity, 1951, The Book, Collier Books, 1966, Beyond Theology, Meridian Books, New York, 1966

Watts, Duncan J., Six Degrees, The Science of A Connected Age, W. W. Norton & Company, New York, 2003

Wegner, Daniel M., Implicit Psychology, Oxford University Press, New York, 1977

West, Diana, The Death of the Grown-Up, St. Martin's Press, New York, 2007

White, Michael, The Pope & The Heretic, Story of Giordano Bruno, William Morrow, New York, 2002

Whitman, Walt, Leaves of Grass, Barnes & Noble, New York,

1993

Wilson, Edward 0., Naturalist, Island Press, Washington, D.C., 1994.

Wittenberg, Rudolph, Common Sense about Psychoanalysis, Funk & Wagnalls, New York. 1962

Zilbergeld, Bernie, The Shrinking of America, Little Brown & Co., Boston, 1983.

James R. Fisher, Jr., PhD.

ABOUT THE AUTHOR

Dr. James R. Fisher, Jr. is an industrial/organizational development psychologist with a diverse work record. He writes from this background in the genre of work, workers and the workplace.

Over his career, in the complex organization, he has served in the US Navy, worked in the chemical and hi-tech industry, acted as consultant to Fortune 500 companies, been an adjunct professor at several universities, and written more than a score of books in nonfiction and two in fiction.

He makes his home in Tampa, Florida with his wife, Betty, and can be reached by e-mail at thedeltagrpfl@cs.com or peripateticphilospher.blogspot.com

www.ingramcontent.com/pod-product-compliance
Lightning Source LLC
Chambersburg PA
CBHW030421290526
45786CB00001B/85